Behavioural As

The Marketing Series is one of the most comprehensive collections of books in marketing and sales available from the UK today.

Published by Butterworth-Heinemann on behalf of the Chartered Institute of Marketing, the series is divided into three distinct groups: *Student* (fulfilling the needs of those taking the Institute's certificate and diploma qualifications); *Professional Development* (for those on formal or self-study vocational training programmes); and *Practitioner* (presented in a more informal, motivating and highly practical manner for the busy marketer).

Formed in 1911, the Chartered Institute of Marketing is now the largest professional marketing management body in Europe with over 22,000 members and 25,000 students located worldwide. Its primary objectives are focused on the development of awareness and understanding of marketing throughout UK industry and commerce and on the raising of standards of professionalism in the education, training and practice of this key business discipline.

Other titles in the student series

Behavioural Aspects of Marketing

KEITH C. WILLIAMS
BSc (Econ), DipM, MInstM, MCAM

Published on behalf of the Chartered Institute of
Marketing and the CAM Foundation

Butterworth-Heinemann Ltd
Linacre House, Jordan Hill, Oxford OX2 8DP

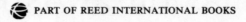 PART OF REED INTERNATIONAL BOOKS

OXFORD   LONDON   BOSTON
MUNICH   NEW DELHI   SINGAPORE   SYDNEY
TOKYO   TORONTO   WELLINGTON

First published 1981
Reprinted 1982, 1984, 1985 (twice), 1987, 1990 (twice), 1992

ISBN 0 7506 0608 8

Printed and bound in Great Britain by
Redwood Press Limited, Melksham, Wiltshire

CONTENTS

PREFACE

The aim of this book is to present as clearly as possible a review of the main behavioural concepts and theories and to demonstrate their application in the marketing arena. Although behavioural scientists have long been associated with marketing, it is only comparatively recently that behavioural science *per se* has become recognized as an essential component of the marketer's repertoire of skills. Even so, most books on the subject written to date have concentrated on consumer behaviour and have tended to ignore the behavioural aspects of employee interaction and motivation. This to me has been a matter of regret, since marketing is not only concerned with consumer purchasing behaviour but also with the orientation of products or services to the market. This requires an integrated marketing-orientated approach by the organization. To be effective, marketing must be a planning, co-ordinating, and controlling function and this necessitates certain organizational skills on the part of the marketer.

As a step towards redressing this situation, I have, in writing this book, attempted to show the relevance of the concepts and theories of behavioural science to all aspects of marketing. It is clearly impossible to provide a comprehensive treatment of the vast amount of knowledge now available, but I hope that the introduction provided by this book will stimulate readers to explore further the subject area. To facilitate further study, all sources are fully referenced at the end of each chapter.

As an introductory text to the subject, this book has been designed to meet the requirements of both students and teachers of the Chartered Institute of Marketing and CAM Certificate syllabuses. It should also be useful to honours degree business students at universities and polytechnics.

Few books are the product of one person's efforts and this work is no exception. In preparing this book I have unashamedly sought the help and advice of friends and colleagues and I am particularly indebted to Peter Sampson for his considerable assistance, especially in respect of Chapter 8. I must also record my thanks to the readers appointed by the Chartered Institute of Marketing and by CAM and to John Westlake for their valuable comments and suggestions. Ted Jenner and Edgar Hibbert of the Chartered Institute of Marketing provided support and encouragement at various stages during the preparation of the text. John Quinton did a marvellous job of typing the final manuscript in record time. But most of all my thanks to my wife, Sue, to whom this book is dedicated. Without her very active support and help this text would not have been written.

1. *THE BEHAVIOURAL BACKGROUND*

'Profit is made from people, not products.'

Anon.

1.1 Introduction

This book is about people, or more accurately, the systematic study of their behaviour patterns in a marketing context. This is not a readily comprehensible subject area for man is a complex animal whose behaviour is often apparently illogical. But nonetheless an understanding of the individual's needs and wants is a cornerstone of the marketing concept and marketers are increasingly turning to the behavioural sciences for knowledge, not only of how the individual relates to his environment, but also to suggest new market opportunities. Marketers are no longer content to analyse and segment markets in terms of conventional demographics such as age and socio-economic groupings, but are taking advantage of behavioural concepts such as attitudes, motives, and life-styles.

However, whilst consumer behaviour is of vital importance since marketing is, by definition, consumer-orientated, it must not be overlooked that products and services are produced and distributed by people. If the company's objectives are to be met through the application of the marketing concept, then it follows that a key ingredient determining success is the extent to which the efforts of the entire organization are co-ordinated, controlled, and motivated. The factors that influence and constrain individual behavioural patterns within the organization are hence of legitimate concern to the marketer. To deny this is to ignore the fact that marketing managers are responsible for the selection, training, and motivation of staff; do have responsibility for communication and co-ordination functions; and often do have a major input into reorganization decisions.

The aim of this book is to review the main areas of behavioural knowledge that are applicable to marketing in order to provide the reader with a better understanding of the forces that produce specific behaviour. It must be appreciated that it would be impossible in a book of this length to cover in depth all aspects of the behavioural sciences applicable to marketing. Even so, the intention has been to go beyond the traditional and more restricted area of consumer behaviour since, as explained above, the marketing concept should embrace aspects of organizational structuring and functioning. Chapters 9 and 10 are consequently devoted to the topics of organizational behaviour and employee motivation.

1

There is, however, a major caveat. There is no discrete body of knowledge which we can label 'marketing behaviour'. Whilst there have been attempts to produce comprehensive explanations of consumer behaviour, as shown in Chapter 8, marketing has usually relied on borrowing concepts and theories from the behavioural sciences. Most of the research carried out in marketing uses techniques and theoretical bases that were developed outside the marketing arena. As a result, marketers have sometimes spent far too much effort, and given too much emphasis, to areas that currently have little practical application to marketing, as is shown in Chapter 7 when we deal with the topic of personality. This situation is slowly changing with the realization that the study of consumer behaviour is not merely a subset of that of human behaviour, but is a discipline in its own right; albeit one that is multi-disciplinary in the sense that it utilizes the perspectives of the other behavioural sciences.

The following chapters examine the knowledge gained mainly from the disciplines of psychology and sociology. Much of this knowledge the average reader may have encountered previously in the popular press, or will think obvious from his daily interaction with others. Man has always been interested in his fellow man and through observation has developed his own, albeit subjective, views on the way he relates to his environment. But by systematically studying human behaviour using the principles and methods of scientific analysis, we try to free our observations from subjective bias. In this way we aim to identify relationships which are generally applicable rather than unique to the individual observer. It is therefore appropriate, before examining the major areas of behavioural knowledge, to look briefly at the main behavioural sciences and to examine the principles of scientific method.

1.2 The Behavioural Sciences

'Behavioural sciences' is the collective term given to a number of disciplines which focus on the study of the behaviour of humans. These disciplines differ in the ways they study behaviour, the aspects of behaviour with which they are concerned, the concepts they use, and even their basic units of analysis. But since the general area of study is that of behaviour it is not surprising that as knowledge expands it becomes increasingly difficult to establish boundary lines between the various behavioural sciences. There is now considerable overlap between the various disciplines and each can contribute significantly to the others.

Although, as stated above, the subject matter of this book is taken mainly from the disciplines of psychology and sociology, a useful perspective can be obtained by a brief examination of the principal behavioural disciplines.

1.21 Economics

This has been defined as 'the study of allocation of scarce resources to unlimited wants', a definition that appeared to lose popularity but one that is today probably very appropriate, as may be inferred from the discussion in Chapter 11. The central concept is that of value as measured by money and the main topics of study are those of the production, exchange, and consumption of goods and services. The units of analysis are both the individual consumer and organization (the micro-economic approach) and the aggregate of these (the macro-economic approach).

Marketing has made great use of the theories and principles of economics, but its 'black box' approach (*see* Section 1.31) provides merely a broad picture which can only be completed through knowledge provided by the other behavioural sciences. For example, in micro-economics the theories of marginal utility and revealed preference are based on the assumption of rational economic man. Each consumer is credited with the ability to measure the utility, or satisfaction, he derives from each commodity consumed and, given a total rationality, will select a combination of goods and services that will maximize his total utility. This ignores, however, the questions of why and how need preferences arise in the first place. In any case, man is seldom rational and the assumption 'other things being equal', whilst useful in determining the relationship between variables, does not offer a satisfactory explanation of behaviour, although it provides a very good starting point. This can be seen in Chapter 8 where we examine the 'trade off' model, a technique based on utility theory.

1.22 Psychology

This is the study of human and animal behaviour. It is a broad science that includes many areas of enquiry and has resulted in a multitude of general principles and basic methodologies. The individual is the basic unit of analysis and all aspects are studied, ranging from the physiological (for example, examining how the brain functions) to the social (for example, examining the effect of group influence on the individual). As a result there are a number of specialized subdivisions in psychology. For example, social psychology studies how individuals influence and are influenced by group pressures; industrial psychology studies the effect on the individual of working environments; organizational psychology studies the functioning of the individual within the constraints of the organization.

The individual and the ways he relates to his environment are of vital importance to marketing and Chapters 2, 3 and 4 examine topics which pertain to the individual *per se*, whilst Chapters 6 and 7 examine the individual in his social environment. But whilst an understanding of such topics as perception, motivation, and attitudes is very useful to the marketer, it must not be forgotten that they should be related to the market as a whole, and also to their influence on economic behaviour. A major reason for the marketer's interest in individual differences is to ascertain whether a sufficient number of individuals display similar psychological characteristics to direct a specific marketing effort at this particular group. This, of course, is segmentation analysis; and whilst the technique has long been used in marketing, it is only comparatively recently that concepts such as attitudes have been used as segmentation variables. Again, if such variables are to be of use it will be largely as a result of their influence on the creation of utilities and in this sense the broader framework of economic analysis must not be neglected.

1.23 Sociology and Anthropology

These two disciplines are often treated jointly because of their similarity in
subject matter, concepts, and methods employed. They are both concerned
with the study of the collective behaviour of people in groups. The basic unit
of analysis is, therefore, the group, although this can range from the family
unit living together to a society as a whole. It is fairly obvious that a group of
people will assume an identity that is different from the aggregate of the individuals it comprises. This group identity will determine relationships with
other groups and will also have an effect on the behaviour of individual
members. The way in which this happens, the resulting social structures and
trends, and the influence of culture is the subject matter of sociology and
anthropology. Typically, the sociologist studies modern literate societies,
whilst the anthropologist, being mainly interested in cultural determinants of
behaviour and cross-cultural comparisons, studies more primitive societies.

Marketing has not yet made any great use of the knowledge gained by these
two disciplines, although social trends are often monitored; and social class,
in terms of socio-economic grouping, has formed a useful, if incomplete,
basis for segmentation. We examine sociological concepts in Chapter 5.

1.24 Geography

Although not the subject matter of this book, it should be noted that geography has contributed much to an understanding of man's behaviour. The
two main aspects that are of greatest relevance are human geography, which
is concerned with spatial analysis of human activity, and economic geography, which is concerned with basic resources and human activities in
relation to these resources. Human geography examines where people live
and why, and their physical communication patterns; it is thus closely allied
with sociology. It is important for marketers to know where markets are
located and what form they take. When we talk of dynamic market environments, we are not only referring to changes in attitudes or socio-economic
classifications, but also to physical migrations. An urban area that at one
point in time may be predominantly AB can change to predominantly $C_1 C_2$
two decades later. This has important implications for the kinds of goods and
services that can be sold in that area.

1.25 History

Finally, something should be said about the role of history. Whilst not on a
par with the other behavioural sciences in terms of its methods of enquiry,
history is a systematized body of knowledge concerned with the recorded
behaviour of people. The importance of studying past events is that they may
teach us valuable lessons that may benefit us in the future. Alternatively,
there may be trends which we can identify and use to make predictions about
future events. Lessons can be learned, for example, from the failure of
marketing efforts and, in this respect, case study analysis is now recognized

as an important teaching aid. Even so, the tendency for companies to repeat the mistakes of others indicates that the lessons of history have still to be learned by many.

The trends revealed by historical data are often capable of analysis and can be used to formulate theories about societies which may usefully be applied to our understanding of current events. For example, analysis of population changes over time has resulted in the sociological Demographic Transition Model, which postulates various stages of population development in relation to economic development, and which can be used to study the population events now occurring in certain areas of the world. A projection from this model suggests that the danger of world overpopulation may not be as great as is sometimes thought.

1.3 Scientific Method

A science is a body of systematized knowledge which has been gathered by observing and measuring events according to certain rules. These events are systematized in various ways, but principally by classifying them and establishing general principles that describe, explain, and predict them as accurately as possible. This seems fairly straightforward, but unfortunately there are numerous problems arising from the methods used to collect information, the ways in which observations are measured, the methods used to manipulate data, and the inferences that can be made from data. These methodological issues are at the core of the problem of using behavioural science principles in marketing. Since the reader's attention will be drawn to problems of methodology in the chapters that follow, it is useful to have an understanding of the way in which science seeks to expand the frontiers of knowledge. The discussion that follows is a traditional, if simplified, view of scientific method; philosophical problems concerning the nature of certainty and the problem of knowledge are beyond the scope of this book.

Science starts with ideas or notions about events which may, or may not, have been triggered by an observation of a particular event or study in a related area. An idea might arise from a simple question such as 'Why are soap sales decreasing?', or from an examination of the relationship between events such as rainfall and cloud cover. From this basic idea we can formulate an hypothesis; this is a statement unsupported by facts, which can be refuted by facts. The extent to which we are able to collect facts will depend on our ability to define what we are investigating and on our ability to categorize and measure our observations. Through the process of firsthand observation, survey, statistical analysis, or experiment, we collect facts to test the hypothesis and as a result it is refuted or gains credibility. From a verified hypothesis, or a number of verified hypotheses, we can propose theories to explain the relationships between variables demonstrated by our hypothesis. This theory is then tested further to ascertain those circumstances under which it holds good and those under which it can be refuted or may require modification. This, in essence, is the scientific method. To provide an insight into the methodological problems involved we shall examine further the nature and importance of the terms introduced above.

1.31 Variables and Concepts

There are many factors or variables impinging on any behavioural situation and the researcher is concerned to identify these variables and to ascertain those that are dominant in producing a situation, those that play little or no part, and those that are affected by the situation itself. The researcher will therefore try to simplify situations so that, ideally, all variables apart from two are held constant. He will try to produce a black box situation from which he can observe the effect of one variable, the *stimulus variable*, on the other variable, the *response variable*. This situation can be represented as shown in Figure 1.1.

Figure 1.1 Representation of a 'Black Box' situation

Thus, in supply and demand analysis in economics, price is manipulated and the effect on the quantity sold is observed. In other words, the response variables are the observable activities of individuals that are elicited by stimulus variables. One problem is that this seldom actually happens, for the effects of stimulus variables are modified by the influence of what are known as *intervening variables*. These intervening variables are internal to the individual and cannot be observed or measured directly, but can only be *inferred* from behaviour. Two of the most important intervening variables dealt with in this book are motives (Chapter 4) and attitudes (Chapter 6).

Related to the problem of intervening variables are the concepts to be used in behavioural science. When an observer identifies an intervening variable he will invent a name for it and define precisely to what it refers. A clear definition is essential for there is often disagreement between researchers, even regarding the meaning of terms such as motive and attitude. It will be found that care has been taken in the following chapters to define clearly the concepts studied. Another important reason for defining the concepts we use is that if they are not precisely defined they are seldom capable of measurement.

1.32 Measurement

The ability to assign numbers to events is of crucial importance in any science. Variables have to be assessed in an objective and precise manner and manipulation of data is often only possible if they are in quantitative form. Measurement is, however, arbitrary in the sense that a particular measure (for example, a metre length, a kilogram weight) has to be defined by man. But once a standard has been defined, all measurements are made in terms of that standard. In the behavioural sciences, and particularly psychology, we are dealing with concepts that are extremely difficult to measure and no single standard is generally applicable. In practice, therefore, one of the following four measurement scales is used[1]:

1. *Nominal scale*. This is simply the assignment of numerals for labelling different individuals or classes. To place person 1 in category 3, and person 2 in category 1, is an example of the use of a nominal scale.
2. *Ordinal scale*. This is the ranking of a variable or object according to some attribute it possesses. The scale indicates whether an object possesses more or less of an attribute than another object, but not how much more or how much less. Ordinal scales are frequently used in attitude measurement and some of the difficulties arising here are presented in the discussion of attitude scaling in Chapter 6.
3. *Interval scale*. This provides a measure of the magnitude of difference between one object and another. The important point is that the intervals are equal and this enables us to determine by how much the one object differs from the other. But whilst these scales provide a measure of the true difference between two objects, they are not anchored to absolute zero and this places a limitation on the degree of statistical manipulation we can apply. For example, a temperature scale is an interval scale and 50°F is not twice as much heat as 25°F.
4. *Ratio scale*. This is similar to the interval scale except that it is anchored to absolute zero. As a result, ratios that are equal actually refer to equal proportions. For example, 3 is to 6 as 6 is to 12. Examples of ratio scales are a ruler and a stopwatch.

Obviously the more precise measurements enable a greater degree of manipulation of data and permit the use of more sophisticated statistical techniques. The scale used will, however, depend on the degree of sophistication required. For example, if we wish to know whether extroverts are more likely to cope with a particular training programme than introverts, then a nominal or ordinal measurement may be as useful as the more precise interval measurements.

1.33 Methods of Data Collection

Facts are important to the behavioural scientist in the search for meaningful relationships between variables. These facts are obtained by a variety of methods, but the extent to which they are reliable will depend on the amount of control exercised by the researcher in obtaining those facts. The main methods employed are the following:

1. *Analysis of existing data*. Facts regarding the concept in which we are interested may already exist in a readily usable form. They may have been collected as part of a general data collecting exercise, for example as part of a government survey. Such data can be manipulated statistically to indicate the relevance of a variable to a particular study. For example, given two sets of data the statistical technique of correlation can indicate whether there is any degree of association between two variables. Without going into detail on this particular technique, it must be pointed out that a

high degree of association could be established between the stork population of Scandinavia and the birth rate in the United Kingdom. The
researcher must therefore exercise some care in his choice of variables.
Nonetheless, the results from such analysis can be a useful starting point
for a research programme.

2. *Survey Techniques*. The use of questionnaires and personal interviews is
well established in marketing and the range of such techniques and their
advantages and pitfalls are catalogued in numerous market research textbooks. It should be noted that the method is widely used in sociological
enquiry and indeed modern survey techniques owe their origins to the
social surveys of Booth and Rowntree[2] in England at the end of the last and
beginning of the present centuries. Whilst surveys do not allow the
manipulation of variables, they do enable facts to be collected in areas that
are not amenable to direct observation or experimental method.

3. *Observation*. This technique attempts to study behaviour in naturally
occurring situations. It is widely used in anthropology to study primitive
tribes and has been used in marketing to study shopping behaviour. The
idea is that the researcher observes overt behaviour, catalogues it, and
attempts to make inferences regarding the influence of different variables.
The method can be combined with survey techniques; for example, by
later asking people why they behaved in a certain way. It can also be combined with experimental techniques in the sense that certain variables can
be manipulated. For example, when studying the effects of group influence on the individual, the effect of certain behaviour on the subject can be
studied by getting other members of the group to behave in a certain way
and observing his reactions. There are, however, two problems with this
technique: first, if people are aware that they are being studied they may
alter their behaviour as a consequence, a factor that is discussed in
Chapter 9 when we examine the Hawthorne Studies; second, there is the
danger that the researcher may project his own subjective feelings when
recording observations and as a result may record interpretations rather
than descriptions.

4. *Experiment*. This is the heart of scientific method for it is concerned with
controlling conditions so that relationships among variables can be ascertained. The idea is to eliminate, or at least minimize, the effects of all but
two variables or two groups of variables. One of these, the stimulus or
independent variable, is then altered and the effect on the other, the
response variable or *dependent variable*, is noted. For example, in studying the relationship between motivation and performance of a task we
could alter the motivation as represented by a reward of some kind (the
independent variable) and observe the effect on task performance (the
dependent variable). A problem arises, however, in that we may not have
taken account of all factors and the result may be influenced by a variable
other than the independent variable. To take account of this difficulty we
can use a *control group* which is comprised of people who have similar
characteristics to that of the experimental group (for example, age, sex,
intelligence), but for this group we do not alter the independent variable.
By comparing and analysing the results of the two groups we can deter-

mine whether the independent variable had an effect on the dependent variable. These two designs are summarized in Figure 1.2.

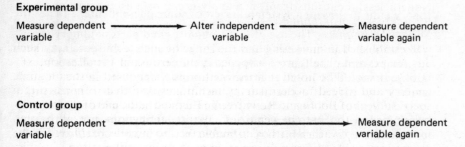

Figure 1.2 Summary of experimental and control group designs

The extent to which results of such designs will support hypotheses will depend on the skill and imagination of the researcher in choosing appropriate variables. But even when there appears to be no relationship emerging, progress can result if the researcher investigates other possible explanations. The history of science abounds with examples of discoveries being made because of experiments that did not produce the expected results. For example, Faraday discovered the principle of electrical induction (which led to the creation of the dynamo for generating electricity) as a result of investigations on an unexpected experimental result.

Of course, the experimental method was developed for use in the physical sciences where it is relatively easy to control variables. In the behavioural sciences it cannot always be used, for people and animals are not always willing to co-operate and, because there are many intervening variables, it is often difficult to determine causal relationships. Experiments are usually conducted in laboratories or in laboratory-type situations and since these are artificial environments they can of themselves alter behaviour. However, experiments are sometimes conducted in natural environments, such as work places, often with very unexpected results. One of the first large scale industrial behaviour experiments was that conducted by Elton Mayo at the Hawthorne Plant; the comparatively lengthy account of this study presented in Chapter 9 will, it is hoped, serve to illustrate many of the principles outlined above.

Before leaving the topic of experimental design, a word of caution is appropriate. Regrettably there have been cases, in both the physical and the behavioural sciences, where results have been falsified to support hypotheses that a researcher believes to be correct. This is one of the reasons why experiments are always reported in full; it allows other people to repeat the experiment and obtain the same results. In fact, the greater the validation of experimental results, the greater the certainty that a hypothesis is correct.

1.34 Theory

A theory aims to present a systematic view of some phenomenon and has the following functions.

1. *Description*. This involves characterizing the nature of something such as, for example, the factors involved in the process of socialization.
2. *Explanation*. This involves attempts to understand the causes of some event or activity. If a causal relationship is established it means that a particular phenomenon directly resulted from one or more specific variables. For a variable to be a cause of a particular phenomenon, we have to establish that the variable is a *sufficient* and *necessary condition* for the phenomenon. If the phenomenon cannot occur without the variable, then the variable is a necessary condition for the phenomenon. If the phenomenon is produced whenever the variable occurs, then the variable is a sufficient condition for the phenomenon. For example, consider the relationship between rainfall and cloud cover. Are clouds a necessary condition for rain? Are clouds a sufficient condition for rain? Our own experience tells us that the answer to the first question is yes, but to the second question it is no. Further research is therefore required to determine the causal elements of rainfall.
3. *Prediction*. This refers to our knowledge of the probability of various outcomes given our knowledge of the relationships among variables. The extent to which we are able to predict events will depend on the completeness of the explanation we have of the causal relationships involved. However, prediction is a vital aspect of theorizing, for if we have adequately explained the relationships among variables then further events resulting from this relationship can be predicted. Additional research can validate the prediction. If the events predicted do not occur then the theory must be modified to take account of the new observations.

Allied to the question of prediction, is that of the generalization of results. The extent to which results obtained in one situation, or for one group of subjects, can be thought to hold true in a different situation, or for a different group of subjects, is a contentious issue. For example, animals are frequently used in psychology to find answers to many general questions about behaviour. In Chapter 3 it will be seen that theories of human learning have been developed from experiments conducted using animals. Under laboratory conditions animals display, or can be taught to display, albeit at a simple level, some of the behaviours displayed by humans. The extent to which these results can be held to be generally representative of behaviour, whether human or animal, is a difficult question. Using animals does provide the opportunity of eliminating many intervening variables and, whenever possible, experiments are repeated using human subjects. The results have been useful in explaining differences and similarities between human and animal behaviour and in many cases provide support for the use of animal experiments to explain human behaviour.

It should also be noted that an increasingly important aid to the development of theories is the construction and use of the model, a term that is often used synonymously for theory. This topic forms the subject matter of Chapter 8.

It must, however, be emphasised that there are no 'final' answers in science. The explanations that are proposed today may tomorrow be shown to be invalid. Just as the Phlogiston Theory in chemistry, which held sway for many years, was shown to be untrue, so many of the currently held theories of behaviour may yet be shown to be ill-founded. Theories may be inadequate because the nature of the variables involved is not fully understood or because not all the relevant facts are available. It is for this reason that the same data can often be used to produce different explanations and hence theories about a phenomenon. Behavioural science is very much in its infancy and has a long way to go before it achieves the respectability of physics. More sophisticated methods of data collection, analysis, and explanation may result in many of the theories discussed in the following pages being shown to be irrelevant, superficial, or even untrue. They are, however, all that we, as marketers, are offered by the behavioural sciences; let us make the maximum use of them.

1.4 Summary

1. The topic of behavioural aspects of marketing consists of contributions from a number of interrelated disciplines in the behavioural sciences. Consumer behaviour and employee behaviour are determined by multiple influences. The contributions of these disciplines and the analysis of these influences are the subject matter of this book.
2. Behavioural science is the collective term given to a number of disciplines which focus on the study of human behaviour. The main behavioural sciences are economics, psychology, sociology, anthropology, geography, and history. All attempt to utilize the principles of scientific method in acquiring knowledge.
3. Scientific method is the way in which events are systematically observed and measured according to certain rules. However, the way in which concepts are defined and measured may give rise to methodological problems and care must be taken in accepting a given result as being valid or reliable.
4. The main issues of concern in science are the variables and concepts identified and defined, the way in which facts about them are collected, the way in which they are measured, and the theories proposed to account for their functioning and their interrelationships.
   (a) Variables may be classified as stimulus, response, or intervening. We cannot directly observe or measure intervening variables but can only infer their existence and operation.
   (b) Facts can be collected by means of an analysis of existing data, survey techniques, observation, or experiment.
   (c) Facts are measured in terms of nominal scales, ordinal scales, interval scales, or ratio scales.

(d) Theories attempt to account systematically for knowledge about variables and their interrelationships. Theories have the function of being descriptive, explanatory, predictive.
5. There are no 'final' answers in science. Thus, many of the theories presented in this book may over time be considerably modified or shown to be inappropriate to an understanding of consumer and employee behaviour. As behavioural science advances its contribution to marketing is likely to become more significant.

References

1. Stevens, S.S. 'Mathematics, Measurement, and Psychophysics', *Handbook of Experimental Psychology*, Stevens, S.S.(ed) (New York: Wiley, 1951).
2. Moser, C.A. *Survey Methods in Social Investigation* (London: Heinemann, 1958).

2. *PERCEPTION*

'Part of what we perceive comes through our senses from the object before us, another part . . . always comes . . . out of our own head.'

William James

2.1 Introduction

Individuals are not merely passive receptors of stimuli but actively process and reorganize the information they receive. *Cognition* is the term given to the mental processes that enable us to give meaning to our environment and experiences. These mental processes are of prime importance during learning and perception. In this chapter we are concerned with perception and the way in which we select and organize sensory data presented by our environment. Learning, as will be shown in the next chapter, both depends on, and influences perception since it involves changes in behaviour which necessitate meaning and order being given to sensory data.

Perception may be defined as 'a complex process by which people select, organize and interpret sensory stimulation into a meaningful picture of the world' (Markin[1]). From the multitude of stimuli constantly bombarding our sensory organs we select certain stimuli to which we attend. We then organize these stimuli so that they become understandable. But our interpretation of sensory stimuli involves more than just receiving and processing information. It is a dynamic process, and is as much influenced by our attitudes and beliefs, motives, and past learning as it is by the character of the stimuli themselves.

An understanding of perceptual processes is important to the marketer as a customer's decision to purchase a product will be influenced to a large extent by the way he perceives the product. His perception will be affected not only by the quality of the product itself, but also by the attributes which the successful marketing manager is able to lend to the product through advertising, packaging, and other promotional techniques.

Much of the research on perception has been undertaken by the *Gestalt* psychologists who argued that perception involves more than the grouping together of a series of discrete stimuli. In this chapter we will look at perception under two broad headings − selection and organization. Attention will, however, be drawn to other influences on perception. It is hoped that by the end of the chapter, the reader will be able to appreciate what is meant by *Gestalt*, and the phrase 'the whole is greater than the sum of the parts'.

13

2.2 Sensation

Although we commonly refer to five senses – vision, hearing, touch, taste, and smell – there are at least five other senses which we tend to forget. These are pain, temperature, the organic senses which provide information about pressure, pain, and temperature within the body, the kinesthetic senses which provide information on the position of our limbs and the tension in our muscles, and lastly the vestibular sense which gives information about the position of the head and is primarily responsible for maintaining balance. These senses together provide us with the information we receive about the world around us. If there is no sensation then there can be no perception or understanding.

Each sense organ responds to a particular type of physical energy whether it is light, air pressure, or chemical substance. Specialized cells or groups of cells, called *receptors*, respond to small changes in these physical stimuli and transmit messages via the central nervous system to the brain. It is the way in which the brain organizes and interprets this information which marks the distinction between sensation – the collection of information – and perception – the way in which we interpret this information.

Some receptors such as the eye and the ear are highly specialized, while others are merely relatively unspecialized ends of nerve fibres. They each respond to specific stimuli within fairly restricted limits. For example, the eye is sensitive to that part of electromagnetic energy which we call light; it does not respond to gamma rays, X-rays, ultraviolet rays, infrared rays or radio waves. Our ears only respond to air vibrations of between 20 and 20,000 cycles per second and are less sensitive than those of many other animals. The sensory system of the human animal is therefore limited. It is not surprising that many of the advances in modern science had to await the development of specialized instruments capable of measuring minute changes in physical stimuli that are not discernible by man.

The minimum stimulation of sense organs required before there is any sensory experience is known as the *absolute threshold*. This varies considerably between individuals and also depends on the individual's physical condition and motivational state. The absolute threshold is difficult to measure because of these variations but some approximate values are shown below.

Approximate Values for Absolute Thresholds

Sense	*Threshold*
Vision	A candle flame seen at 30 miles on a dark clear night.
Hearing	The tick of a watch under quiet conditions at 20 feet.
Taste	One teaspoon of sugar in two gallons of water.
Smell	One drop of perfume diffused into the entire volume of a six-room apartment.
Touch	The wing of a fly on your cheek from a distance of one centimeter.

Source: Galanter[2]

As well as an absolute threshold, there is also a *difference threshold* which is the minimum amount of stimulation needed to tell two stimuli apart or *just noticeable difference*. The difference threshold is not a constant but depends on the intensity of the original stimulus. Thus, for example, when a 100 watt bulb is substituted for a 50 watt bulb in a room there will be a noticeable increase in illumination. If, however, a 150 watt bulb is substituted for a 100 watt bulb the increase in illumination is less noticeable, even though the amount of energy added to the room is the same. This is explained by the fact that, for all but extreme intensities of stimulation, the difference threshold tends to be a constant fraction of the stimulus intensity. This is known as *Weber's Law* and can be stated mathematically as:

$$\frac{\Delta I}{I} = K$$

Where ΔI is the amount of energy that must be added to reach the difference threshold and I is the intensity of the original stimulus.

Weber's Law is of interest to the marketer who wishes to establish whether his product is noticeably different from competing products. It suggests, for example, that a food manufacturer who wishes to make his product taste just noticeably spicier than a competing product would have to add disproportionately more spice if the product was already spiced than if it were unspiced. Equally, a manufacturer who wishes to make his product appear larger than that of a competitor would need to increase its size by a factor of four to obtain double its impact.

2.21 Sensation and Perception

Perception is not, however, solely influenced by the direct input of immediate sensory data, but is conditioned by the manner in which stimuli are presented, and by other cognitive influences such as past experiences and learning.

There is, for example, a great deal of research evidence to show that for a number of products exhibiting strong brand loyalty, where taste would appear on face value to have a strong influence on buying decisions (beer, cigarettes, cola), there is little noticeable sensory difference. For instance, Husband and Godfrey[3] found that identification of brands of cigarettes under blind test conditions (a research technique where the test subject is given no information regarding brand names, packaging, pricing etc.) was little better than could be expected by chance. This suggests that the stimulus factors excluded by the blind test technique — brand names, packaging, pricing — have a more important effect on product perception and buying decisions in such cases than the factor of taste taken in isolation.

Even where there are noticeable sensory differences between products, the consumer can easily be confused by the manner in which they are presented. It is, for example, very difficult for a consumer to compare two 'hi-fi' systems if he is distracted in some way, perhaps by the salesman, between listening to the competing systems. Differences in packaging can also make it difficult to compare two products, particularly if they are placed apart.

It is often the job of the marketer to emphasise those differences between products that may not be immediately apparent to the consumer or to minimize unfavourable comparisons. He will usually do this by creating an image for his product – 'BMW: the ultimate driving machine' – or by convincing the consumer that there is a difference between his product and others by themes such as 'the difference you can taste'. To do this effectively he must appreciate the complexity of the perceptual process and the factors influencing the way in which sensory stimuli are perceived. But before examining these factors it is helpful to examine briefly the two principal sensory systems: vision and hearing.

2.22 Vision

In many respects the eye is like a camera. Light enters the eye through the transparent cornea, passes through the lens, and is focused on the light-sensitive surface of the retina. The amount of light entering the eye through the pupil is controlled by the autonomic nervous system through expansion and contraction of the iris. This analogy should not, however, be taken too far. Unlike the camera the eye has a double lens system, as the cornea also plays an important role in light refraction. Secondly, the eye is not a passive receiver but is constantly moving. Thirdly, and more importantly from the point of view of this chapter, we do not see directly the small images that form on the retina. Rather, the light falling on the retina is transmuted through nerve impulses to the brain and the visual impression we experience is quite different from the light patterns on the retina.

2.23 Hearing

The ear responds to pressure changes in the atmosphere caused by sound waves. These waves are characterized by their frequency and amplitude; the frequency of the wave determines pitch, while the amplitude determines loudness. When sound waves enter the ear they activate the eardrum and in turn three small bones in the middle ear. The sound is then conducted through a fine membrane called the oval window to the inner ear and the cochlea, which houses sensitive cells which transmute the auditory stimulus through the central nervous system to the brain. Most tones are not pure and are composed of a number of differing frequencies superimposed one on the other. The ear is able to identify these different tones and provides a wide variety of sensory data about the external environment.

Although important for our daily survival the other senses lack the complexity of vision and hearing. We give meaning to our environment through what we see and what we hear, and have evolved a complex symbolic system, called language, which helps us organize the sensations we receive through our eyes and our ears. There is no comparable symbolic system for coding odours, taste, and touch.

The remaining sections of this chapter will mainly be concerned with our perception of light and sound, and with the way in which we organize the sensations brought to us through our eyes and ears. This does not mean that we do not organize the experiences of our other senses each in our own individual ways. Indeed, one only has to think of the various likes and dislikes of food in the average family to realize the differences in the ways that chemical stimuli brought to us through our noses and taste buds are interpreted by the brain. Equally it does not mean that these other senses should be ignored by the marketer. For many products the sense of touch, for example, has importance and a great deal of attention may need to be given to their texture and shape.

2.3 Selectivity of Perception

At any one point in time our sensory organs are being bombarded by a multitude of different stimuli, yet only a few are clearly perceived. We are able to focus our attention on only a selected number of stimuli while others are either not perceived or are only dimly perceived. Take for example the experience of watching a Wimbledon tennis final. While we will be dimly aware of the rest of the crowd, the ball boys, and the umpire, our attention will be concentrated on the movement of the ball and on the position of the next player to hit the ball. At the same time we will be bombarded by a number of other stimuli: the conversation of the couple behind, the sun on our backs, and hunger pangs from our stomachs. While play is going on we may not be aware of these sensations at the margin of our attention. Only when play is finished will we realize how warm it is, and that we are hungry.

But although we can focus our attention on specific stimuli at any one point in time, our attention is constantly shifting. One activity might dominate our attention but other stimuli will, from time to time, impinge on our consciousness and keep us alert to what is going on around us. What is at the focus of our attention one minute may be marginal the next.

Our perception of the stimuli constantly bombarding our sense organs is therefore highly selective. We are also constantly shifting attention from one set of stimuli to another. But what determines the choice of stimuli that come to the focus of our attention? It cannot be a completely random process or we could not carry out any extended activity.

Psychologists have succeeded in identifying a number of factors that are important in determining the direction of attention. They can broadly be classified under the headings external and internal. External factors relate to the physical characteristics of the stimulus, while internal factors include our motives and expectations. A knowledge of these factors is of obvious importance to the marketer, since one of his key tasks must be to attract the attention of the consumer to his product.

2.31 External Factors Influencing Attention

Humans rapidly adjust to the stimulation surrounding them. The ticking of a clock may be immediately noticeable on entering a room but after a while we adapt to it and it lapses into the margin of our attention. Daylight appears particularly bright when we come out of a cinema, but after a few minutes we have adjusted completely to the new light level. This process is known as *habituation* and refers to the fact that after a period of prolonged exposure to a continuous stimulus, the stimulus may cease to produce its characteristic sensation.

We become habituated to everyday objects which we experience or see regularly and may cease to perceive them directly, although they will still be part of the backdrop at the margin of consciousness. If, however, there is a change in a familiar stimulus it will immediately be noticeable. Thus we will be aware if the clock in a room stops ticking, even though the sound of it ticking was not previously noticed. If we are driving a car we will, after a while, cease to be aware of the sound of the engine. But if the sound of the engine changes in any way it will immediately be noticed and will become the focus of our attention. Thus, to some extent, we perceive by exception; that is, our attention is drawn to objects or situations which are in some way different from our prior level of adaptation or habituation.

Physical properties of the stimulus important in gaining attention include intensity, size, position, contrast, novelty, repetition, and movement. These factors are widely used in advertising to attract the attention of potential customers.

1. *Intensity and Size.* The brighter a light or the louder a sound the more likely a person is to attend to it. Similarly, large sizes and bright colours generally attract more attention than small sizes and muted colours. But a doubling in the size of an advertisement, or doubling the brightness or loudness of a stimulus, will not double the likelihood of gaining attention. Extensive research has shown that there is, in fact, an exponential relationship between the magnitude of the stimulus and attention value[4]. This means that a doubling of the size of an advertisement will only lead to a 50% increase in attention. A doubling of the attention value of an advertisement would therefore require a fourfold increase in size.

   It will be noticed that this relationship bears a close resemblance to Weber's Law on sensory difference thresholds. Like Weber's Law, the relationship between stimulus magnitude and attention value is relative rather than absolute. Thus a full page advertisement in a tabloid newspaper may be given twice the attention of a quarter page advertisement in the same newspaper. If, however, a similar size advertisement is placed in a broadsheet, its impact will not be as great given the larger overall format of the broadsheet newspaper. Similarly, the sound of one heavy lorry in congested city traffic may not be noticed, but the presence of the same heavy lorry on a rural road will immediately be apparent.

2. *Position.* There has been some interesting research on the role of position in advertising in newspapers and journals. It has been shown that where cultural values involve reading the printed page from left to right, the upper part of the page gains greater attention and the left-hand page obtains more attention than the right-hand page[5]. There is, however, little evidence to suggest that this has any significant influence on the readership of advertisements; the content of the advertising message being the primary factor determining whether or not an advertisement is read. Indeed it has been shown that in newspapers the upper right-hand page

offers some advantage in terms of readership. Position within newspapers does not appear to be a crucial factor because of the speed with which the average reader passes from page to page. In magazines, however, greater readership is usually obtained by advertisements placed on the covers or first 10% of the pages. Readership of both newspapers and magazines is enhanced when an advertisement is placed adjacent to compatible editorial features[6].

3. *Contrast*. As we have seen, a change in the level of stimulation to which we have become habituated will arouse our attention. Thus the deliberate use of contrast can be a useful means of capturing attention. The alternating use of large and small sizes, loud and soft tones, and primary and pastel shades can be most effective in advertising and will produce greater attention than any one stimulus alone. Thus although colour advertisements are generally more effective than black and white advertisements, an isolated black and white advertisement in a publication full of colour advertisements may attract more attention because of its contrast value. Contrast can also be evoked by taking an object out of its normal setting. A car, for example, may be shown travelling across dunes or along a beach, or a giant box of breakfast cereal may be placed in the middle of a country scene.

4. *Novelty*. Anything that is different from what we would normally expect will tend to attract our attention. It may be a differently shaped package or a lovable monster. Advertisers are constantly looking for new novel ways of presenting their products. The problem is that once a new theme has been discovered other advertisers may also choose to exploit it. Novelty also tends to wear off after two or three exposures and the advertiser must then look for a new idea.

5. *Repetition*. A stimulus that is repeated has a greater chance of gaining attention than one that is presented only once. Our attention is constantly shifting from one stimulus to another and the likelihood that the stimulus will catch us while our attention for one task is waning will be greater if the stimulus is repeated several times. Our sensitivity or alertness to the stimulus will also be enhanced if it is repeated. Thus in television advertisements a key phrase, which sums up the attributes of the product, may be repeated a number of times in a short space of time.

6. *Movement*. As part of our bodily defence mechanism our eyes are involuntarily attracted to movement. Advertisements that involve movement are therefore likely to be more effective than those which do not. Point of purchase displays and outdoor billboards often incorporate moving features as a means of attracting attention. Indeed, local authorities have strict regulations governing the use of moving displays by the roadside as they can constitute a traffic hazard. Skilful artwork in printed advertisements can also be used to inject a semblance of motion into the two-dimensional page. This often involves the use of horizontal and curved lines.

Although the factors discussed above have been considered, for simplicity, as distinct variables, in practice they interrelate and the effect of one factor can often be negated by another. In any promotional situation it is unlikely that one factor will be dominant and the marketer must take care not to apply specific research findings rigidly to generalized situations.

A glance through the pages of any magazine or at any series of television advertisements will, however, show the reader how successful advertising makes use of stimulus factors to attract the attention of the consumer. Advertising material, however, readily habituates and the marketer must constantly be on the search for new ways of demonstrating how his product differs from competing brands. There is little to be gained in designing packaging and advertising material which in isolation gains attention, but when placed on the supermarket shelf or alongside other advertisements appears very similar to the competition.

It should be noted that in the case of some products, habituation to certain themes in advertising and particular types of packaging can be a useful tool which the marketer can apply to his advantage. For example, a company which has a brand leader in one product area may find it helpful to use a similar style of packaging for his other products in the hope that consumers' positive perceptions of the successful product will be transferred to his other products. Similarly, a competitor may attempt to emulate the advertising style or packaging used by the brand leader as this might lead the consumer to perceive the two brands as being similar.

2.32 Internal Factors Influencing Attention

Our attention is not only involuntarily drawn to stimuli which in some way stand out against others present, but is also voluntarily influenced by our interests, needs, motives, and expectations.

Interests, Needs and Motives: Our needs and interests determine not only what will arouse our attention, but also what will hold it. Two people may experience exactly the same situation but their perception of that situation may be completely different because of their differing interests and motives. Consider, for example, an engineer and an accountant visiting the same factory. The engineer will probably notice the layout of the factory floor, the type of machinery used, and the arrangements made for the flow of materials. The accountant, on the other hand, may notice how many people are employed, how many tea breaks they have, and the amount of material scrappage. Both will have experienced exactly the same tour, but because of differences in their interests, their attention has been drawn to different aspects of the same situation.

Interests may be either long term or short term. Long term interests, as in the case of the engineer and accountant above, influence the choice of those stimuli which are received and command attention, and those that are rejected. Short term interests, such as the conversation into which we may be drawn at a party have a more transitory impact on perception.

Our needs also affect perception. If we are hungry we will be more likely to attend to food stimuli, and if we are thirsty we will be more likely to notice drink stimuli. It is well known that the hungry shopper will be likely to load his supermarket trolley with more food items than the shopper who has just eaten.

Advertisers frequently appeal to motives when trying to attract attention to their products. Women, for example, tend to notice advertisements including babies or children, irrespective of other external stimulus factors, while men tend to notice fast cars, sport, and attractive women. Our motives are, however, not constant and will vary according to time and place. A businessman, for example, may not perceive an advertisement for a new type of photocopier in his weekend newspaper although he may notice an advertisement for a lawnmower. If the same two advertisements are placed in his Monday morning newspaper his attention may well be reversed. Emotional state can also influence perception. For example, the jealous husband is more likely to notice a compliment paid to his wife than a less jealous husband.

Consumers will tend to pay more attention to advertisements for products in which they have an interest. If the consumer has developed a brand preference then he will tend to notice advertisements for that product and may well overlook advertisements for competing products. Thus the interest of the owner of a Ford car is more likely to be aroused by an advertisement for a new Ford model than it is for, say, a new BMW. This factor must be taken into account when trying to measure the effectiveness of a new product promotion. Commercial advertising effectiveness ratings generally compare a given advertisement with others in the same product class to eliminate the effects of basic product interest, but the brand leader will generally be noticed more frequently than less popular brands.

In general, if the consumer is interested in a product then it is usually worthwhile to present more information about the product. For example, most car advertisements include details on performance, fuel consumption, and other special features in the hope that the consumer reading the advertisement will be stimulated to pay a visit to his dealer's showroom. For necessity products, such as washing powder, where consumer interest in the product itself is low, the marketer will need to pay more attention to stimulus factors in both promotional material and packaging.

Thus an individual's interests and motives may lead him positively to select certain information from his environment. This is known as *selective attention*. They will also influence the kind of information to which he is exposed. For example, a person with deep political convictions is more likely to attend political meetings of the party to which he is affiliated than he is to attend meetings of opposing parties. Such meetings are therefore more likely to reinforce the beliefs of the already committed than they are to bring about a change in attitudes. Through *selective exposure* we avoid coming into contact with information which may be contradictory to our strongly held beliefs and attitudes. This process has been termed *cognitive consistency* and was summarized by Katz[7] as follows:

(a) . . . an individual self-censors his intake of communications so as to shield his beliefs and practices from attack;
(b) . . . an individual seeks out communications which support his beliefs and practices; and
(c) . . . the latter is particularly true when the beliefs or practices in question have undergone attack or the individual has otherwise been made less confident of them.

Humans also exhibit *selective reception*. This was demonstrated by Mc Ginnies[8] in an experiment involving the use of a tachistoscope (a device which allows stimuli to be presented to a subject for brief controlled periods of time). Mc Ginnes exposed a mixture of neutral words (eg. dog, chair, book etc.) and emotional words (eg. raped, bitch etc.) to a number of subjects and gradually increased the exposure time until the subject correctly reported the word. At the same time he measured the subject's galvanic skin resistance (the resistance of the skin is thought to decrease as emotion increases). He found that significantly longer exposure times were needed when emotional words were presented than when neutral words were presented; the subjects' skin resistances were also lower in the case of emotional words. From these results he deduced that the subjects' emotional responses to certain words delayed their recognition. This process has been termed *perceptual defense*, and refers to a tendency not to report the presence of threatening or unpleasant stimuli under conditions when neutral or non-threatening stimuli are reported.

In this context it is interesting to note that appeals to fear either enhance or inhibit the response to an advertisement. In some cases, the consumer is motivated to follow the advice given in an advertisement in order to avoid an unpleasant situation. He may purchase a deodorant to avoid the stigma of body odour or buy insurance against fire or flood to his property. In other cases the use of fear can cause a defensive reaction and the consumer may avoid the advertisement (selective exposure) or repress its content (perceptual defense). Source credibility is important in fear appeals, and they are unlikely to be effective if the presenter is not considered sufficiently expert. Well-known and respected personalities are therefore often used to present such advertisements; for example, ex-Metropolitan Police Commissioner Sir Robert Mark has promoted the products of a tyre company.

Reactions to fear appeals, however, vary from individual to individual. Generally they are more successful with people who feel able to cope with a threatening situation or who do not see themselves as being vulnerable to a particular situation. But the more a consumer identifies with a threatening situation the more likely he is to adopt a defensive reaction and the less effective will be the use of fear. This was shown by Robertson[9] in a controlled study of the effect of advertisements for seatbelts which depicted particularly unpleasant scenes of accident victims.

If a message threatens an individual's strongly held preconceived attitudes or beliefs he may rationalize it in several ways. He may miscomprehend the message in such a way that it appears to fit in with his own beliefs. Alternatively he may reject the source and/or the content of the message as being biased. The marketer must be careful to avoid, as far as possible, such misinterpretations of his message by varying his promotional techniques. Media advertisements may need to be backed up by information leaflets, demonstrations and, in some cases, by a personal approach.

Expectations, or set: Expectancy, or set, plays an important part in the selection of what we perceive. It refers to a readiness to respond in a certain way to a given situation or set of stimuli, and may be the result of either known or unknown past experiences. Thus the engineer in our previous example, when walking around the factory, would probably have paid greater attention to factors influencing the cost of production if he had been told beforehand that this was to be discussed after the tour.

The influence of expectations on perception was demonstrated by an experiment carried out by Kelly[16]. A group of students were told that their normal lecturer would be away for their next class and a brief description of his replacement was circulated. Half of the students received a description of a 'rather cold person, industrious, critical, practical, and determined'. The rest of the students received a similar description except the words 'very warm' were substituted for 'rather cold'. During the lecture the reactions of the two groups of students were noted and at the end of the lecture the students were asked for their impressions of the replacement lecturer. Analysis of the results showed that the group of students that had received the description including the words 'very warm' described him as being 'more considerate of others, more informal, more sociable, more popular, and more humane' than the other group of students who had received the description including the words 'rather cold'. It was also noted that the students who had been told that the lecturer was very warm participated more in the discussion than the other students. The expectations aroused by the descriptions of the stand-in lecturer had clearly influenced the students' perception of him as a person, and had affected both their reported experience and behaviour. Our expectations are to a large extent a function of personality, attitudes, and cultural norms and values. We learn through the process of socialization to expect people to behave in certain ways in given situations. If a person smiles we will tend to react positively towards him, but if he scowls we may think twice before talking to him. These influences on behaviour are discussed in more detail in Chapters 5, 6, and 7.

Past learning also plays a significant role in the establishment of set responses. This is important to the marketing manager in view of the growing body of opinion which suggests that brand choice does not depend only on brand awareness but also on the consumer's evaluation of the product into distinct groups or sets. Faced with a number of product groups comprising a multiplicity of relatively similar brands, consumers will try to simplify their purchase decisions. Howard and Sheth[11] argue that consumers will select, from the brands of which they are aware, a smaller range of brands from which they will make their actual brand choice. This group is called an *evoked set*. Thus for any given product range there will be a number of brands of which the consumer is aware – the *awareness set* – and within this awareness set there will be a smaller number of brands which the consumer would actually consider purchasing – the *evoked set*. It is therefore not sufficient for a brand to feature in a consumer's awareness set; it must be included in the consumer's evoked set if it is to have any chance of being chosen.

It has also been suggested[12] that brands included in a consumer's awareness set, but which do not feature in his evoked set, can be subdivided into an *inert set* and an *inept set*. Brands included in a consumer's evoked set stand a high chance of being selected and must therefore be positively evaluated. The *inert set*, however, comprises brands for which the consumer has neither a positive or negative evaluation. This may be because of insufficient information about the product or the consumer may not perceive it to be in any way better than the brands in his evoked set. Brands included in the *inept set* are negatively evaluated by the consumer. This may be because of an unfortunate past experience or because he has heard bad reports of the product.

The relationship between awareness set, evoked set, inert set, and inept set is illustrated in Figure 2.1.

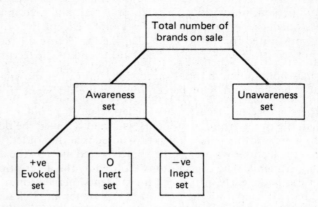

Figure 2.1 Relationship between awareness set, evoked set, inert set, and inept set

Only limited research has been undertaken to test this hypothesis but the results achieved suggest that consumers do try to simplify their purchase decisions by categorizing available brands into groups which they either consider or reject. The concept of evoked set can be useful as a market research technique since it may help the marketer to clarify the competitive position of his product and identify what the consumer perceives as being competing products. It is the consumer who decides which products are placed into a particular evoked set and this may not always be in accord with the marketer's own conception of the competition.

The concept of evoked set is also of interest because it suggests that the strategies that might be adopted by the marketer differ according to the way in which a brand is categorized by the consumer. If a brand does not feature in the awareness set of most consumers then a considerable amount of effort must be expended in drawing the attention of the consumer to the existence of the brand; this may involve a nationwide media campaign. If a brand features in the inert set of most consumers this will signal the need to provide more information about the product and to highlight its positive features. The marketer might therefore consider providing free samples or undertaking comparative advertising. For a product in the inept set of consumers more drastic action may be required. The advertising and promotional strategy may need to be revamped and possibly the product itself will need to be changed. For evoked set brands the promotional strategy would be defensive; the consumer would need to be reminded periodically of the brand's key features as this will serve to reinforce the consumer's buying decisions.

2.4 Organization of Perception

When we attend a concert we do not hear or see a number of discrete stimuli representing loud or high-pitched sounds, patches of colour, and variations in brightness, but rather rhythms and melodies, people, and objects. We hear music and words, and see musicians and instruments. Our raw sensory input has therefore been organized in some way and the perceived output is ordered and understandable to us. When we go to the cinema we do not see a number of separate snapshots shown in rapid succession, but rather moving figures against a stable background. Our perception is quite different from what would be expected from the stimuli received. Perception cannot therefore involve just the passive receipt of a number of different sensory stimuli. The *Gestalt* psychologists argued that perception is a dynamic process which results in more than would be expected from a simple summation of our sensory experiences. Their view is often expressed by the phrase 'the whole is greater than the sum of the parts'.

    Gestalt psychologists have shown that perception involves several different organizing tendencies. These tendencies rarely operate in isolation and in certain circumstances one may overrule another. It is, however, possible to categorize them under four broad headings : figure-ground; grouping; closure; contour.

2.41 Figure-ground

Perception of figure and ground is the simplest but most important organizing tendency. Our perception of the world consists of a number of objects which appear to stand out against the general background of our experience. Trees stand out against the sky and words against the page. Trees and words are seen as figure, while the sky and the page are seen as ground. The organization of stimuli into patterns of figure and ground is not confined to recognizable objects. For example, Figure 2.2 does not resemble any known object but nonetheless it is seen as an entity which is distinct from the page. It has a definable shape and appears to stand out from the page even though we

Figure 2.2 An unrecognizable blob appears as figure against the ground of this page

know it is only printed on the surface. By comparison, the ground seems formless and appears to extend continuously beyond the figure. Although it may just be possible to concentrate exclusively on the ground, our attention will keep returning to the figure.

Perception of figure-ground relationships is not confined to visual stimuli. When we watch a television interview, the words of the speakers appear to stand out against other sounds and noises in the room. The general posture of the speakers may be seen as ground, while movements of their hands or eyebrows to emphasise a point will be seen as figure.

In some circumstances there will be a reversal of the figure-ground relationship and the contour that previously bounded the figure becomes part of the ground. This is illustrated by Figure 2.3, which can be perceived either as a goblet or as two profiles. The goblet is seen as figure against a dark ground, while the two profiles can be seen as figure against a light ground. It is virtually impossible to see both the goblet and the profiles simultaneously.

Reversal may occur spontaneously, as in the case of Figure 2.3, or voluntarily, for example when one decides either to listen to the soloist or the orchestra at a concert.

Figure 2.3 Reversible figure and ground

2.42 Grouping

Objects which are close to one another tend to be grouped together. Thus when several different stimuli are presented together we tend to perceive them as a kind of pattern. Figure 2.4 shows a number of different examples of such groupings.

Figure 2.4 (a) illustrates the role of *proximity* or *nearness*. Instead of six separate parallel lines we see three pairs of parallel lines. The lines closer to one another are perceived as belonging together and constituting a group.

Similarity is also important in the patterning of stimuli. In Figure 2.4 (b) we see one large square formed by sixteen separate dots. A similar grouping is shown in Figure 2.4 (c), but in this case we see one large square made up of dots and a smaller square made up of circles. The dots are seen as one grouping and the circles another. The importance of similarity can be demon-

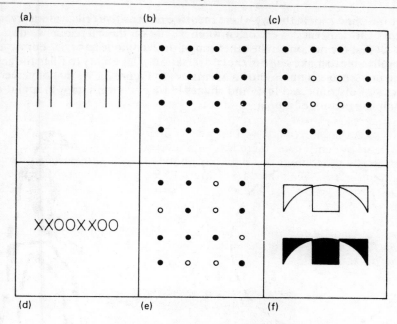

Figure 2.4 Perceptual grouping

strated by a simple experiment. Ask any of your friends to copy out Figure 2.4 (d). In the majority of cases you will find that they will unconsciously draw two Xs close together followed by a space and then two Os close together.

Grouping according to similarity only takes place, however, if there is some logic in the grouping. In Figure 2.4 (e) there is a mixture of both dots and circles but we do not perceive them as two separate groupings. The principle of *symmetry* or *good figure* takes precedence.

A final example of grouping is shown in Figure 2.4 (f). In this illustration we perceive a sine wave superimposed on a square wave and not the enclosed elements of the figure. This shows the importance of good *continuation*.

Grouping also occcurs with our other senses. Human speech involves a patterning of a number of sounds or phonemes, while the rhythm of music depends on the grouping of various tones over time. This capacity to group the stimuli presented by our sense organs according to proximity, similarity, symmetry, and continuation, lends structure to our environment and provides a good illustration of what is meant by *Gestalt* psychologists when they say that the whole is different from the sum of the constituent parts.

2.43 Closure

Our sense organs often do not provide us with complete information but we make sense of the information provided by filling the gaps. For instance, there is a blind spot in the eye where there are no sensitive cells, yet we are not aware of its existence. Very often when we are on the telephone we do not hear all that the person on the other end of the telephone has said, but we are generally able to make sense of the conversation. This ability to fill in the gaps left in our sensory input is known as *closure*. In Figure 2.5 we do not perceive a series of disconnected lines and shapes but a circle with gaps in it and an incomplete picture of a man.

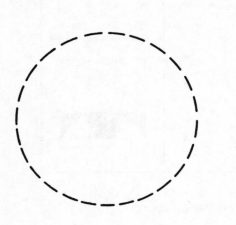

Figure 2.5 Closure – filling in the gaps

2.44 *Contour*

When we see an object such as a chair it appears to be surrounded by a line or contour. Contours give objects shape and are normally formed when there is

Figure 2.6 Two different faces shaped by the same contour

a marked change in colour or brightness. Shape and contour are not however the same, as shown in Figure 2.6. Our ability to perceive contour is closely related to closure as in many cases, for example when sunlight is shining on an object, there is little difference in colour or brightness between figure and ground.

The organizing tendencies of perception identified by *Gestalt* psychologists can work together or in opposition. The curves of Figure 2.7 (a) will appear to resemble Figure 2.7 (b) if grouping according to proximity takes place but Figure 2.7 (c) if closure occurs.

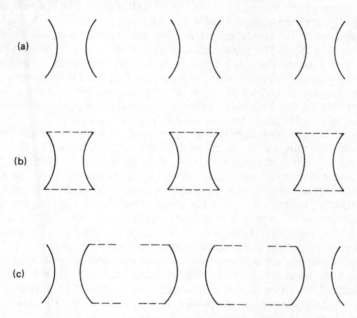

Figure 2.7 Opposing organizing tendencies

An understanding of the organizing tendencies of perception can be helpful to the marketer when devising promotional strategies. The principle of figure and ground can, for example, be used effectively in printed promotional material and in billboard displays to draw the attention of the consumer to important parts of the message. Grouping also may be used to encourage, or discourage, associations between a product and specific attributes. Fast foods, for instance, are often shown being enjoyed by fun-loving people who value convenience, while the low price of certain brands of cigar is inferred by advertisements which show them being enjoyed by ordinary people. Closure is a device that is frequently employed in advertising, particularly of well known brands, for example 'Sch . . . you know who', as it encourages the consumer to become involved in completing a message that might otherwise quickly habituate. Contour, again, is important in the design of certain products, particularly where a number of different materials are used, such as in a motor car.

It must be noted that there is a limit to the amount of information we can perceive at any one time. If two or more people are speaking simultaneously, we are unlikely to grasp all that is being said. Generally we will select one speaker and filter out others; our chosen speaker becomes figure and the others ground. *Channel capacity* is not, however, absolute and will depend on the nature of the stimuli and the way in which they are presented. If, for example, we are listening to two speakers and one begins 'Jack and Jill went up . . .' we might be led to expect that he intends to recite the familiar nursery rhyme. We would have developed a set and would only need to attend to the occasional word to assure ourselves that our expectation was correct — closure would fill in the gaps. Additional channel capacity would then be available to listen to the other speaker. Similarly, the words printed on this page are grouped for convenience in a pattern that has been recognizable to us since we learned to read. If, however, the information was presented in a less convenient form 'thecatsatonthemat' instead of 'the cat sat on the mat', the reading speed of most people would drop considerably.

As Woodworth and Schlosberg[13] comment: 'When the requirement is simply that the number of objects shall be correctly reported . . . the average span for keen adults is about 8 objects . . . Individual averages range from 6 to 11, and every individual varies about his own average . . .' In normal circumstances our channel capacity will be even lower and our attention will be constantly shifting. It is therefore important that the marketer trying to attract attention to his product keeps his message as simple as possible. A billboard or television advertisement which is seen for only a short space of time should ideally contain one clear message. The inclusion of additional extraneous information will only confuse the consumer and the principal message may be lost. Even when more time is available, such as in a salesman's presentation, only two or three principal themes should be developed. If at the end of the presentation the potential customer has clearly grasped these few key ideas then it can be judged a success.

2.5 Subliminal Perception

Although it has been established for some time that, under controlled laboratory conditions, individuals can perceive stimuli which are presented below their absolute threshold, there is continuing controversy regarding the existence of subliminal perception under normal uncontrolled conditions. Outside the laboratory the individual is forced to select between numerous stimuli occurring above the absolute sensory threshold. Is it therefore possible that he will attend to a stimulus presented below his sensory threshold?

Much concern regarding subliminal perception was aroused in the 1950s when a cinema owner claimed that flashing the words 'Eat popcorn' and 'Drink Coca Cola' on the cinema screen below the visual threshold had led to an increase in consumption of both popcorn and Coca Cola. During the six weeks of the experiment, sales of popcorn increased by 57 per cent, and sales of Coca Cola by 18 per cent[14]. Subsequent investigation failed to verify the claim that the increase in sales was a direct result of subliminal perception; certain changes in the physical arrangements inside the cinema had also taken place.

So far no convincing evidence has been obtained to suggest that subliminal perception can be effective in influencing individuals. In 1970, Hawkins[15] showed that people can be motivated by subliminally presented stimuli but the effect was very small and could easily be swamped by other stimuli presented under normal conditions. This is not surprising because a subliminal message must be brief and we know that, unless there is some interest or motivation on the part of the individual, stimulus factors must be strong. This, and the existence of perceptual defence against unwelcome stimuli, make it unlikely that subliminally presented information could influence a consumer to do anything against his will. Furthermore, even if subliminal perception could be effective in reinforcing existing attitudes, it would be difficult to exploit. As explained earlier, individuals' sensory thresholds differ and a stimulus which is below the threshold of one individual will be above the threshold of another. Thus unless the stimulus is so weak as to be below the absolute threshold of all individuals, and therefore so low as to be ineffectual on most individuals, some individuals would see or hear the message presented.

It is probably as well that the evidence in support of effective subliminal perception is not strong as otherwise there would rightly be concern about the ethical implications of influencing individuals without their being aware of such manipulation.

2.6 Implications for Marketing

A number of examples have already been given of the importance of perception to product evaluation. Consumers may try to evaluate directly a product's attributes by physical cues such as taste, smell, size, and shape. However, in some cases those physical differences that do exist between competing products may not exceed consumers' sensory thresholds. In other cases, even though the consumer is capable of discriminating between brands, he may not be sufficiently expert to determine which product differences are important in achieving satisfaction. This means that for a wide range of products the consumer is not able to make a judgement purely on the basis of a product's physical characteristics.

It is not surprising, therefore, that research evidence has shown that, for a number of products, brand preferences are based on non-product characteristics. Brown[16], for example, found that housewives perceived bread wrapped in cellophane to be fresher than equally fresh bread wrapped in waxed paper. Similarly, most disinfectants are purchased on the basis of smell, even though this has no connection with the ability of a particular brand to kill germs. For the marketer, consumers' use of surrogate indicators in product choice decisions means that a great deal of research may be needed to identify those indicators that are commonly used in purchase decisions for a particular product. As many of these indicators are illogical from the basis of fact, it is often the case that they can only be identified by intensive testing.

Price is often used as an indicator in product choice decisions, particularly in the perception of quality. Although micro-economic theory suggests that the lower the price the greater the satisfaction, or utility, obtained by the consumer, studies have shown that consumers judge the quality of some products by their price; a higher price being related to higher quality. The price-quality relationship, however, varies between products and appears to have most influence where the risk of the consumer making a wrong decision is great and where the consumer is least able to judge directly the quality of competing brands[17]. The price-quality relationship appears to be less important in the case of products where there are established brand names and where there is a high degree of product experience[18].

The marketer must always remember that perception is a process that is not only affected by direct sensory cues but is also influenced by individuals' past experiences, learning, and attitudes; and the surrogate indicators used by one individual to differentiate between brands may be quite different from those used by another. It is therefore important that the marketer researches his market fully before embarking on any major changes in product strategy. He should identify the attributes of particular market segments and be fully aware of any conflicting variables. There is no point in introducing a product promotion which appeals to one market segment but which alienates another. He must also take care to ensure that his strategy works in the buying situation. An advertisement involving a subtle play on words may appeal to the marketer in the seclusion of his office, but may be completely lost on the consumer who glances briefly at an advertising display.

One area in which particular caution must be exercised is the use of sex in advertising. Few studies have been undertaken in this area but the available results suggest that the market is comprised of different groups who react in varied ways to the use of sexual themes. Older people and feminists, in particular, are against the use of sex appeals in advertising[19]. Morrison and Sherman[20] found that sexual-romantic and non-sexual themes in advertisements appeared to be more successful in gaining attention than advertisements involving nudity. Similarly, Stedman[21] found that brand names accompanied by sexual illustrations were recalled correctly less often than those unaccompanied by such illustrations.

Marketers have long recognized the importance of projecting a favourable image for their product, as they realize that perception involves more than a rational evaluation of sensory data. Increasingly, however, companies are beginning to realize that their corporate image can be just as important in securing sales, particularly where new products are involved. A great deal of time and money may have to be spent by a company in establishing a reputation for quality and reliability for its various branded products. Why not capitalize on this investment? By drawing consumers' attention to the fact that several well known and respected brands are made by the same company, the consumer may generalize his preferences for these brands to other products produced by the same company. One way in which this can be done is by promoting an image through a corporate slogan, for example 'BP: Britain at its Best'.

Similarly, consumers' patronage of retail stores can be influenced by their perception of store image or 'personality'. Lazer and Wyckham[22] showed that not only do stores have identifiable images, but that these images appeal to specific socio-economic groups and to specific age groups. The images of individual stores not only arise from functional attributes such as location, convenience, and price and merchandise selection, but are influenced also by variables such as architecture, interior design, and decor. Retailers should therefore devote attention to the ambience of their premises, and may find that they will be more successful in appealing to a specific target market than to the mass market. Product marketers should also bear in mind store image when deciding on their distribution policy to ensure that there is no conflict between product image and the image of the outlets through which they are sold.

2.7 Summary

1. Perception involves the selection and organization of sensory data into a form that has meaning for the individual. It is influenced not only by direct experience of sensory data but is conditioned by past experiences, learning, and attitudes.
2. Attention is an important determinant of what is perceived. External factors controlling attention are intensity and size of the stimulus, position, contrast, novelty, repetition, and movement. These factors may be used in promotion campaigns as an aid to gaining consumers' attention.
3. Attention is also influenced by individuals' interests, needs, motives and expectations. To a considerable extent we perceive what we want to perceive. By a greater understanding of consumers' needs and expectations in the buying situation the marketer will be in a better position to devise appropriate marketing strategies for his products.
4. Perceptual processes organize the world around a person into objects and groups of objects. An awareness of these organizing tendencies, such as that provided by the *Gestalt* psychologists, can help the marketer to create an appropriate image for his product and draw the attention of the consumer to its positive attributes.

References

1. Markin, R.J. *Consumer Behaviour* (New York: Macmillan, 1974).
2. Galanter, E. 'Contemporary Psychophysics', *New Directions in Psychology*, R. Brown,(ed) (New York: Holt, Rinehart & Winston, 1962).
3. Husband, R.W. and Godfrey, J. 'An Experimental Study of Cigarette Identification', *Jour. App. Psychol.* 1934, 18.
4. Rudolph, H.J. *Attention and Interest Factors in Advertising* (New York: Funk & Wagnalls, 1947).
5. Yamanaka, J. 'The Production of Ad Readership Scores', *Jour. of Advertising Research*, 1962, 2.
6. *Media/Scope*. 'How Important is Position in Consumer Magazine Advertising?', June 1964.
7. Katz, E. 'On Reopening the Question of Selectivity in Exposure to Mass

Communications', *Theories of cognitive consistency: A source book.* Abelson, R.P. et al, (eds.) (Chicago: Rand McNally, 1968).

8. McGinnies, E. 'Emotionality and Perceptual Defence', *Psychol. Rev,* 1949, 56.
9. Robertson L. et al. 'A Controlled Study of the Effect of Television Messages on Safety Belt Use'. *Amer. Journal of Public Health,* 1974, 64.
10. Kelly, H.H. 'The Warm-Cold Variables In First Impressions of Persons' *Journ. Person,* 1950, 18.
11. Howard, J.A. and Sheth, J.N. *The Theory of Buyer Behaviour* (New York: John Wiley & Sons, 1969).
12. Narayana, C.L. and Markin, R.J., 'Consumer Behaviour and Product Performance: An Alternative Conceptualization' *Journ. Marketing,* 1975, 39.
13. Woodworth, R.S. and Schlosberg, H. *Experimental Psychology* (New York: Holt, Rinehart & Winston, 1960).
14. Brooks, J. 'The Little Ad that Isn't There', *Consumer Reports,* January 1958.
15. Hawkins, D. 'The Effects of Subliminal Stimulation on Drive Level and Brand Preference', *Journ. Marketing Research,* 1970, 7.
16. Brown, R.L. 'Wrapper Influence on the Perception of Freshness in Bread', *Journ. App. Psychol.* 1958, 42.
17. Lambert, Z. 'Price and Choice Behaviour' *Journ. Marketing Research,* 1972, 9.
18. Peterson, R.A. 'Consumer Perceptions as a Function of Product Colour, Price, and Nutrition Labelling'. *Advances in Consumer Research.* W.D. Perkeault Jr. (ed.), (Atlanta Association for Consumer Research, 1977).
19. Wise, G.L., King, A.L., and Merenski, J.P. 'Reactions to Sexy Ads Vary with Age', *Journ. Advertising Research,* 1974, 14.
20. Morrison, B.J. and Sherman, R.C. 'Who Responds to Sex in Advertising?', *Journ. Advertising Research,* 1972, 12.
21. Stedman, M. 'How Sexy Illustrations affect brand recall', *Journ. Advertising Research,* 1969, 9.
22. Lazer, W. and Wyckham, R.G. 'Perceptual Segmentation of Department Store Marketing' *Journ. of Retailing,* 1969, 45.

Further Reading

Gregory, R.L. *Eye and Brain* (London: World University Library, 1972).
Myers, J.H. and Reynolds, W.H. *Consumer Behaviour and Marketing Management* (Boston: Houghton Mifflin, 1967).
Vernon, M.D. *Experiment in Visual Perception* (Harmondsworth: Penguin, 1966).

Past Examination Questions

1. To what extent is perception influenced by motivation? What are the implications of this relationship to the design of an advertising

campaign? (IM 1975).
2. Discuss the effectiveness of the use of fear as an appeal in advertising. (IM 1976).
3. How might selective perception affect the organizational behaviour of a marketing manager in his interaction with general management? (IM 1979).
4. How can an understanding of the process of perception help the executive make better marketing and advertising decisions? (CAM 1977).
5. What an individual 'perceives' is conditioned by both inborn characteristics and experience. Give examples of both types of factor and indicate their possible value to the marketing executive. (CAM 1976).

3. *LEARNING*

'Since learning is such an important factor in what man is and does, a greater understanding of the learning process would go far toward increasing his self-knowledge.'

Winfred F. Hill.

3.1 Introduction

In common usage the term 'learning' refers to the acquisition of knowledge or skill, generally through the deliberate memorizing of information (in order, for example, to pass an examination) or set patterns of mechanical actions (in order, for example, to drive a motor car). In behavioural science, however, the term has a far more general meaning and refers to *any relatively permanent change in behaviour occurring as the result of experience or practice*. The following elements of this definition should be carefully noted:

1. learning results in a *change in behaviour* and can take place without awareness on the part of the individual. It can also take a positive or negative direction;
2. the change in behaviour must be *relatively permanent* and thus excludes changes in behaviour that may result directly from temporary conditions such as drug intake or fatigue;
3. the change is the *result of experience or practice* and as such excludes changes that result from maturation, physical damage, or disease.

In attempting to influence or manipulate behaviour it is important to understand how learning occurs. Unfortunately, learning, like most other behavioural topics, is a complex phenomenon but an insight can be gained by examining the basic elements of the learning process.

3.2 Factors in Learning

In every simple learning situation there are three factors that can be identified as being important. These are *association*, *reinforcement* (or reward) and *motivation*.

3.21 Association

The most basic form of learning is that arising through an association or connection in time and place between two events. Associations are formed between two stimulus objects (for example, cigarette and lighter) or between an action and its results (for example, an analgesic will alleviate pain). These associations develop from frequent repetitions of an action and can lead to

36

the formation of habits, which are more or less automatic responses to familiar situations or encounters. Thus, most shoppers rely on habit to ease the problem of choice presented by numerous brands and tend to buy the same brand of tea, butter or cornflakes that they bought last time.

It is the idea of association that underlines the concept of branding in modern marketing — advertising aims to develop an association between product and brand. Associations may be built by the simple repetition of a product's slogan with the brand name: for example, 'Beanz Meanz Heinz'. The shopper responds to the stimulus of a brand name simply because it is what has been learned in that particular stimulus-response association.

This simple association building, the association between stimulus and response (or the building of S-R bonds), is the central theme of the basic theories of learning, classical conditioning and operant conditioning, which are discussed below.

3.22 Reinforcement

Reinforcement is an important factor in building associations and was first formally recognized by Thorndike[1] in 1911 when he postulated his 'Law of Effect' which states, 'of the responses made to a situation, those which satisfy the organism's needs tend to be retained while those which fail to satisfy these needs tend to be eliminated'. In other words, if one obtains satisfaction from a particular act one will tend to repeat that act. But if satisfaction is not obtained then one will tend not to repeat that act. Thus the cold relief remedy which reduces cold symptoms most effectively and for the longest time period will reinforce the association between that particular brand and the alleviation of cold effects. The strength of reward or reinforcement is important in determining the strength of the association in learning. Being extremely satisfied with a particular product strongly predisposes the consumer to make a repeat purchase.

3.23 Motivation

Motivation is important because of its role in reinforcement. The concept of reward arises because the individual is learning to respond in order to achieve a need reduction. If there is no motivation, there is less need to learn associations. But if purchase of a particular product results in satisfaction or need reduction, a consumer will continue to respond to the same stimuli because of this satisfying experience.

The satisfaction acts as an incentive motivation for reducing the drive by purchasing the same product or brand which produced the satisfaction. The consumer has learned that this response results in the satisfying of a drive.

3.3 Connectionist Learning Theories

Although there is more to learning than the association of one event with another, it is useful to consider the basic learning theories and so we shall begin with an examination of classical and operant conditioning.

3.31 *Classical Conditioning*

Classical conditioning takes place when two stimuli are paired. One neutral stimulus initially elicits no response; this is called the *conditioned stimulus*. The second stimulus, the *unconditioned stimulus*, is one which always produces a reflex-like response, termed the *unconditioned response*. As a result of pairing the unconditioned stimulus with the conditioned stimulus, the previously neutral conditioned stimulus will give rise to a response which is similar, but not necessarily identical, to the unconditioned response. This is called the *conditioned response*.

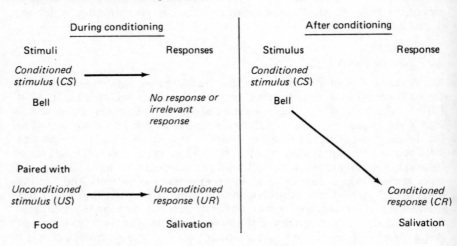

Figure 3.1 Summary of the classical conditioning process

The concept of classical conditioning was developed by the Russian physiologist Ivan P. Pavlov[2] during the late 1890s. Pavlov was primarily interested in the digestive systems of animals but his experiments with dogs established many of the basic principles which are today associated with classical conditioning.

One of his most famous experiments involved the association of the sound of a bell with the presentation of food. A dog was placed in a sound-proofed room in an apparatus which allowed a food pan to be swung out, by remote control, within the dog's reach. A bell was sounded and was followed immediately after by the presentation of food. The amount of saliva secreted by the dog (the unconditioned response) was then measured. After pairing the two stimuli, the food (the unconditioned stimulus) and the bell (the conditioned stimulus), a few times, only the bell was sounded and no food presented. Pavlov found the dog had begun to associate the sound of the bell with the presentation of food and salivated in response to the sound of the bell (the conditioned response). The experiment was resumed with the paired presentation of the bell and the food for a few more times and then with the bell alone. As the experiment proceeded Pavlov found the amount of saliva secreted in response to the bell alone gradually increased. He plotted the results as a learning curve. Figure 3.2 shows that the strength of the conditioned response increases with successive pairings of the conditioned and the unconditioned stimulus. The curve gradually flattens out towards a maximum response.

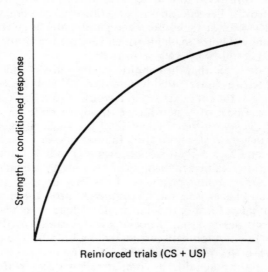

Figure 3.2 The Pavlovian learning curve

In similar experiments involving animals and humans Bekhterev[3] used a shock to the forelimb or hindlimb as his unconditioned stimulus. This produced an unconditioned response of arm or leg flexion. Just before the shock was delivered a conditioned stimulus, a tone for example, was presented. After repeated pairings of the tone followed by the shock, the subject animal promptly flexed its limb when the tone alone was presented. This *flexion response* to the previously neutral stimulus is the conditioned response in this experiment.

An important feature of this latter experiment is that the subject cannot escape the shock; he always receives it following the presentation of the conditioned stimulus. Also, unlike the Pavlovian experiment, no test trials were employed. In Pavlov's experiments trials were needed to establish whether salivation occurred with the conditioned stimulus alone. This is not necessary in flexion conditioning because the conditioned response anticipates the presentation of the shock.

Classical conditioning is not just a laboratory novelty but can be seen operating in everyday life. The housewife who purchases a new product, because of a price discount scheme, may continue to purchase the product even when the sales promotion scheme has ended. An association is established between the desirable price reduction (unconditioned stimulus) and the product brand (conditioned stimulus). If the product is of comparable quality and performance to competing brands, the association initially established by means of a sales promotion scheme may persist and in the short run the product may be selected despite the absence of further sales promotion.

Classical conditioning applies to many aspects of our daily lives. Children are conditioned to respond to a raised eyebrow, a frown, or other signs of parental disapproval. The salesman is conditioned to respond to changes in a potential buyer's voice or facial expression and many large companies have extensive training schemes through which salesmen are taught to respond automatically in certain ways to given situations.

It must be understood that the conditioned response is seldom identical to the unconditioned response. Pavlov discovered that if he conditioned an animal to salivate at the sound of a bell, it would also salivate at the sound of a buzzer or to the beat of a metronome, though to a lesser extent. This is termed *stimulus generalization*. The greater the similarity between stimuli, the greater the degree of generalization that occurs.

Stimulus generalization is of importance in product promotion since a positive association established through advertising a particular brand can be generalized to other similar products unless care is taken to differentiate between the brand advertised and its competing products. For example, an advertising campaign for a particular brand of lager may lead to a general increase in sales of lager beers. 'Knocking copy' can be used as a means of encouraging differentiation between competing brands. The advertising for the U.K. launch of the Fiat 127 in 1978, for example, stressed the positive design features of the Fiat model by comparing it with competing models produced in France, West Germany and the United Kingdom.

A conditioned response will not last indefinitely if it is not reinforced by the unconditioned stimulus. If the conditioned stimulus is repeatedly presented without being followed by the unconditioned stimulus, there will be a gradual weakening of the strength of the conditioned response. This is known as *extinction*. If, for example, a person has been conditioned to blink in response to a light, as a result of puffing air into the eye each time the light is presented, the conditioned eyeblink response can be extinguished by presenting the light without the puff of air.

A conditioned response that has been extinguished may, however, *spontaneously recover* some of the strength lost in extinction after an interval of rest following extinction. Thus after a period away from the experimental situation the person whose eyeblink response has been extinguished might react positively to a light. Usually by repeated re-extinctions, the conditioned response will eventually be extinguished more or less permanently. This is a technique used by psychologists to erase irrational phobias that might have been created by the generalization of a response to a particular stimuli.

The degree of spontaneous recovery after extinction will depend on the strength of the association developed between the conditioned and unconditioned stimulus and on the time interval between successive conditioning processes. This can be of critical importance to the marketer who has a limited advertising budget. Should he have one or two campaigns in a year or should he spread his budget through smaller but more frequent advertising campaigns throughout the year? If he is launching a new product it will generally be worthwhile to spend his budget on an intensive campaign in order to build up a strong association for his product. For an established brand the problem is more difficult and will depend on the type of product and on the activities of competitors.

Pavlov's experiments also established the existence of *higher order conditioning*, where one conditioned response is used to generate another conditioned response. A dog was first conditioned to salivate to the sound of a metronome. A card with a black square on it was then thrust in front of the dog just before the metronome was sounded. No food was given to the dog during this second stage. After several pairings of the card and the metronome, the dog started to salivate when the card with the black square was presented. The card was never paired with food but nonetheless it came to elicit the same response, salivation.

Higher order conditioning can be seen in the associations established between social groups and life-style. These associations are used by advertisers who wish to promote their products to particular social groups. It would clearly be inappropriate to show a prestige car against the backdrop of a council estate but rather with the trappings associated with wealth — a large house, a large dog, and an attractive woman. Where an advertiser wishes to widen the market for his client's product, he will often show it being used in a number of different settings, each aiming to appeal to a particular social group.

The existence of higher order classical conditioning is important as it seems probable that many of our subjective emotional feelings are conditioned responses. We are often not able to identify the origins of particular emotional responses to certain situations, but their roots may lie in classical conditioning situations.

3.32 Operant Conditioning

Operant conditioning (sometimes called instrumental conditioning) occurs when a response by the learner is instrumental in producing a reinforcing stimulus. The response producing the reinforcement becomes stronger, whereas that not reinforced becomes weaker. Operant conditioning differs from classical conditioning in two main respects. First, the learner is active and emits responses rather than having responses elicited from him by an unconditioned stimulus. Second, reinforcement is contingent upon certain responses. The response may be to obtain something that the individual needs — *positive reinforcement*, or it may allow the learner to escape from a painful or fear-producing situation — *negative reinforcement*.

Much of the work on operant conditioning has been undertaken by B F Skinner[4,5] in the United States. He developed what is known as a 'Skinner Box'. This has a lever at one end operating a food delivery or water delivery mechanism. A hungry rat is placed in the box and after an initial period of inactivity the rat begins to explore the box and eventually presses the lever.

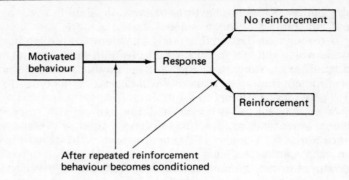

Figure 3.3 Summary of the operant conditioning process

After a time the rat begins to associate the depression of the lever with food. A cumulative and continuous record of responses is plotted against time and a graph similar to that shown in Figure 3.4 is obtained.

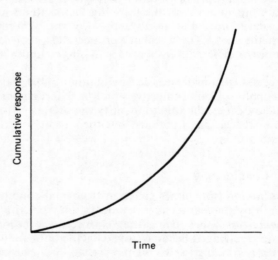

Figure 3.4 The operant learning curve

This simple experiment illustrates the basic features of operant conditioning. The rat first of all was motivated towards a goal — he was hungry. General exploratory activity takes place and in the course of this activity a response happens to be made which is instrumental in the rat achieving the food — he presses the lever and obtains a pellet of food. After a while the rat begins to associate pressing the lever with the attainment of his goal (his behaviour is reinforced) and pressing the lever becomes a learned response to his hunger motive. The essential feature of operant conditioning is that *reinforcement follows a specific response*.

As in the case of classical conditioning, stimulus generalization takes place with operant conditioning; the extent of the response being dependent on the degree of similarity between the original learning situation and the changed stimulus situation. It is also possible to obtain discriminatory behaviour through operant conditioning by, for example, presenting food to a hungry rat in a Skinner Box only when the box is illuminated. After a period of *selective reinforcement* the rat will learn only to press the lever when the light is on, but not when it is off. The light in this case acts as a *discriminative stimulus* controlling the response.

Answering the doorbell is an example of operant conditioning. A person is not forced to react to the sound of the bell ringing; it is a voluntary response − the individual is operating on his environment. He has, however, through experience learned that answering the door will fulfil a need for social contact or for information. In other words, his behaviour (answering the doorbell) will be reinforced. If he does not wish to have social contact he can decide not to react to the bell and leave the door unanswered. In this case, the bell also acts as a discriminative stimulus as previous experience will have taught the individual that there is little prospect of his behaviour being reinforced if he answers the door without the doorbell having first been rung.

Operant conditioning can be used to *shape* behaviour through the appropriate use of reinforcement. For example, a young puppy may be trained to walk to heel by being given a titbit or praise each time he undertakes desirable behaviour, thus reinforcing this behaviour. At first the puppy might be rewarded for walking rather than running and jumping. After a while reinforcement will only be given if the dog walks by the owner's side. The dog eventually comes to associate the approval of his master with walking quietly by his side.

As we have seen a reinforcing stimulus or event of some sort is essential in instrumental learning. A distinction is sometimes made between primary and secondary reinforcing. *Primary reinforcers* are those which reduce some innate or physiological need, such as the need for food or water, or to escape pain. *Secondary reinforcers* become effective as a result of previous stimulus-response situations. For example, prior to being placed in a Skinner Box a rat is given a sip of sugar water every time a buzzer sounds. The rat is then put into the Skinner Box, but instead of reinforcing the rat with sugar water, it is reinforced with the buzzer that had previously been paired with sipping water. The buzzer is found to work very well as a secondary reinforcer and increases the rate of lever pressing.

Secondary reinforcement is an important feature of everyday life and an integral part of the process of socialization of the child as is shown in Chapter 5. Parents rarely use primary reinforcers to shape behaviour. Instead, secondary reinforcers such as praise, encouragement, and threat of punishment are used to shape new learning and to maintain learned behaviour. To be effective, a secondary reinforcer requires prior association with a primary reinforcer. In the socialization process the child may initially have come to associate parental approval with a primary reinforcer such as food, as most mothers will smile and give encouragement when they are feeding a young baby.

Reinforcement need not be given for every response. Where reinforcement is given for some, but not all, responses (known as *partial reinforcement*) learning is usually found to be slower than under *continuous reinforcement*. However, behaviour learned as a result of partial reinforcement is maintained for far longer in the absence of any reinforcement – that is, the learned behaviour is more difficult to extinguish. There is a danger that partial reinforcement according to a prescribed schedule may lead to discriminatory behaviour. For this reason, random partial reinforcement is usually the most effective way of maintaining learned behaviour. The respondent will be encouraged to gamble that his actions will be rewarded the next time he responds in a certain way to a given situation.

Random partial reinforcement is used as a basis for sales promotion schemes such as competitions. The consumer is encouraged to purchase a certain product because it provides the opportunity to enter a competition and satisfy a need, perhaps to own a motor car. Only a minority of those entering the competition will obtain reinforcement and win a prize. A large number of people will, however, have been persuaded to buy the product. If they find it satisfactory, its purchase could become a learned response.

Sales promotion schemes of this type need not be directed at a particular product or brand but can be used, for example, to promote a particular chain of stores. All customers shopping at the store within a specified period are given the added incentive of a chance to win a prize. For example, the supermarket chain 'Keymarkets' have used a bingo promotion where every shopper is given a bingo ticket which could win him a prize.

Operant conditioning has a powerful influence over our daily lives and is responsible for most voluntary behaviour. Responses to certain situations are learned because they result in need fulfilment, the response being instrumental in bringing about a reinforcing stimulus. The need that is fulfilled may be either positive or negative – that is, *positive reinforcement* or *negative reinforcement*.

Positively reinforced behaviour is goal-directed. Negative reinforcement, by comparison, is directed towards escaping or avoiding a particular event or situation. An aversive stimulus may be avoided either by making no response – *passive avoidance* – or by making a specific response which prevents the occurrence of the aversive stimulus – *active avoidance*. Active avoidance may, for example, involve a person who dislikes travelling in lifts taking a positive decision to use the stairs. A person who has experienced an aversive reaction to heights, however, may avoid the aversive stimulus of being at the top of a hill or building by refraining from climbing hills or buildings. In passive avoidance the aversive stimulus can sometimes be termed punishment. A child is taught to avoid certain behaviour under the threat of punishment by the aversive stimulus of a smacked bottom.

When a consumer purchases a particular product and is satisfied, his behaviour will be positively reinforced and there is a high probability that he will buy the product again. If he continues to obtain satisfaction from the product its purchase may become a learned response and brand loyalty will be established. However, if through a manufacturing problem the product is found to be faulty, or if the customer feels that the product does not live up to its manufacturer's claims, the purchase of the product will be negatively reinforced and the customer may consciously avoid purchasing it again. This can create serious problems for the manufacturer concerned as it may be difficult to extinguish a negatively reinforced response. If, for example, the cars produced by a particular manufacturer develop a reputation for rust, it may take many years to overcome this reputation even though corrective action was taken soon after the fault had been discovered.

3.33 Comparison between Classical Conditioning and Operant Conditioning

There are two essential differences between classical and operant conditioning. These are:

1. classical conditioning involves unconscious (involuntary) learning, while operant conditioning involves conscious (voluntary) intent on the part of the learner;
2. in classical conditioning the learner's responses do not influence the delivery of the reinforcing stimulus, while in operant conditioning reinforcement is contingent upon a certain response.

Classical conditioning can be seen as a kind of stimulus substitution. By pairing two stimuli, the previously neutral conditioned stimulus is seen to emit a response similar to that previously associated with the unconditioned stimulus. (Pavlov's dogs learned to salivate at the sound of a bell). Operant conditioning, on the other hand, is drive-related and behaviour that is reinforced is encouraged to persist. (Skinner's rats found that pressing the lever would lead to the presentation of food).

Neither classical nor operant conditioning will persist in the absence of reinforcement (that is the learned responses can be extinguished) and in both cases generalization will occur to other similar situations. The positive involvement of the learner in operant conditioning, however, also permits discriminatory behaviour and shaping of the response.

The key feature of classical and operant conditioning is that both involve the establishment of an association or connection between stimulus and response. This is why they are termed connectionist theories or S-R theories. They say nothing about the learner himself and how he can influence the learning process. For this reason they are sometimes referred to as 'black box' theories as in their crudest form they assume the individual is not able to influence his environment and is, therefore, open to manipulation by various stimuli.

But each individual and each learning situation is different. The individual's perception of a particular stimulus will depend on his personality, motivation, past experiences, and emotional response to that stimulus. If we are to further our understanding of the learning process we must move on from the simple S-R theories, which work well under controlled laboratory conditions, to the real world and take account of cognitive variables which intervene between the occurrence of a stimulus and the given response.

Stimulus-Response theories, as applied to marketing, assume a passive role on the part of the consumer. But buying is a problem-solving situation, especially for durable and infrequently purchased goods. The consumer here plays an active role in the purchasing response. This appears to be recognized, for example, in the advertising of products such as motor cars where a great deal of information about style, comfort, and performance is presented.

The next section of this chapter is therefore largely concerned with what are known as S-O-R theories. The 'O' which intervenes between S (stimulus) and R (response) is called the *organizing force* and represents the cognitive variables inherent in the individual and the learning situation.

3.4 Cognitive Learning

Although extremely useful in demonstrating the relationship between variables involved in the learning process, the problem with connectionist learning is that it may lead to too much concern for piecemeal activities and give far too little attention to organized relationships and meaning. Learning cannot be satisfactorily explained in terms of conditioned associations; attention must be given to the roles of cognitive processes such as perception and knowledge. The studies in this area have lead to the formulation of the concepts of 'insight learning' and 'latent learning'.

3.41 Insight Learning

This concept originated with the work of Kohler[6] in a series of experiments with chimpanzees that involved solving complex problems. At some point in working on a problem the chimpanzees appeared to grasp its inner relationships through insight; that is, they seemed to solve the problem not by trial and error, as in conditioning experiments, but by perceiving the relationships essential to the solution.

A moderate degree of insight is so common to human experience that we tend to take it for granted. Occasionally insight comes dramatically and then we have what has been called the 'Eureka' experience: the solution of a problem becomes immediately clear as though a light had suddenly been turned on in the darkness. Although the variables that influence insight learning are not well understood the following factors seem to be important:

1. insight depends on the arrangement of the problem situation. Past experience does not guarantee a solution and insight will come easily only if the essentials for solution are arranged in such a way that the relationships can be perceived. (This is directly related to the organizing forces of perception referred to in the last chapter);
2. once a solution occurs with insight, it can be repeated promptly;
3. a solution achieved with insight can be applied in new situations. Insight does not involve the learning of a specific set of conditioned associations but rather a cognitive relationship between a means and an end.

3.42 Latent Learning

Latent learning refers to any learning that is not demonstrated by behaviour at the time of the learning situation. Such learning goes on in the absence of reward but when a suitable reward appears use is made of information previously learned.

The major contribution to the theory of latent learning was made by Tolman[7,8] whose research was concerned with the problem of rats learning their way through a complex maze. To Tolman, a rat running through a maze was not learning a sequence of right and left turns, but rather was developing a *cognitive map*; that is, a mental picture of the layout of the maze. If a familiar pass became blocked, the rat adopted another route based on the spatial relations represented in its cognitive map. In explaining how rewards and punishments influence behaviour Tolman distinguished between learning and performance. In the latent learning situation the rat learned something about the spatial arrangement of the maze but this learning was not evident until reward motivated the animal to perform.

Tolman's work suggests that, for learning, reward and punishment serve to convey information rather than imprinting specific behavioural responses and eliminating others. Performance (i.e. responses), on the other hand, is determined by knowledge about rewards and punishments learned through past experience. The response with the greatest expectation of reward is likely to be the one that is chosen. Part of Tolman's theory is the concept of 'sign − *Gestalt* − expectation'. This is the individual's expectation that the environment is organized and certain things will lead to others. These expectations are about stimuli which are signs of certain things, rather than about responses. *Gestalt* (a term the reader encountered in the Chapter on perception) indicates that these signs must be considered in the context presented; it is the whole pattern of stimulation that is important.

Tolman's ideas go far beyond those of the 'black box' connectionist learning theories. Tolman was attempting to consider the intervening variables that occur between the stimulus and response. The individual forms many kinds of cognitions about the way the world is structured, about how goals can be achieved, and about what things go together. Cognitions from several different learning experiences may thus be put together so that the individual can respond adaptively to new situations and thus achieve his goals.

However, the major problem with Tolman's theory is that in introducing more variables than are found in the comparatively simple S-R series, the effect of each variable on the outcome becomes far more difficult to understand with the result that prediction, a main aim of theory, becomes far more difficult. But in marketing we are very much concerned with a complex mix of variables that constitute a product or brand. As Clarke and Roe[9] pointed out: 'It would be apparent that the "model" on which we are working looks something like the diagram on the left, when what it should actually be is the one on the right' (of Figure 3.5).

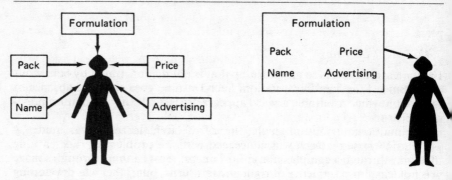

Figure 3.5 Mix Model

Source: Clarke, K. and Roe, M. 'The Marketing Mix Test — Relating to Expectations and Performance', MRS Conference Papers, 1977. (By kind permission of the authors and the Market Research Society)

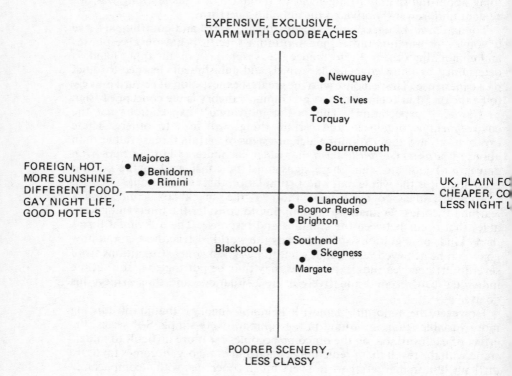

Figure 3.6 Perceptual mapping of certain constructs of holiday resorts

Source: adapted from Riley, S. and Palmer, J. 'Of Attitudes and Latitudes', *Journ. MRS*, April 1975. (By kind permission of the authors and the Market Research Society)

Another difficulty with Tolman's work is that the term 'cognitive map' places too much emphasis on spatial information when the concern is for all types of knowledge structure in memory. At the time Tolman conducted his research it was difficult to study and understand fully the extent and influence of these intervening variables. However, computers now allow the use of multidimensional scaling techniques to construct perceptual maps. These allocate objects to space; and by using attribute vectors or points, it is a simple process to define that space, indicating the degree that attributes are distributed amongst the objects or brands occupying the product space. A perceptual map of different holiday resorts is shown in Figure 3.6.

From Figure 3.6 it can be seen, for example, that the West Country resorts are perceived as being the most expensive and exclusive while the eastern coast resorts are perceived as being less classy.

The possibility of conceptually mapping consumers' cognitions in a quantitative manner has many implications for marketing practice. Sampson[10] draws attention to the following:

1. the interpretation of maps provides descriptions of, and insights into, the system of perceptions that different groups of consumers use to compare, contrast and evaluate a set of brands. Such knowledge about positioning can be useful in the planning and determination of focused and selective communication strategy. The use of an 'ideal' brand for a given market or a market segment can aid the new product development planning and screening process. Moreover, just as spatial proximities provide some indication of closeness of competition, so the absence of points in a space may indicate a market opportunity. Thus mapping may be a basis for gap analysis . . .
2. from the standpoint of usefulness of mapping to advertising planning, an advertiser may seek to move his advertised brand towards some more favourable position with or without some formulation change (e.g. using advertising to reposition the brand).

3.5 Memory and Forgetting

It is fairly obvious that all learning must imply memory (that is the storage of previously acquired information). If nothing could be remembered from previous experiences, then nothing could be learned.

3.51 Memory

There are three essential stages in the memory process. These are:

1. *encoding* – the transformation of sensory data into a code that is acceptable to the memory process;
2. *storage* – the retention of that code in the memory mechanism;
3. *retrieval* – the recovery of the information from storage.

Research indicates that these three stages of memory do not operate in the same way in all memory situations. This has led to the view that there are two types of memory:

1. *Short term memory* where material is stored for a matter of seconds.
2. *Long term memory* where material is stored for longer intervals (even for a whole life time).

Short term memory has been said to correspond to the active part of total memory whereas long term memory corresponds to the passive part of total memory.

A neurophysiological or biochemical explanation of the differences between these two types of memory is beyond the scope of this book, but it is useful to consider the processes involved in each and also the relationship between them.

1. *Short term memory*: Encoding requires that information must be given attention. Selective perception ensures that only certain information will be encoded and stored. Thus very little of the vast amount of information to which the individual is exposed at any one time ever enters memory. Short term memory storage capacity appears to be very limited. Most adults seem to have a capacity for seven items plus or minus two. That is, some people are capable of storing as few as five items whilst others can store as many as nine. An item is the largest meaningful unit that can be found in the information presented and can consist of digits, letters, words or even phrases. But whatever the nature of the unit employed, the storage capacity is approximately seven units. When this limit is reached a new item can enter short term memory storage only by replacing one already held. Retrieval takes place by means of a search process in which each item held is examined in turn.

2. *Long term memory*: The extent to which information is encoded appears to depend on the extent to which that information is meaningful or the extent to which meaning can be given to it. Thus in encoding a person's name, meaning might be provided by simultaneously encoding a mental picture, or image, of that person. Although imagery appears to be important, there is also much evidence that a semantic code is involved in encoding. Storage capacity for long term memory appears to be almost unlimited but retrieval appears to be dependent upon an appropriate retrieval cue; that is, anything that can trigger the retrieval of information held in long term memory storage. In a normal adult, poor memory is probably the result of retrieval failure rather than storage failure and it may be a truism that the better the retrieval cues, the better the memory.

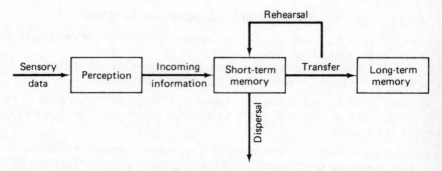

Figure 3.7 The relationship between short term and long term memory

Although there are alternative viewpoints on the relationship between short and long term memory, a typical theory is that of Atkinson and Shiffrin[11]. This theory assumes that information enters short term memory but cannot stay there without 'rehearsal'; this being the term given to the recycling of the same items in short term memory. For example, in studying a foreign language a new word is repeated over and over again. (It must be noted that rehearsal is silent, inner speech and must not be confused with mere repetition — rehearsal in fact implies an active, conscious interaction with the incoming information). Information that is rehearsed is then transferred to long term memory. This process is illustrated by Figure 3.7.

3.52 Forgetting

As shown above, forgetting in short term memory is a function of the limited capacity of the storage mechanism. Since storage capacity is limited to seven items, plus or minus two, a new item can only be stored if an existing one is displaced. For long term memory, forgetting appears to be a function of the lack of appropriate retrieval cues. However, there are other factors that inhibit the individual's ability to retrieve information. These are:

1. *retroactive inhibition* — the memorizing of new information inhibits the recall of previously memorized information, for example, when a salesman finds that a customer has changed his telephone number. After memorizing the new number the salesman may find it difficult to retrieve the old number since the storage of the new one inhibits retrieval of the old one;
2. *proactive inhibition* — previously memorized information inhibits memorizing of new information. For example, a supermarket has a new manager, the previous one having been there for several years. A salesman used to dealing regularly with the previous manager may find it difficult to remember the new manager's name;
3. *emotional factors* — whereas excitement (positive emotion) can assist retrieval, anxiety (negative emotion) can inhibit retrieval. Thus, a student's anxiety about failing an examination may inhibit his attempts to retrieve information in the examination situation;
4. *repression* — this was first identified by Freud and postulates that the individual will subconsciously avoid retrieving information associated with unpleasant events. Thus, a salesman might forget he has been asked to visit a certain customer because of some particularly traumatic experience previously connected with the customer.

3.53 Methods of Improving Memory

Since this book is primarily written for students whose aim is to pass an examination, which in turn requires them to memorize information, it is appropriate, given the above discussion of memory, to indicate some of the methods by which memory may be improved.

As has been shown, the capacity of short term memory is fixed for each individual and, therefore, the only way to increase the amount of information that can be held in short term memory storage is to group items into more easily manageable pieces. Thus, for example, the number 24543842 (8 digits) can be more easily handled by being broken into the manageable pieces 24-54-38-42 (4 items). It is, however, obvious that there is a distinct limit on the extent to which short term memory can be improved.

Long term memory, on the other hand, can be greatly improved by the individual becoming more efficient in the way he encodes and retrieves information. One method is to organize the information so it is more easily encoded and retrieved. For example, in studying the Law of Contract, instead of attempting to memorize a list of terms it is far more effective to memorize the fact that there are six major elements and that these may be represented by the word LACICO (being made up of the first letters of the terms legality, acceptance, consideration, intention, capacity, offer). Another useful tool is to give meaning to information by the use of imagery. For example, in memorizing the theory of classical conditioning outlined above, rather than attempting to memorize the words contained on the page, it is more effective to memorize an image of what happened in the experiment – the dog being presented with food, a bell ringing etc.

A method which combines both organization of material and imagery is that of patterning information rather than organizing information in tabular form; this is a method promoted by Buzan[12] and for interested readers it is recommended that his book *Use Your Head* is consulted. Another imagery retrieval method is that of using context. For example, in trying to recall who was at a particular social event it is often more effective to try to visualize the room in which the event took place rather than just to recall a list of names. Finally, a factor known as depth of encoding can be very effective in improving retrieval. This, quite simply, entails expanding on the meaning of information. For example, in relation to Pavlov's experiments, elaboration of the information given could be achieved through asking what kind of dog was the subject of the experiment, or what kind of food was provided for the dog, or what kind of bell was rung. The greater the elaboration of information, the better the chances that memory of the basic story should improve.

3.6 Implications for Marketing

A prime task for marketers is to inform consumers, through advertising and promotion, about the merits of particular products in an attempt to influence purchase; and this obviously involves a learning process on the part of the consumer. Although a great deal of research has been undertaken on various aspects of the learning process, our knowledge is far from being complete. The above sections have outlined some of the processes identified by psychologists as affecting the learning situation. It is now useful to review how the learning process appears to operate on the purchase behaviour of the consumer.

Simple Stimulus-Response (classical conditioning) theory tells us that a stimulus will bring about a response. In this sense advertising or promotion seeks to establish a connection for the consumer between the product or brand and the consumer's attitudes and needs. But this in itself may not motivate the consumer to buy the particular product. Operant learning theories suggest that behaviour that is reinforced will be repeated. Thus, if consumers are reinforced (that is, they are rewarded through being satisfied with the product or brand), then they are likely to repeat that purchase behaviour with regard to that particular brand. Continual reinforcement results in consumers perceiving that the consumption of one brand is more rewarding than the consumption of another, and consequently forming a habit of buying the chosen brand. Habit is therefore an important feature of product purchase and in the building of brand loyalty. Every decision to purchase a particular brand that is reinforced will strengthen the association between the brand and the consumer's needs until its purchase becomes an automatic and unconscious learned response. For this reason, it is often very difficult to get consumers to try a new product and the marketer may find it helpful to offer free samples or conduct in-store demonstrations of his product.

If the product or brand lacks distinctive features, however, there is a danger that consumers might generalize and buy a similar product. It is therefore important that marketers ensure that brands appear as distinctive as possible through advertising, promotion, packaging, product performance etc. If a brand is similar to other products and has no distinctive attribute then a major task will be to create a unique selling point and thereby ensure a perception of value for uniqueness even where there is none. This can explain why retailers' own label products, whilst cheaper, do not generally enjoy significant market share. For example, in 1979, Heinz had approximately a 45% share of the U.K. baked beans market even though own label brands were 10% cheaper. Although distribution coverage does much to explain Heinz domination of the U.K. baked beans market, it is obvious that there is a perceived advantage, whether real or imaginary, for many consumers with regard to the Heinz label.

Connectionist theories of learning demonstrate the importance of time and frequency of product exposure to purchase. A product must be available to a customer at the time he is motivated to buy it, as otherwise he may find some other way to fulfil his need or he may leave it unsatisfied. This highlights the importance of distribution in product marketing and explains why manufacturers of confectionery and cigarettes make use of vending machines in public places. Frequency of product exposure, through advertising and other forms of promotion, is also important, particularly in the case of less frequently purchased items, as periodic reinforcement is essential if a learned response is not to become extinguished.

Whilst providing a valuable contribution to our understanding of the basic variables involved in learning, connectionist theories are an over-simplification of what happens in a very complex process. They can, however, be useful in understanding simple buying situations, for example regular good purchases, where one brand may easily be substituted for another. But for more important purchases, for example consumer durables such as refrigerators and motor cars, intervening variables play a significant role. A person's past experience may influence his perception and behaviour and therefore the response of consumers to marketing stimuli may differ considerably. As Levy[13] stated:

> . . . the things people buy are seen to have personal or social meanings in addition to their functions. Modern goods are recognized as psychological things, as symbolic of personal attributes and goals, as symbolic of social patterns and strivings.

Thus consumers learn in different ways and a promotional strategy that works for one consumer may not work on another.

3.7 Summary

1. Learning is a relatively permanent change in behaviour occurring as the result of experience or practice.
2. The important factors involved in the learning process are association, reinforcement, and motivation.
3. Theories of learning can be classified as connectionist and cognitive.
   (a) Connectionist theories involve the establishment of an association between a stimulus and a response. The best known theories are classical conditioning (work of Pavlov) and operant conditioning (work of Skinner).
   (b) Cognitive theories attempt to take into account all variables that impinge on the learning situation. Such theories are influenced by the principles of *Gestalt* psychology (work of Kohler) but the most important contribution comes from the work of Tolman.
4. Memory, which is necessary for learning to occur, has three stages: encoding; storage; retrieval. Memory can be divided into short term and long term.
5. Learning is important to marketing because of its influence on product perception and brand loyalty. Consumers associate particular brands with the fulfilment of particular needs. Through an understanding of learning theory the marketer can plan product and promotional strategies more effectively.

References

1. Thorndike, E.L. *Animal Intelligence* (New York: Macmillan, 1911).
2. Pavlov, I.P. *Conditioned Reflexes* (G.V. Anrep, trans., London: Oxford University Press, 1927).
3. Bekhterev, V.M. *General Principles of Human Reflexology* (New York: International, 1932).
4. Skinner, B.F. *The Behaviour of Organisms* (New York: Appleton-Century-Crofts, 1938).
5. Skinner, B.F. *Science and Human Behaviour* (New York: Macmillan, 1953).
6. Kohler, W. *The Mentality of Apes* (trans E. Winter) (New York: Harcourt Brace, 1925).
7. Tolman, E.C. *Purposive Behaviour in Animals and Men* (New York: Appleton-Century-Crofts, 1939).
8. Tolman, E.C. 'Cognitive Maps in Rats and Men', *Psychol. Rev.* 1948, 55.
9. Clarke, K. and Roe, M. 'The Marketing Mix Test-Relating Expectations and Performance' *MRS Conf. Papers*, 1977.

10. Sampson, P. 'Some Experiences with Mapping' *MRS Conf. Papers*, 1977.
11. Atkinson, R.C. and Shiffrin, R.M. 'The Control of Short-term Memory' *Scientific American*, 1971, 224.
12. Buzan, Tony. *Use Your Head* (London: BBC Publications, 1974).
13. Levy, S.J. 'Symbols by Which We Buy' *Advancing Marketing Efficiency*, L.A. Stockman, ed. (Chicago: American Marketing Association, 1959).

Further Reading

Bolles, R.C. *Learning Theory* (London: Holt, Rinehart & Winston 1975).
Hilgard, E and Bower, G.H. *Theories of Learning* (New Jersey: Prentice-Hall, 1975).
Hill, W.F. *Learning : A survey of Psychological Interpretations* (London: Methuen, 1964).
McLaughlin, B. *Learning and Social Behaviour* (New York: Free Press, 1971).

Past Examination Questions.

1. 'The stimulus-reponse theory as applied to marketing suggests that stimulus (product) should provoke a response (purchase)'. Why can this statement at best only be regarded as naive and oversimplified? (IM 1974).
2. A number of factors affect the learning process. Which of these factors do you consider have immediate application to marketing practice? (IM 1975).
3. What do you understand by the term 'learning'? Briefly outline any one learning theory and discuss its relevance to an understanding of consumer behaviour. (IM 1978).
4. What do you understand by the stimulus-generalization concept? How might a retail chain make use of it? (IM 1979).

4. MOTIVATION

'I take the view that human motives are not only usually impossible to ascertain, but are in any case seldom unmixed; it is therefore best to avoid making value judgements about them, and to leave the facts to speak for themselves.'

Professor Leonard Schapiro

4.1 Introduction

Marketing seeks to satisfy consumers' needs and aims to persuade consumers that the use of a certain product or service will satisfy a particular need or group of needs. Marketing managers must ensure that their staff perform at a high level, and consequently often spend much effort in designing elaborate incentive schemes. However, if the motivational patterns of consumers and employees cannot be adequately identified and exploited then effort will be wasted and may even be counterproductive.

There has been a great deal of research undertaken in the field of motivation, but few studies have provided an adequate basis for the development of a comprehensive framework necessary for an understanding of the subject as a whole. The main problem is that of attempting to study not only apparent and conscious motives, but also the unconscious and hidden motives of a highly complex social animal who exists in a dynamic environment. Since the economic, social, and political climate is constantly changing, so are the needs of consumers and employees, and appeals that may provoke action today may not do so tomorrow. Thus there is a constant requirement for the marketer not only to be aware of all the motives governing action at any one point in time and their interrelationships, but also to be able to predict the nature and extent of changes. A complete picture is unlikely to emerge until research techniques become more sophisticated.

It is therefore the aim of this chapter to describe the nature of motivation and the ways in which it can be studied and explained, given existing knowledge and technology, and to discuss its application to marketing.

4.2 A Classification of Motives

Motivation is the general term used to describe the interrelationship between needs, behaviour aimed at overcoming needs, and the fulfilment of these needs. It is a dynamic process which, in its simplest sense, can be thought of as having three separate stages. Firstly, the states that motivate behaviour, such as being thirsty or cold. These are generally referred to as motives, drives or needs. Secondly, the behaviour motivated by these needs or drives. This is often called instrumental behaviour since it is usually instrumental in achieving the third stage, namely the attainment of an objective or goal. In its simplest form motivation can be illustrated by the Figure 4.1.

Figure 4.1 A simple model of the motivation process

A person who has been without food for a day will experience hunger. The hunger drive will result in behaviour directed towards obtaining food. Having eaten, the individual will no longer pursue the need for food since he will have achieved his goal.

While food can easily be identified as having the qualities which correspond to the biological motivation of a hungry man, in complex modern societies the process of eating and drinking has taken on a much wider social significance. The type of food a person eats, the place where he eats it, and the people with whom he eats, will depend on a complex interrelationship of economic and social drives. A person who regularly takes his lunch in a pub may do so from a need for human contact, whilst another may wish to conform to certain group norms – that is, to be 'one of the boys'. Yet another may do so because he can often meet useful business contacts and so enhance his career prospects.

Motives may be *learned* or *unlearned*. *Unlearned* motives include the basic *physiological drives* and *primary drives* that appear to have no obvious physiological basis. *Learned* or *secondary motives* arise where, through learning, previously neutral stimuli arouse motive states. Social motives are the most important learned motives.

Motives can also be positive or negative. *Positive goals* are those which a person strives to attain, an example being the desire to join an exclusive club. *Negative goals* are those which a person tries to avoid, such as difficult or unpleasant situations.

Thus a broad classification is possible, enabling motives to be categorized into four main types, as shown by the matrix in figure 4.2

	Learned	Unlearned
Positive	Getting married	Eating
Negative	Visit to dentist	Childbirth pains

Figure 4.2 A broad classification of types of motive

4.21 Physiological Drives

These include hunger, thirst, temperature regulation, and sleep. It is essential to the survival of the body that a balance is maintained among internal physiological conditions. The general term given to this concept is *homeostasis*. An imbalance in any of these physiological conditions will lead to automatic physiological responses to minimize the imbalance and these responses may often be the stimulus to further behavioural reactions by the individual. For example, if body temperature becomes too high the body will perspire. In addition, the onset of perspiration may cause the individual to behave in such a way as to achieve a more comfortable temperature; he may take off his coat or open a window.

Sexual motivation and the maternal drive are also examples of unlearned physiological motives. They are very powerful motivating forces, yet unique as biological motives in the sense that the survival of the individual does not depend upon them in any way. They are, nonetheless, essential to the survival of the species.

4.22 Primary Drives

An examination of the everyday behaviour of animals, children, and adults indicates that there are several primary drives which appear to be unlearned yet are not related to any physiological stimuli. All are, however, essential if a person is to be effective in interacting with his environment. Primary drives include the need for activity, for perceiving and exploring the environment, for manipulating things, and for contact with other people and other objects. For example, before they have learned to talk, small babies are active in exploring their environment. They take interest in strange noises and shapes, and like to handle strange objects.

Primary drives, like other motives, can be satisfied. Interest in a novel object or situation tends to diminish over time. Children may play exclusively for many hours with a new toy and then completely lose interest in it.

4.23 Learned Motives

Socialization, a topic which will be reviewed in the next chapter, has an important influence on the expression of physiological and primary drives. Religious norms, for example, modify the expression of the hunger drive; Roman Catholics may still abstain from meat on a Friday, while Jews and Moslems are forbidden to eat pork. The need for physical activity is socially acceptable when expressed in the form of team games such as rugby or soccer, but socially unacceptable if expressed in street corner brawling.

Learning plays an important part in motivation by the creation of secondary drives and secondary goals. As we saw in the last chapter, secondary drives will often result from classical conditioning. A person who works long hours in order to feed, clothe, and house his family may for instance find that working hard provides the opportunity for human contact and also improves his social prestige. In time he may acquire the secondary goals of human contact and prestige and will continue to work long hours even though the need to provide a basic standard of living for his family is no longer apparent.

Instrumental learning is also a factor in the creation of secondary goals. If a person is constantly reinforced for certain actions, those actions and ideas will become dominant. For example, a child that is regularly rewarded by parental praise every time he makes an achievement statement, such as 'I want to be a doctor', will be reinforced and in time a secondary goal, for achievement, is learned. Many of the secondary goals acquired through instrumental learning involve other people. These include social values such as courtesy, respect for superiors, honesty, law obedience, and cleanliness. Such social values govern relationships between people, and determine the material and social objectives which they strive to achieve or preserve.

Human behaviour is characterized by complex motives such as the need for prestige, power, achievement, and social approval. Many of these complex goals are secondary goals acquired while learning how to obtain primary goals. Thus, the millionaire who seeks power may have found that in his earlier days the material rewards he sought to satisfy his basic physiological drives depended upon his ability to influence the actions of others.

Human drives and goals are connected in diverse ways and each individual combines them uniquely. Several secondary goals may be related to a single primary drive and conversely several drives may be satisfied by a single goal. Two individuals with the same goal may be satisfying quite different drives, while those with the same drive may satisfy it with different goals. Prestige may, for example, be satisfied by one person through being successful in his job, while for another the goal is that of being a pillar of local society.

Learned goals, as was shown in the last chapter, have to be reinforced periodically if they are to survive. However, it is often the case that motivated behaviour will continue long after the original primary or secondary goal has been achieved, a further secondary goal having taken its place. For example, in the case of the millionaire mentioned above, the satisfaction of physiological needs has ceased to be a primary goal and has been replaced by the secondary goal of power.

Motives are often classified as being conscious or unconscious. But while physiological drives are often consciously acknowledged, it is more difficult to categorize primary and secondary goals in this way. A person may not know his real motive, even though he may think he does, because several drives and goals are inextricably intertwined. In other cases, an individual may not wish to recognize some of his motives and may repress them, perhaps because they were fashioned under unpleasant conditions or because they are in conflict with other deeply held personal or social values.

4.3 Theories of Motivation

Research on motivation has mainly been concentrated on exploring the detailed behavioural responses to common motive states. The results obtained have mainly served to illustrate the complexity of motivation and the interrelationships which exist between drives and goals.

A number of theories of motivation have been proposed, but most of these appertain to particular motive states in specific contexts, or form part of more general theories. For example, the theories proposed by Hertzberg and Vroom, which are discussed in Chapter 10, were developed from studies of the work situation. Freud's Psychoanalysis Theory, discussed in Chapter 7, whilst being known as a theory of personality, has also a great deal to say about motivation since motive states are important determinants of an individual's personality.

In this section, we shall examine two general theories of motivation. Maslow's Theory takes into account both unlearned and learned motives, and is important because it offers an explanation of the individual's pursuit of certain goals in preference to others. McClelland's Theory, on the other hand, is concerned with complex motives and is important because it does much to explain man's behaviour in advanced societies.

4.31 Maslow's Theory of Self-Actualization

Maslow[1] characterized human needs into five groups which are arranged in a hierarchy of importance. The five groups of needs, arranged from lower to higher levels are:

physiological needs, such as hunger, thirst, sex, and activity;
safety needs, such as security, order, and stability;
belonging needs, such as love, affection, affiliation, and identification;
esteem needs, such as prestige, success, and self-respect;
self-actualization.

The ordering of these groups of needs is of significance, firstly, because it is the order in which needs tend to appear during development, and secondly because it is the order in which they need to be satisfied. As soon as the needs on a lower level of the hierarchy have been fulfilled, those on the next level will emerge and demand satisfaction. Thus people in poor societies will tend to be principally concerned with the satisfaction of physiological and safety needs and will not be particularly interested in the higher needs. In more affluent societies, however, the basic needs will usually be easily satisfied and greater emphasis will be placed on esteem needs and self-actualization.

Maslow's hierarchy of needs has often been illustrated by means of a pyramid structure (see Figure 4.3) which shows the relationship between the various groups of needs, not only in terms of their position in the hierarchy but also in relation to their importance.

Maslow's theory also distinguishes between needs according to whether they fulfil a deficit or growth function. All the needs included in the first four levels of Maslow's hierarchy are *deficit needs*. They are stimulated by the absence of something required; for example, a lack of food, a lack of security, a lack of affection, or a lack of prestige. Meeting these needs results not in satisfaction but the reduction of dissatisfaction.

Many writers have seen Maslow's fifth need for self-actualization as an

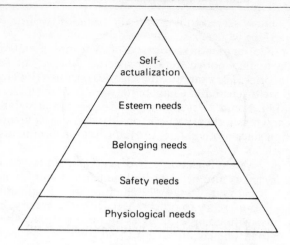

Figure 4.3 Maslow's hierarchy of needs

extension of the esteem needs and have overlooked the fact that according to Maslow self-actualization is the only source of real satisfaction. Self-actualization, an inner need to develop one's full capabilities, is the only growth need and sole potential source of happiness. It means different things to different people, as each individual has his own potentialities. For some it will mean achievement in creative or scientific fields, for others it will mean bringing up a well-balanced family. It is a feeling of accomplishment and of being satisfied with oneself.

Maslow's theory implies that motivation must be cyclical in nature. As soon as one group of needs is fulfilled, other drives become predominant. These higher level drives will modify goal directed, or instrumental, behaviour at lower levels. For example, a person who has fulfilled a physiological need for shelter and a safety need for security by finding somewhere to live may begin to look on his abode as a means of satisfying social or esteem needs. He may become concerned about the type of house in which he lives and its location and will consequently strive to obtain a better house in a more desirable locality. Thus Figure 4.1 needs to be modified to take account of this cyclical pattern as shown in Figure 4.4.

Maslow's theory can be a useful tool for the marketer. Physiological needs are the most basic needs, requiring satisfaction before all other needs. A feature of the physiological needs is that they have to be satisfied regularly and provision often has to be made in advance for their satisfaction. Consumption of products related to these needs tends therefore to be high and easy access by the consumer is important. Advertising can be used to emphasize either the physiological benefits of the product, such as its nutritional value, or its convenience as a means of satisfying these needs.

A food or drink manufacturer marketing a luxury product may however find that, rather than appeal to the physiological need for food and drink, it is

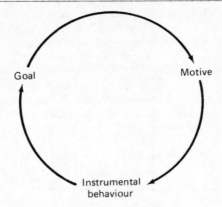

Figure 4.4 The cyclical nature of motivation

preferable to identify his product with the satisfaction of one of Maslow's higher needs. He may, for instance, appeal to belonging needs and display his product in a social context. Alternatively, he could appeal to esteem needs and suggest that by serving the product to friends the social status of the consumer will be enhanced.

As a generalization, income and social status will determine the position of consumers in Maslow's hierarchy. The marketer should therefore aim to project his product in terms of those needs yet to be satisfied by his target market.

Maslow's theory also has important implications in the job situation. For most people in industrialized countries, the money earned through employment provides the means of satisfying physiological needs and most safety needs. Job security and pension provisions are therefore important because without them the means of satisfying the basic needs is threatened. A major error in industry, however, is an oversimplification of human motivations. Too often it is assumed that the only reason that people work is to earn money. But whilst money can be an aid to the attainment of the higher needs in Maslow's hierarchy, it cannot necessarily fulfil all safety, belonging, and esteem needs.

Security needs can be fulfilled if workers know that hasty decisions will not be made by management: if it is clear what is expected of them; if they are aware of all the relevant rules and regulations affecting job performance; and if they can predict with reasonable accuracy the behaviour of their immediate superiors. Belonging needs can be satisfied by a friendly working atmosphere, good communications, and some attempt to involve workers' families in the job situation through open days, social clubs, and children's Christmas parties. Esteem needs could be satisfied by merit awards, advancement programmes, and by the encouragement of respect for others' abilities, whatever their position in the company.

The satisfaction of these deficit needs will not, however, necessarily lead to high job performance. People will only perform at high levels if they find their work interesting and challenging and if it provides an opportunity for self-actualization. It is therefore essential that employees are conscious of the contribution that they make to the company's performance and this requires adequate feedback on the results of their efforts. Employees should be encouraged to identify with the goals of the company and have some discretion over the way in which the goals attached to their own jobs are achieved. In this way the individual will be provided with the opportunity to link the company's success to his own efforts and experience a sense of achievement.

4.32 McClelland's Theory Of Need Achievement

McClelland, in contrast to Maslow, did not study the whole range of human needs, but concentrated on the learned motives for achievement, affiliation, and power. He is best known for his work on the achievement motive[2].

McClelland argues that people can be broadly classified into two groups: those that have a high need to achieve and are challenged by the opportunity to succeed; and those who have little or no ambition to be successful. Individuals having high achievement motivation prefer situations in which they can take personal responsibility for a particular task. They show a tendency to set moderate achievement goals and are prepared to take calculated risks to achieve them. If a problem is too simple, the person with high achievement motivation will obtain little satisfaction from success, while a very difficult problem will usually carry a higher probability of failure and provide less chance that the individual's achievement need will be fulfilled. People with a high need to achieve tend to learn faster and make decisions more quickly than those with low achievement motivation. They are also active seekers and users of information. It is important, however, to people with high achievement motivation that they receive feedback on the results of their efforts, for without this they are unable to derive satisfaction from these efforts.

The strength of the achievement motive varies from individual to individual – not, according to McClelland, because of innate differences, but because of variations in childhood training, parental attitude, cultural values, and education. This latter point was particularly significant for McClelland and his associates who were interested in the problems of underdeveloped countries and the relationship between economic growth and entrepreneurial activity. High achievement motivation is an important factor in entrepreneurial activity and, as it appears to be a learned motive, this suggests that training can be used to reinforce the achievement motive learned in the course of socialization.

McClelland's work on the achievement motive is of importance to the marketer who wishes to motivate his staff to a high level of performance. It suggests that careful consideration should be given to the identification of work targets so that they provide the achievement-motivated individual with sufficient challenge and opportunity for satisfaction. Attention must also be given to the feedback of information on an individual's performance. McClelland's work further suggests that jobs requiring innovative skills would be best performed by those having high achievement motivation, while repetitive tasks, which would provide little satisfaction for the achievement-motivated individual, might be better performed by those with low achievement motivation.

McClelland himself has drawn attention to the dilemma facing achievement-motivated individuals in large complex organizations. Such individuals are primarily concerned with personal improvement and on doing things for themselves. While this may be possible in a small organization, the manager in a large organization could not personally tackle all the tasks necessary for the successful performance of his job. He must direct the work of others and this may delay and obscure the feedback he obtains on the results of his efforts. For this reason, he may find it difficult to delegate work to others. This may partly explain why a number of people who perform well in one job may be totally unsuited to the managerial position to which they are promoted as a result of their successes elsewhere. This phenomenon forms the basis of the book *The Peter Principle*[3].

McClelland's more recent researches[4] suggest that power, or the need to influence the actions of others, is probably the most important attribute for the successful manager. The need for affiliation, that is the need to interact with others, is even less appropriate than the need for achievement. Effective managers, however, score high on inhibition as well as power, and this suggests that the power motive for such individuals is directed towards the organization and the people for whom they work, rather than towards personal aggrandizement.

Little empirical evidence is available on the role of need achievement in buyer behaviour, although research by Landon[5] has indicated that men with high achievement scores tend to prefer products that are considered virile and masculine, for example boating equipment, straight razors, skis, and manual lawn mowers. Men with low achievement scores, on the other hand, preferred products of a more fastidious nature, such as automatic dishwashers, headache remedies, mouthwash, and deodorant. The results were less distinct for women and this suggests that the need for achievement is more closely related to the male sex role than to the female sex role.

4.4 Frustration

Frustration occurs when there is perceived interference with the attainment of a goal. It can arise as a result of both internal and external barriers preventing the satisfaction of a particular need. External causes of frustration are those arising from the environment; for example, a traffic jam preventing an individual from keeping an appointment or an apparently pointless government regulation which prevents the sale of a product in a particular market. Internal causes of frustration are twofold. Firstly the choice of goal may be inappropriate. This is often the case when an individual sets his sights too high and there is a discrepancy between his level of aspiration and his ability or level of performance. The second cause of internal frustration is conflict between two or more motives, where satisfaction of one goal means frustration of another.

The intensity of frustration experienced by an individual will depend on the relevance and significance of perceived needs at a particular time and on the nearness of the individual to his set goal. Reactions to frustration are many and varied and will depend both on the individual and on the frustration situation. An individual's ability to cope with frustrations will be affected by his maturity, his time perspective, his values, and the social pressures upon him to achieve his goal.

4.41 Responses to Frustration

The most common responses to frustration are learned adjustments to behaviour. Upon experiencing interference with the attainment of a goal, a frustrated person will usually vary his behaviour until he hits upon a response which is reinforced. As a result of such *problem-solving behaviour* he may see his way round the barrier and achieve his goal. If this does not work, he may seek an alternative solution to the problem by redefining his need or goal. He may lower his level of aspiration or seek alternative ways of satisfying his needs or goals. A person seeking to fulfil achievement needs through academic success for which he lacks ability, may instead pursue creative goals to which he is better suited. This is known as *sublimation*.

If there is no easy way of overcoming a frustration situation through learned adjustments, the individual may seek to minimize or withdraw from the conflict situation. He may come to terms with the situation, resign himself to failure, and substitute new needs or goals for those that have been thwarted. Such reaction to frustration is known as *compensation*. This differs from sublimation in that it is normally associated with a sense of failure or loss of self-esteem. In an attempt to reduce this feeling of failure, the drive to succeed in the new venture is often very strong. Alternatively, an individual may lose interest in his desired goal and experience *apathy*. In other cases he may retreat from the conflict situation either physically, for example, by leaving his job or by experiencing a real or imagined temporary illness, or mentally, by resorting to *fantasy*. Here, he may have stimulating daydreams of assisting in the downfall of his enemies. Closely related to fantasy is *regression*, when behaviour becomes childlike in an attempt to simplify or escape from a conflict situation.

Aggression is a common reaction to frustration and can be displayed in a number of ways. It can be *constructive*, leading to renewed and more persistent effort to achieve the desired goal, or *destructive*, aimed at the elimination of the persons or barriers perceived as interfering with the attainment of a goal. Destructive aggression can take a number of forms. It may be *direct* verbal or physical assault aimed at the perceived cause of the frustration. Alternatively, it can be *displaced* and directed towards an available scapegoat or turned back on to the individual himself or on to things he values. *Displacement* is related to the concept of generalization which was discussed in the previous chapter. When aggression cannot be satisfied directly it becomes aimed towards situations perceived to be in some way similar to the frustration situation. A man who gets angry with his boss, but is afraid to argue with him, may go home and shout at his wife on the smallest of pretexts. The increase in child and wife battering is seen by many psychologists as a disturbing example of displacement as a reaction to the frustrations of modern life. Another example of a generalized response to a particular situation is *fixation*. In such cases, behaviour is repeated even though it is known that it will not lead to the attainment of the desired goal.

Repression usually occurs when there is no apparent escape from a frustration situation. It is a reaction common when frustration results from motivational conflict involving one or more negative goals and where there is fear attached to the attainment of these negative goals. A conflict between two negative goals will arise, for instance, when a person is faced with the choice between doing a job he intensely dislikes or leaving his job and facing a loss of income which will prevent him from satisfying other desirable goals. Repression is a form of forgetting through which the individual stops thinking about the conflicts involved. It may not, however, be completely successful as a means of reducing the fear associated with such situations. Even though the reason for the conflict may be repressed, there still remains a general feeling of uneasiness, known as *anxiety*.

In an attempt to reduce anxiety a person may disguise a motivational conflict in a number of ways. He may convince himself that his motive is exactly the opposite to his real motive. Often when a person appears to be too friendly or unduly affectionate towards another, it is likely that he harbours hostility or other negative feelings towards that person, which are being disguised by the opposite kind of behaviour. This defence mechanism is known as *reaction formation*. Another common defence mechanism is *projection*. This arises where an individual ascribes his own motives to others. For example, a student who feels a strong desire to cheat in order to get good marks, but is prevented from doing so because of his own moral code, might become unduly suspicious of others and accuse them of cheating even though they are innocent.

An individual may also disguise conflicting motives by *rationalization*. Here, he conceals an unacceptable motive by convincing himself that his behaviour results from some other socially acceptable motive. A salesman who is an alcoholic may rationalise his heavy drinking by convincing himself that it is a necessary part of his job in winning new clients.

4.42 Uses of Frustration

There is nothing abnormal about frustration or about the defence mechanisms used to relieve it. Only when these defence mechanisms fail to be effective and when a person continues to experience a great deal of anxiety does abnormal behaviour such as neurosis or paranoia result.

How then can knowledge of frustration aid the marketer? Frustration can be usefully employed in the job situation when it results in problem-solving behaviour. In such situations a limited degree of frustration will provide a challenge which makes the attainment of the goal more rewarding. High degrees of frustration will however result in misdirected effort and can lead to the loss of good personnel. Managers must therefore be aware of the frustrations inherent in a particular job situation and seek a balance between the positive and negative side effects on behaviour. There is no simple rule of thumb, as individuals' reactions to frustration will vary according to their personalities. While one individual may appreciate the challenge of a highly frustrating job environment, another will work better if he is given a succession of limited goals, each of which he feels capable of fulfilling.

In advertising, a product can be portrayed as a means of overcoming potentially frustrating situations. TV dinners are shown as a simple way of resolving a conflict between hunger and a favourite television programme. Again, sitting back and enjoying a good cigar may be shown as a way of opting out of a conflict situation.

4.5 Motivation Research

The basic tenet of successful marketing is knowledge of the target market and the identification of factors common to that market which can be used to promote a particular product. But marketing takes place in a human arena in which behaviour is governed by a complex interrelationship between different drives and goals. No number of facts and figures on the size and profile of a market will explain *why* an individual purchases one product in preference to another. This is the aim of motivation research.

Motivation research is not concerned with overt behavioural responses but rather with the reasons why individuals behave as they do. It aims to provide an insight into the attitudes, beliefs, motivations, and environmental pressures that influence purchasing decisions. These influences may not be apparent from conventional market research, either because they are not consciously appreciated by the consumer or because the consumer feels that an honest answer would create an unfavourable impression. Some years ago, an American company marketed the ultimate in convenience products; a cake mixture to which only water needed to be added. After an initial flurry, sales fell to a low level. It was not clear why the product had failed so abysmally as all market trends indicated that consumers were demanding convenience products. Motivation research revealed that the housewife needed to feel that she had made a contribution to the success of the final cake and felt cheated when only water needed to be added. As a result the company changed the product by making it necessary to add an egg as well as water to the cake mixture. Sales increased and the product was a success[6].

The techniques of motivation research are derived from experimental methodology used in social psychology and clinical psychology and their application in marketing was pioneered by Dichter. Two techniques borrowed from social psychology are the depth interview and the group discussion. The depth interview takes place in an informal atmosphere and the respondent is encouraged to talk about a subject rather than answer a list of specific questions. The group discussion is a similar technique in which groups of up to ten persons are asked to discuss predetermined aspects of a product buying or ownership situation. The general flow of the interview or discussion and the emphasis given to various aspects of the subject all reveal a great deal about the subject and the way it is perceived by the participants. It may not always be desirable to inform participants in depth interviews or group discussions of the real subject of the research. Where this is the case, the discussion is usually kept on a broad level at first and gradually directed by the researcher to the core of the problem.

Group discussions are often more fruitful than individual depth interviews, as the interrelationship between the group members usually results in individual participants reviewing their own initial reactions to the subject and adding new perspectives to the discussion. However, where the subject matter is delicate and one on which individuals may feel embarrassed to disclose their views to strangers, a personal interview will be more appropriate. Difficulties can arise in group discussions when one or more of the participants are revealed to be opinion leaders, a topic that is discussed in Chapter 7. Whilst the researcher should in these circumstances encourage the other members of the group to air their own opinions, it is often the case that they will conform with the views put forward by the group leaders. It may therefore be difficult to ascertain whether the group leaders are stating generally held views which the remainder of the group are afraid to express or whether the conformists in the group have modified their views in line with those expressed by the opinion leaders.

Depth interviews and group discussions require highly skilled researchers to conduct the interviews and to interpret the results. If there is to be comparability between the results of a series of interviews or discussions, the researcher has to ensure, through prompting, that each discussion covers the same aspects of the subject. If this is not done, bias will be introduced into the results. But even using highly qualified staff, the problem of bias cannot be totally eliminated. Each researcher is governed by his own attitudes and beliefs and these will influence his interpretation of the results of the interviews or discussions. The choice of participants is also a potential source of bias and objective criteria must therefore be established regarding the selection of participants in motivation research. In recent years, tape and video recorders have been used to reduce the risk of bias in the interpretation of results. They enable a number of researchers to review the data obtained and each can give his own assessment of the salient points.

From clinical psychology, motivational researchers borrowed projective techniques. The basic idea behind these techniques is to present a person with a situation which will make him unknowingly reveal some of his personality characteristics by projecting them into the presented situation. Some of the principal projective techniques are:

1. *Thematic Apperception Test (TAT)*: the subject is shown a picture or photograph of a situation that is open to a number of interpretations. Most people tend to identify with one of the characters in the picture and reveal feelings and desires about the depicted situation which they might otherwise be unwilling to discuss openly or might be unwilling to admit to themselves.

   A variation on the Thematic Apperception Test is to ask the subject to fill in a blank 'balloon' or caption in a cartoon. This can be a useful technique for obtaining attitudes regarding social interaction situations.

2. *Rorschach Test*: the subjects are shown ink blots and asked to assign

meaning to them. The interviewer will then probe more deeply to ascertain why that particular response was given. This technique has only limited use in marketing as a means of investigating the personalities of specific groups of people.

3. *Word Association Test*: here a subject is required to give a single word response to each word presented to him by the researcher. The words mentioned will include 'test' words related to the product, interspersed between neutral words. Those responses associated with the test words will provide an insight into the way in which the consumer views the product. One of the problems in using such a test lies in semantic differentials; that is, the different emphasis and connotations of words to different social groups. There are many variations on this test such as word matching, sentence completion, and story completion.

The problem with projective techniques is that convincing proof of their validity is lacking and too much depends upon the interpretation given by the researcher. Whereas there was a considerable vogue for the use of such tests in the 1950s, emphasis is now placed on the group discussion and depth interview as the foundation for further quantitative research. That is, qualitative research is generally used as a basis for defining the parameters of the research problem and not as a means of providing a solution to the problem. The main variables in a buying situation, or advertising awareness situation, can be ascertained through depth research. Those variables are then used to form the basis for a structured questionnaire.

There is, as yet, no conclusive evidence on the value of motivation research techniques to marketing, and opinions on the subject vary widely. Advocates of the technique argue that it has provided valuable insights into consumers' underlying motivations and that it can be particularly helpful in the formulation of hypotheses that can later be verified by quantifiable research techniques. Dichter, one of the staunchest advocates of motivation research, stressed the role of emotion in the buying process and argued strongly that products must convey to consumers a feeling of emotional security, and appeal to subsurface motivating factors such as the need for conformity. Critics of motivation research as a practical research tool in marketing point to the difficulty of interpreting with any clarity the results of such research and the ease with which bias can affect these results. On a different level, Vance Packard[7] raises the moral and ethical problems of probing into individuals' subconscious motivations. He writes 'The most serious offence many of the depth manipulators commit, it seems to me, is that they try to invade the privacy of our minds'.

4.6 Implications for Marketing

For the marketer, an understanding of the process of motivation is of fundamental importance, for our motives not only inspire us to take action but they also provide direction to that action. In primitive societies, individuals' motivations are primarily directed to the fulfilment of the basic needs for food, warmth, shelter, and security. However, as societies advance and incomes rise, human motivations become more complex. The producer is no longer in the position of meeting readily identifiable needs, but of providing a product that captures the attention of the consumer as a means of satisfying an unconscious need. We move from a production-orientated economy to a consumer-orientated economy.

As motives become more complex, the individual is less able to appreciate the motivational basis of his behaviour. Indeed, it appears that many consumers see the acquisition of a particular product, for example a car or a mink coat, as a goal in itself, and do not realize that it is only a means of satisfying a complex need. By understanding the basis of higher order motives, the marketer is better placed to influence the consumers' goal-directed behaviour to the purchase of his product.

Motives also serve as a means by which consumers evaluate competing products, either consciously or unconsciously. For example, the car buyer who is motivated by the need for security, may be particularly attracted by safety features such as child-proof locks, head restraints, and a collapsible steering wheel. On the other hand, the car buyer motivated by convenience may instead be attracted by electric windows, central door locking, and electronic speed control. If the car manufacturer can identify whether both these needs are shared by his target market, or whether one predominates, he will be in a better position to design his product and decide upon an appropriate promotional campaign.

In any product choice decision, the consumer is faced with the task of evaluating whether the purchase of a particular brand will be more likely to satisfy his needs than the purchase of another. Bauer[8] has pointed to the consumers' need to minimize risk in the buying situation and argues that the consumer acts to minimize this risk. He seeks support for his buying decision and this may come from the strong corporate image of the company marketing the product or from the information contained in promotional material. The marketer is therefore in a position to influence decision-making and may do this by pointing to product features that the consumer may otherwise have overlooked. For example, the manufacturer of a range of crockery may point out in its literature that it is suitable for use in a dishwasher and, by so doing, may add to the consumer's evaluative criteria a product feature that was previously not considered. Such a strategy may have particular impact on consumers who aspire to own a dishwasher as a means of meeting status needs.

As pointed out earlier, an understanding of motivation is vital to the marketing manager who wishes to maximize the efforts of his staff. The factors influencing employee motivation are considered further in Chapter 10.

4.7 Summary

1. An understanding of the process of motivation is of fundamental importance to the marketer, not only because of the implications for product formulation and promotion strategy but also because of the implications for the manager who aims to achieve a high level of job performance by his staff.

2. Motivation is the term given to describe the interrelationship between needs, behaviour aimed at overcoming needs, and the fulfilment of these needs (i.e. the attainment of specific goals). It may be described as being cyclical in nature since as one need is satisfied, others become predominant.
3. Motives may be classified into the unlearned physiological and primary drives and the higher learned or secondary drives. Within this classification they can be further categorized as being positively or negatively directed.
4. Secondary goals become more important to individuals as societies progress. Their acquisition is a product of socialization and learning. Theories such as classical and operant conditioning do much to explain their development.
5. Theories of motivation attempt to provide a conceptual framework for the understanding of the existence and development of various motive states.
   (a) Maslow has proposed a general theory which orders various need types into a hierarchy and offers an explanation of the reasons for certain goals being pursued in preference to others.
   (b) McClelland is concerned with higher-order needs and concentrates his work on the concept of need achievement.
6. Frustration results from the situation where there is perceived interference with the attainment of a goal. Reactions to frustration may be positive (for example, problem-solving behaviour) or negative (for example, aggressive behaviour).
7. Motivation research aims to provide insight into the attitudes, beliefs, motivations, and environmental pressures that influence purchasing decisions. Although projective techniques have been used in the past the main techniques are now the depth interview and the group discussion. Although very useful to marketing, care has to be taken in interpreting the results of such research because of the bias that can be introduced by the researcher.

References

1. Maslow, A.H. *Motivation and Personality* (New York: Harper and Row, 1954).
2. McClelland, D.C. et al. *The Achievement Motive* (New York: Appleton-Century-Crofts, 1953).
3. Peter, L.J. and Hull, R. *The Peter Principle* (New York: William Morrow, 1969).
4. McClelland, D.C. and Burnham, D.H. 'Power Is The Great Motivator', *Harvard Business Review*, 1976, March/April.
5. Landon, Jr., E.L. 'A Sex Role Explanation of Purchase Intention Differences of Consumers Who are High and Low in Need for Achievement'. *Proceedings of the 3rd Annual Conference, Association for Consumer Research*, Venkatesan, M., ed., 1972.

6. Della Femina, Jerry *From Those Wonderful Folks Who Gave You Pearl Harbour* (London: Pitman, 1971).
7. Packard, Vance *The Hidden Persuaders* (London: Longmans, Green, 1957).
8. Bauer, R.J. 'Consumer Behaviour as Risk Taking' *Proceedings of the 43rd National Conference of the American Marketing Association* Hancock, R.S., ed. (Chicago: American Marketing Association, 1960).

Further Reading

Evans, P. *Motivation* (London: Methuen, 1975).
Vernon, M.D. *Human Motivation* (London: Cambridge University Press, 1969).
Vroom, V.H. and Deci, E.L. eds. *Management and Motivation* (Harmondsworth: Penguin, 1970).

Past Examination Questions

1. Describe the structure of human motivation. Which motives do you think are fundamentally important in understanding consumer behaviour? (I.M. 1974)
2. What do you understand by the term 'frustration'?
   What are the major characteristics of frustrated behaviour? (I.M. 1975)
3. What is motivation research? To what extent can the effect of bias be eliminated from this type of research? (I.M. 1977)
4. Maslow's Theory of motivation postulates five general types of needs. Define these needs and explain with examples how their economic importance can be exploited by advertising. (I.M. 1978)
5. 'The object of motivational research is often to discover the soul of the product' (Ernest Dichter).
   (a) What do you think Dr. Dichter meant by this?
   (b) Describe some qualitative research techniques which might be of use in this context. (CAM 1978)

5. SOCIAL INFLUENCES ON BEHAVIOUR

'The tendency to conform to cultural requirements and social expectations cannot be seen as "normal", but must be taken as problematical; it is not something to be assumed, but a fact to be explained.'

Ely Chinoy

5.1 Introduction

Although the marketing process is directed at the individual consumer, it must not be forgotten that its aim is to satisfy as many consumers as possible if a profitable business is to result. In studying a national market, or society, as a whole, it is apparent that we are not looking at a homogeneous entity but rather at a body composed of various social groupings, the individuals within each grouping having similar life-styles, values, attitudes, and beliefs, and reacting in similar ways to environmental stimuli. Whilst there is scope for individualism within each social grouping or segment, the very important human need for maintaining and improving social contact ensures that social pressures acting on the individual result in a far greater degree of conformity of behaviour than individuals may perhaps wish to admit. It is this conformity of behaviour within social groupings that provides the opportunity to segment markets and tailor products and promotions specifically for these segments. Thus, in determining an appropriate target market for a product or service, it is important to understand the processes that affect society in general and the various market segments in particular.

The social environment can be viewed as an extremely complex network of continuing interrelationships. The highly structured and specialized economic nature of advanced society means that the individual cannot survive in isolation and consequently has to learn to satisfy his needs in a manner acceptable to society. An important prerequisite for social interaction is the acquisition of a system of behaviour patterns that will enable the individual to adapt to his social environment. It is the aim of this chapter to describe and analyse the societal influences on consumer behaviour. The basis for our understanding of these influences comes from both social psychology, that branch of psychology concerned with the behaviour of individuals in relation to their social environment, and sociology, the social science that takes as its subject matter the development and behaviour of groups and of social organization generally.

5.2 Roles

In his continuing interaction with others, the individual is called upon to behave in certain ways according to the nature of the interaction involved. In each interaction the individual is expected to conform to a set of social rules appropriate to the situation involved. In the course of a working day an individual may be called upon to play the part of a loving husband, a caring parent, a shrewd businessman, a demanding boss, a loyal employee, an understanding friend, and an attentive host. The extent to which he is able to play satisfactorily each of these parts will depend on his understanding of the expectations and obligations of his position in each social interaction. As a result, social man can be seen to be a complex animal who is required to slip into any one of a variety of parts depending on the nature of the situation in which he finds himself. The concept of *role*, which can be defined as *an organized system of behavioural expectations*, has been developed by sociologists as a means of explaining the varied and complex interactions between individuals.

5.21 Norms

Central to the concept of role is the idea of *norms*, which are *standards of behaviour expected* in a given social interaction. In other words, they are the rules governing social behaviour. As a result, certain kinds of behaviour are acceptable, resulting in social approval for the individual; others are unacceptable, resulting in social disapproval and possible social punishment. Some norms carry legal sanctions − for example, incest is a legally punishable offence − while others are formally defined and the individual, therefore, must learn what is expected of him in a particular role. Norms are an important attribute of culture and it is useful at this stage to identify the following two important norm-setting agencies:

1. *Institutions*, which may be defined as organized systems of norms relating to a major feature of human existence (for example, the institution of marriage). Institutions serve specific functions or purposes and the norms which comprise them must be recognized by a large number of people and must be sanctioned.
2. *Associations*, which may be defined as a group of people organized for the pursuit of specific tasks. Every association must serve a specific function or purpose and commonly there are principal functions and subordinate functions; for example, a church has as its principal functions religion and worship, while secondary functions are ethics and education. All associations have norms and as a result they have status that in turn helps to determine the social relationships of members of the association.

5.22 Role Performance

Since society is dynamic, role innovation is constantly occurring and this means the individual is facing a continual learning process. The individual who refuses to accept such role innovation may become labelled 'old-fashioned' or 'stuffy' and as a result may find his behaviour becomes unacceptable to certain sections of society. Since role-playing involves a learning process, performance in a role will depend not only on the individual's perception of what is expected of him, but also on the sum total of the variables that make up his personality. This is illustrated by Figure 5.1.

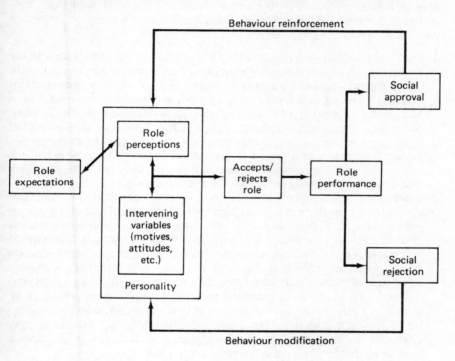

Figure 5.1 The effect of role on social behaviour

Thus, the performance of a role by an individual will depend on his perception of how he is expected to perform that role, which in turn will depend on a number of variables including motivation, attitudes, values, and previous experience. If his performance in the role is acceptable then there is reinforcement to repeat that performance in future similar interactions; but if the performance is not acceptable he will have to revise his performance if he wishes to gain future social acceptance. In performing a new role the individual is constantly searching for cues to tell him whether or not his behaviour is acceptable; this has important implications for advertising. Thus, an individual who is promoted to, or aspires to, an executive position will imitate what he perceives to be 'executive' behaviour in other executives but will also be susceptible to advertisements promoting 'executive cars', 'executive suits', 'executive briefcases'. Such products are often symbolic of the fact that the individual is now playing a sought-after role and this type of consumer behaviour is what some economists have labelled 'conspicuous consumption'. In other words, there are material symbols associated with many roles and an analysis of product usage in terms of role-playing for some products may form a basis for market segmentation.

Throughout his lifetime an individual will accumulate many roles. It is almost inevitable that the performance of certain roles will produce conflicts or strains for the individual. Sociologists identify the following main types of conflict or strain:

1. *Inter-role conflict*, where a performance of one role may interfere with the performance of another. For example, a salesman who is required to travel a great deal for his company might find his role as a conscientious employee coming into conflict with that of parent, a role requiring him to be at home. The greater the number of roles performed by the individual, the greater the potential for inter-role conflict. This type of role conflict may, however, produce market opportunities. The growth of the convenience food and take-away food industries has been to a large extent the product of consumers reducing the conflict resulting from the opposing demands on time made by job and domestic roles.

2. *Intra-role conflict*, where strains result from the conflicting demands of the different requirements of the same role. For example, a sales manager who is expected to reach a specific sales target but is not allowed to dismiss an incompetent salesman will experience intra-role conflict. This type of role conflict may be resolved in a number of ways. *Compartmentalization* occurs when an individual shuts out one facet of a role; for example, a sales manager may thus concentrate on achieving the sales target and refuse to get involved in company politics. *Delegation* occurs where an aspect of a role is assigned to someone else; for example, a doctor may call upon another doctor to treat his wife. Finally, the individual may *eliminate* the role altogether; for example, a person may resign from a committee rather than sit in judgement on a friend.

As mentioned above, the concept of role is of fundamental importance to an understanding of social behaviour. As Chinoy[1] states: 'The importance of social roles lies not only in the extent to which they regulate behaviour, but also in the fact that they enable men to predict the actions of others and therefore to fashion their own actions accordingly'. Roles exist independently of individuals and in many ways may be considered to be basic units for marketing analysis. Many products are purchased because they enhance a role relationship. In the U.K., for example, a high proportion of purchases of after shave lotions is by women as gifts for the men in their lives. Again, the acquisition of a role may give rise to conspicuous consumption behaviour, the nature and extent of which will depend on the status accompanying that role.

5.3 Status

Roles can be classified as being inferior (for example, employee) or superior (for example, boss); and the factor that gives them this aspect is *power*, a concept that may be defined as the *capacity to control the actions of others*. Often, it is the exercise of power that determines whether a person will effectively perform a role. It must be noted, however, that power is an attribute of personality; and the attainment of *authority*, the socially recognized right to exercise power, does not necessarily mean that the person having authority will be able successfully to control others. It is power, wealth, and occupation that determine *status*, which is 'a kind of social identification tag which places people in relation to others' (Chinoy[1]). In other words, status determines the basis on which a particular role is patterned since it places restrictions on the role-playing that can be enacted by the individual. A status may be ascribed or achieved.

1. *Ascribed status* derives from factors over which the individual has little or no control; for example, man or woman. The individual is expected to acquire and conform to the roles appropriate to that status.
2. *Achieved status*, on the other hand, is actively sought after by the individual and he seeks to acquire and conform to the appropriate roles. For example, the professional status of lawyer requires conformity to certain standards of behaviour.

The concept of status is important because status groupings are the basis of social stratification, or social class.

5.4 Social Class

Any particular social class, or social stratum, is composed of a collection of individuals with sufficiently similar status to give them the same sort of command over goods and services. Generally, the members of each class are thought to have similar beliefs, attitudes, and values and these are reflected by their behaviour patterns. There is a distinct positioning of classes and the members of one class may regard themselves as superior or inferior to members of other classes. As a result whilst members of each class mix freely with other members of that class, there may be barriers to interaction between members of different classes.

Although there is little doubt that some sort of class structure exists in every society, its nature and extent, or reality, depends on three factors:

1. Class consciousness; that is, the members of each stratum are demonstrably conscious that they belong to one identifiable unit.
2. The styles of life must be strikingly uniform within each stratum and therefore there is a clear contrast between different groups.
3. Social interaction is strikingly and demonstrably patterned by the social class.

Sociologists have classified societies into open or closed depending on the rigidity of the class system. *Closed societies* are characterized by a rigid class structure with little or no social mobility (i.e. the opportunity to move from one class to another). In these societies, the individual is born into a particular class and thus has an ascribed status. In *open societies*, on the other hand, whereas status may be ascribed there is great scope for achieving superior status through education or the acquisition of wealth or power.

The classic example of a closed society is that of the Indian caste system. Membership in a caste was ascribed at birth and apart from those who lost caste it was fixed for an individual's lifetime. Marriage was usually restricted to those of the same caste and interactions between members of different castes were defined and restricted according to caste rules. Contact with outcasts, 'untouchables', made the caste member unclean and demanded that he purified himself from the effects of such pollution. A member who violated caste rules could be expelled from the caste; the rules being enforced by an organized central body.

Most open societies have evolved from closed societies. Medieval England, for example, had a fairly rigid class structure based primarily on the ownership of land. The process of industrialization, which provided great scope for the entrepreneur to acquire wealth, and the erosion of the ability to inherit wealth, through such means as estate duty, have changed the basis of class determination. Although in open societies status, and hence class, can be determined by inheritance or through family connections, there is the capacity to gain or lose status as a result of changes in occupation, wealth, or power. In this sense, it may be argued that the class system is a very important motivating factor. Given the opportunity for social mobility, the members of the lower classes may aspire to the life-style and membership of superior classes, and will as a result work harder to achieve these ends.

It is interesting to note in this context that the U.S.S.R. has developed into a meritocracy; that is, a class system based solely on achieved status. Despite the egalitarian, classless society ideals of the 1917 Revolution, the U.S.S.R. now has a distinct class structure determined by education, ability, occupation, and position in the hierarchy of the Communist Party. The differential rewards accruing to each stratum of Soviet society have been deliberately introduced in order to provide a motivating stimulus. Thus, for the Soviet Union, the higher the level of achievement, the greater the status symbols that can be obtained. For example, a more responsible position not only gives a higher salary, but carries with it such status symbols as better housing, a car, the opportunity to buy products that are not generally available, and even the use of a country house.

As stated previously, the importance of the concept of social class to marketing lies in the opportunity it presents for market segmentation analysis. Products may be pitched to appeal to the upper classes — such 'up-market' products are usually prestigious and of implied high quality; and because they have a fairly limited target market, in terms of absolute numbers, they require a high profit margin and are consequently expensive. On the other hand, 'down-market' products appealing to the lower classes are relatively cheap, not of such high quality, and confer less prestige. Some products are relatively classless, for example, television sets, and are equally likely to be bought by members of all classes. Thus, class structure must obviously be considered when planning product or advertising strategy. In a closed society, there is little point in appealing to the social mobility motivations of consumers. However, in a relatively open society there could be considerable scope for promoting a product as a prestige item, thereby appealing to the aspirational motivations of people who wish to obtain membership of a superior social class, or to be associated with those they perceive to be its members.

The major problem, however, with social class analysis is ability to define and identify such classes in a meaningful way. In a closed society this is fairly easily solved since the divisions between classes are clear-cut. In an open society, however, not only is there movement between classes but the very openness of the society allows for changes in social factors such as attitudes, beliefs, and values. The process of industrialization in England, for example, is noted for the rise of the middle class, composed of merchants and manufacturers, who tried to emulate the lifestyle of the aristocracy and who attempted to gain admittance to the superior class. The social evolution that has occurred in the U.K. since the time of the Industrial Revolution has meant that the old classifications of upper, middle, and working class have less relevance today than, say, before the Second World War. Whilst status and class position can still be ascribed to the individual through family connections, or inheritance, achievement of status through income and occupation is now far easier to obtain. It is no longer unrealistic for an individual from a working class background to aspire to the job of Prime Minister or to that of head of a major company. In defining social class in the

Table 5.1
Jicnar's Social Grade Definitions

Social Grade	Social Status	Occupation	% of Total Population (1979)
A	Upper Middle Class	Higher Managerial, or Professional	3.2
B	Middle Class	Intermediate Managerial, Administrative or Professional	13.4
C_1	Lower Middle Class	Supervisory or Clerical and Junior Managerial, Administrative or Professional	32.2
C_2	Skilled Working Class	Skilled Manual Worker	31.7
D	Working Class	Semi and Unskilled Manual Workers	20.9
E	Those at Lowest Level of Subsistence	State Pensioners or Widows (No Other Earner), Casual or Lowest Grade Workers	8.6

Source: National Readership Survey, Jan. – Dec. 1979.

U.K., therefore, market researchers have tended to use as their basis a classification based on the occupation of the head of the household. Such a socio-economic grouping is given in Table 5.1. It should be noted that this is only one of several social grade classifications. Because of the social mobility of the population, the percentages for each category may vary noticeably over time.

Table 5.1 shows social grades based on occupation and as a result may have little connection with actual purchasing power. Although one would generally expect an individual occupying a high managerial position to earn more than a manual worker, this is not necessarily the case. The grading does not take account of the extra income brought into a household by a working wife, nor of the number of wage earners in a household. Another problem is that as households are classed according to the occupation of the head of the household, this may not present a true picture. A further problem is that class distinctions are not as clear-cut as such a categorization may imply. For example, there is an assumption that an individual identifies with the social class into which he is placed as a result of such a grading, thereby overlooking the influence of reference groups existing outside the individual's own social class. Allied to this problem is the question of social mobility. An individual with aspirations of moving to a higher class may adopt the attitudes and values associated with that class, whilst an individual who has experienced upward class mobility may still adopt some of the values and attitudes of his previous class. As a result of such deficiencies in the existing socio-economic grading system, researchers have recently focused their attention on studying life-styles as an alternative basis for market segmentation.

5.5 Culture

In common usage, the term *culture* usually refers to the more aesthetic aspects of life; for example, art, music, philosophy. However, sociologists use the term to refer to the sum total of man-designed tools both mental and physical, and all man-defined values, attitudes, and beliefs represented in the patterns of life of the members of a particular group, class, or society. The main characteristics of the concept of culture are outlined below:

1. It is a social acquisition of mankind. It exists to serve the needs of a society.
2. It is learned. Since culture is a product of social interaction, the individual must learn the appropriate responses to a given social situation. To survive he must adopt the values and norms of the culture into which he is born and he does this through a process known as socialization.
3. It is cumulative. Culture is transmitted from generation to generation and whilst there are possibilities for change, many aspects of culture have a distinct historical character.
4. It is adaptive. It changes in response to the needs of society.

Culture provides a means by which people can cope with their physical and social environment. It provides language, a function that is vital for the communication of the knowledge and techniques that allow the human race to survive. In this sense it should be noted that the higher the species, the lower the extent of highly complicated biological behaviour. Man's behaviour is determined by culture and not instinct. One of the vital distinctions between man and other animals is that only man possesses culture.

Since it is such a broad concept, it is useful to analyse culture in terms of its main components: these are institutions, the norm-setting agencies; ideas, the knowledge and beliefs of a society; and materials, the artefacts which man produces and makes available for his needs.

1. *Institutions*, which we have already defined as organized systems of norms, encompass folkways, conventions, mores, and laws.
    (a) *Folkways* is the term given to appropriate patterns of behaviour, such as shaking hands on greeting. They are practices which, though regarded as appropriate, may not be insisted upon; and as a result violations of such norms are not punished severely.
    (b) *Conventions* are standards of behaviour which have over time become accepted as the appropriate social behaviour in a given situation. Examples include the exchange of presents before a business meeting, social etiquette, and the English Sunday lunchtime roast.
    (c) *Mores* are the most significant social norms. They include love of parents, faithfulness to one's spouse, and refraining from killing or stealing. They have strong moral sanction and are often codified in a society's laws and religious teachings.
    (d) *Laws* are the formal recognition of the mores deemed to be necessary for the well-being of a society. Laws can carry sanctions imposed by the society; but they can only reflect the society's views at a particular time. For example, there have been drastic revisions of the U.K. laws on homosexuality and abortion.
   It is often difficult to distinguish between these concepts and they should really be viewed as being a continuum ranging from folkways to laws; the further along the continuum, the greater the severity of the sanction, representing increasing degrees of threat to organized society and the well-being of its members. However, such an analysis is useful in that it helps us to distinguish the origins of various norms and identifies the methods by which they are enforced. In attempting to change buying behaviour it is important to identify the kind of norm governing the behaviour. Thus, it is likely to be far more difficult to bring about the substitution of pasta for the English Sunday roast (that is, changing a convention) than it is to bring about a change in formal apparel (that is, changing a folkway).
2. *Ideas* is a concept that includes beliefs, knowledge, and values; that is, those factors that help to develop the characteristics of people who live in a particular society. *Values* may be defined as standards against which things are compared and seem to be good or bad, desirable or undesirable, appropriate or inappropriate. Some values are more uniformly held within a society than others, depending on the nature and extent of the sub-groups or sub-cultures existing within a particular society. A *belief* is a state of knowledge, or cognition. Beliefs and values are important factors in determining attitudes, as we shall see in the next chapter.

3. *Materials* are the physical manifestations of human existence. Such arte-facts are created because they are physically or psychologically useful to man's survival. It follows that there is a connection between the material aspect of culture and the state of knowledge existing within a culture; the greater the degree of knowledge, the greater the possibilities for tech-nological progress.

Within any particular culture there are various sub-groups or sub-cultures, each having its own norms or values, which produce variations and a dominant pattern of life within the overall culture. In the U.K. we can readily identify four broad sub-cultures based on nationality (that is, ethnic groups), religion, geography, and age.

1. *Nationality groups*. These include not only sections of the indigenous population such as the Welsh and Scots, but also those groups who have migrated to the U.K. Quite often these immigrants will settle in a partic-ular geographical area and will seek to interact with other members of their own nationality. Gradually such immigrants will absorb the norms of their host culture and will be assimilated into the host society, although they might still retain their native language, traditions, and, as far as possible, eating habits and life-styles. In the U.K., for example, there are fair-sized Ukranian, Greek, West Indian, and Indian sub-cultures.

2. *Religious groups*. For believers, organized religion is a very powerful norm-setting agency that can exert considerable influence on their way of life. Jews cannot eat pork or shellfish; Mormons cannot consume alcohol, tobacco, coffee, tea, or other stimulants; Hindus regard the cow as sacred and will not eat beef. But apart from these more obvious norms, religions exercise considerable and more subtle influences on the thought processes and life-styles of their followers, and inculcate values such as brotherly love and charity.

3. *Geography*. Whilst there are considerable cultural variations exhibited throughout the world as a result of physical geographical factors such as climate, it must also be recognized that there are often variations within a culture as a consequence of geography. These usually result from poor physical communication between areas or regions. Prior to the transport developments of the Industrial Revolution, the U.K., for example, could be viewed as a number of distinct regional cultures and economies. The consequent need for regional economic self-sufficiencies resulted in distinct variations in eating habits between areas, whilst the lack of physical contact with other regions resulted in regional life-styles that changed little from generation to generation. Whilst developments in transport and communication have done much to dissipate regional cul-tures, there still remain discriminating cultural variations. Regional accents are still, for example, very much in evidence; and northern eating habits are still slightly different from those in the south. Again, whilst we tend to think of differences as being between regions, it must also be noted that considerable variations can be found within urban areas. For example, life-styles in the East End of London are different from those in

an area such as Ealing. Such differences result from particular social class orientations to different urban areas.

4. *Age*. Within the population there may be variations in cultural values and attitudes between age groups. These variations may reflect differences in socialization processes and behaviour learned as a result of common experiences. For example, many people brought up in the Depression of the 1930s experienced frugal circumstances in their formative years and may share a common attitude towards unnecessary waste.

Probably the most clearly identifiable sub-culture based on age is that of youth; in broad terms this includes those aged between fourteen and twenty-four. People of this age group are poised between childhood and adulthood and are in a position of trying to establish a stable personal identity and to prepare themselves for the various roles they will be called upon to play once they reach full maturity. They are in a transient situation and may, as a result of uncertainty, adopt exaggerated values, attitudes, and behavioural norms. These are often referred to as 'fads' or 'crazes'.

Although these four factors influencing the formation of sub-cultures have been discussed separately, it must be appreciated that they are deeply interrelated. The Welsh, for example, are a national group who have a geographical identity, and whose life-style and outlook have historically been shaped by various Nonconformist Protestant influences. There is a strong youth movement in Wales to re-establish a national identity by preserving the Welsh language and traditions.

By attempting to understand the differences in values and life-styles between cultures, the marketer can do much to overcome potential problem areas when introducing a product into a different cultural environment. Apart from the obvious problem of language, there are marked differences in customs, perceptions, attitudes, and thought processes. The greater the degree of variation between cultures, the more notice tends to be taken by marketers of these differences when applying successful products and advertising to another cultural environment. It is well known, for example, that white is a colour of mourning to the Chinese and should therefore be avoided when exporting to many Asian countries.

The main problem is that there is a tendency to perceive cultures which are at the same technological level as being very similar; but this is seldom the case. In a comparative study of American and French consumer habits and innovator characteristics, Green and Langeard[2] concluded that 'even though France and the United States are similar in many economic respects, the behavioural differences found by the study suggest that marketing programmes may need to be substantially revised if they are to be equally effective in both countries. Most of the differences that were found could be attributed to social and environmental factors that characterize the two nations'. Despite such studies, the cultural influence on behaviour has too often in the past been neglected and marketing literature abounds with failure stories, especially when there is transfer of promotional material from one country to another, often the only concession being to language differences.

Ricks *et al*[3] provide the example, among others, of how the American company General Mills attempted to enter the British breakfast cereal market with advertising based on an 'all American' child, not realizing that this type of promotion would be unlikely to appeal to a culture that possessed a more formal view of the role of children. Griffin, in a talk before the Primary Club of London in 1972, cited the example of Maxwell House who attempted to enter the German market as 'the great American coffee' only to discover, many dollars later, that the Germans had little respect for 'American coffee'[4].

On the other hand, cultural differences can provide marketing opportunities. The exploitation of stereotypes, a concept discussed in the next chapter, could be a useful promotional weapon, whilst the identification of different sub-cultures might be a useful market segmentation variable. For example, it is estimated that the population of Great Britain originating from the New Commonwealth and Pakistan numbered approximately 1.9 million people in mid-1978; this is approximately 3.5% of the total U.K. population[5]. Although this total of 1.9 million comprises various different national and religious groupings (for example, Chinese, Indians, Moslems, and Hindus), there could be significant opportunities for tailoring products and services to the attitudes, values, and norms of these different cultures. Finally, as culture is adaptive, i.e. able to assimilate the life-styles of other cultures, marketers should anticipate the changes that might occur in one culture as the result of exposure to other cultures. As people travel internationally on holiday or on business, they experience new life-styles and may assimilate elements of these into their own life-styles. The incidence of mass tourism in the last few decades has brought about a considerable change in eating and drinking habits in the U.K. Wine drinking has increased significantly and housewives, especially younger ones, have accepted Continental-style convenience foods and are now using far more herbs and spices in cooking. It must be noted, however, that cultural influence is a two-way process; for immigrants tend to absorb the culture of their host country but their own culture also tends to have an impact on that of the host nation.

5.6 Groups

Cultures and sub-cultures are aggregate units for analysis and as such only provide a broad view of the social influences acting on the consumer. In attempting to understand social interaction the basic unit is the group, which Schein[6] defines as 'any number of people who (i) interact with one another (ii) are psychologically aware of one another, and (iii) perceive themselves to be a group'. Groups consist of two or more people and are formed because many goals cannot be achieved by the individual acting alone. Such goals include problem-solving and social interaction *per se*. Characteristics of groups include communication, cohesiveness, and conformity.

1. *Communication*. Individuals in groups interact with each other and the extent to which they are able to do so on a face-to-face basis will depend on the size of the group.
2. *Cohesiveness*. This refers to the extent to which members of a group exhibit solidarity and share common attitudes, values, and beliefs. The

greater the degree of cohesiveness, the more likely are the members of the group to co-operate with one another to achieve the aims of the group.
3. *Conformity*. Groups develop standards of behaviour, or norms, and their members are expected to conform to these, otherwise sanctions are imposed. Whilst some deviation may be permitted as a means of achieving goals, or accepted as evidence of eccentricity, major deviations can result in rejection of the deviant by the other members of the group.

An individual will simultaneously belong to several groups, each having some degree of influence on him. It is useful, therefore, to examine the ways in which groups can be categorized.

1. *Ascribed groups and acquired groups.* An ascribed group is one to which the individual automatically belongs; for example, he is born into a family. An acquired group is one to which he has actually sought membership.
2. *Primary groups and secondary groups.* Primary groups are those in which interaction is usually on a face-to-face basis. The most important primary groups are the family and the friendship group. Secondary groups, on the other hand, are more impersonal in terms of communication and interaction; examples are the Institute of Marketing and CAM. Primary groups are often subsets of secondary groups; an Institute of Marketing branch committee is a primary group.
3. *Formal groups and informal groups.* Formal groups usually have a clearly defined goal or objective and a definite structure or hierarchy. For example, they usually have a chairman and/or secretary. Informal groups may have no particular objective other than social interaction *per se* and may not have a hierarchy, although there may be a recognized leader. Both types of group will have norms governing behaviour and the formal group might have some of these laid down in writing. Informal groups are often subsets of formal groups. The importance of the informal group in the organizational setting was demonstrated by the Hawthorne studies which are discussed in Chapter 9.
4. *Membership groups, aspirational groups, and dissociative groups*: Membership groups are those to which the individual belongs. Aspirational groups are those to which he does not belong but wishes to belong. Dissociative groups are those to which he does not belong and with whose values and behaviour he does not wish to be associated.

Obviously there is a great deal of overlap between these various distinctions but, however viewed, the important point is that any or all may serve as a reference group for the individual. *Reference groups* are those which influence the individual's behaviour and in this sense even a dissociative group influences behaviour, but in a negative way; the individual will avoid the development of attitudes and behaviour associated with such a group. The greater the degree of attraction of a group, whether he belongs to it or not, the greater the influence of that group's attitudes on the individual's own attitudes and behaviour.

That reference groups influence consumer behaviour is very much in evidence. But since each individual is simultaneously a member of several groups the essential task for a marketer is to discover which particular reference group exerts the greatest influence. The first reference group influence is that of the family and later various peer groups. But as the consumer progresses through life and develops new attitudes, beliefs, and aspirations he may be influenced by reference groups with whom he does not regularly interact; that is, from which he is socially distant. Thus, a consumer may be influenced by the life-styles of filmstars and as a result may take note of David Niven's promotion of instant coffee. However, the same consumer may find that serving instant coffee to some groups with whom he interacts does not meet with their approval. The marketer must, therefore, take care that in selecting socially distant reference groups for product promotion they have the maximum appeal to the chosen target market segment. It should be noted, in view of the discussion above on sub-cultures, that every reference group may be regarded as a sub-culture because it has identifiable norms and values which may be distinct from those of the overall culture. Every sub-culture, however, is not necessarily a reference group, for whilst there may be shared beliefs and values, there may be little interaction between members, solidarity may be poor, and norms may be ill-defined and not sanctioned.

Group influence has a considerable impact on consumer behaviour and it is important to understand the reasons for this influence. The vital factor is that a group satisfies a particular need for the individual and, as a result, he is reluctant to deviate from the norms set by the group and incur the disapproval of, and possible rejection by, the other members. The powerful nature of group influence was demonstrated by Sherif[7] (1935), using what is known as the *autokinetic effect*. This is the name given to a phenomenon whereby a small stationary light in a totally darkened room will appear to have movement if a person concentrates on it. The important point to note is that there is no real movement of the light. In his experiment, Sherif asked subjects to judge how far the light appeared to move. Individuals were shown the light in a group situation and each person expressed his opinion aloud. Whereas their judgements at first did not agree very well, as they listened to one another's opinions they seemed to agree about the range of movement of the light. Later, when each group member was asked individually to make a judgement, they still judged the movement to be within the range that had been agreed upon in the group situation. It would thus appear that in the group situation the subjects learned to interpret an ambiguous situation in a given way and that the learning process continued to affect their judgements when they were alone.

This compliance with group norms, apart from the obvious fear of rejection by other group members, seems to stem from four main factors.

1. The degree of the attraction of the group to the individual. The greater the attraction, for example, because membership carries a high status, the more likely is the individual to conform.
2. The amount of agreement existing in the group. If all other members are agreed on a course of action then the individual is more likely to conform with this view.
3. The degree to which the individual is orientated to the group. A task-orientated individual, that is, a person who is more concerned with results than

with relationships, is less likely to be influenced by group norms than is a group-orientated individual.

4. The degree to which the individual needs to be liked and accepted. The greater the need to be accepted, the greater the degree of conformity to norms.

A further aspect of group influence that should be considered is the patterns of interaction between members of a group. People who are liked, or who are respected, will have greater influence and are more likely to emerge as informal group leaders than those people who are less popular. (The topic of opinion leadership is discussed in Chapter 7). Moreno[8] devised the sociometry technique as a means of studying the patterns of interaction among members of a group. At its simplest level, the method involves asking each member of a group privately to choose another member of the group to, for example, share some activity. The question could be 'With whom would you most like to spend a holiday?' or 'Whose dress style do you most admire?'. The results obtained can be depicted by means of a sociogram as shown in Figure 5.2.

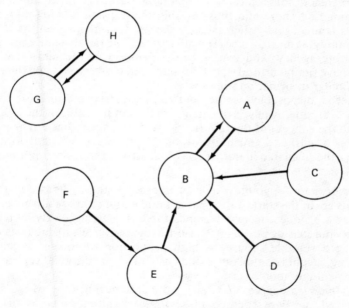

Figure 5.2 A sociogram

The sociogram in Figure 5.2 shows the choices of a group consisting of eight individuals. In sociometric terminology B is a 'star' since he has been chosen by the greatest number of members. G and H are a 'pair', as are B and A, since the choices are reciprocated.

Such an analysis is useful as a basis for the identification of the qualities that make for leadership in certain groups. In the above example it is likely that B will emerge as a leader, if he is not already recognized as such.

5.7 The Family

The family was mentioned above as a primary group, but in terms of influence on the individual the family is probably the most important group. Indeed it has been argued that the family should be the main focus for the study of consumer behaviour. In practice, however, marketers have often failed to consider fully the importance of the family as a decision-making group. The family is both an earning and a consuming unit and it is important for the marketer to understand how purchasing decisions are made within the family structure and also the factors that bring about certain consumption behaviour at various times.

Sociologists classify family units as being *nuclear* (that is, the immediate group of parents and children living together) or *extended* (that is, the nuclear family plus other relatives such as grandparents, uncles and aunts, and in-laws). Whereas in some cultures it is common to find extended families living in the same household and thus forming the decision-making unit, in the U.K. this is not usually the case and the decision-making unit is thus the nuclear family. It must also be remembered that the family is an institution, a norm-setting agency, and consequently members of the same family are likely to have similar attitudes, beliefs, and opinions derived from their exposure to similar information sources.

The needs, disposable income, and consequent expenditure for a family will vary over time. Analysis of changes in the family status of the individual has led to the concept of the *family life cycle*; a concept that can be usefully applied as a market segmentation tool. Engel, Blackwell, and Kollat[9], in reviewing the available literature, have identified the following family life cycle stages.

1. *Bachelor stage* – young single people not living at home. Here individuals are at the start of their careers and earnings are relatively low, but as they are subject to few demands there is generally fairly high discretionary purchasing power. Attention is focused on leisure interests and on finding a suitable spouse. A high proportion of income is spent on clothing, alcohol, eating out, holidays, and leisure durables such as stereo equipment and motor cars.
2. *Newly married couples* – young, no children. Since the wife is usually employed, newly married couples without children are better off financially than they have been previously. Whereas at this stage expenditure on leisure activities is quite high, such couples are particularly concerned with building up a home and this group has the highest average purchase of durable goods, particularly furniture and domestic appliances.
3. *Full Nest I* – young married couples with youngest child under six. The arrival of the first child requires an increase in family expenditure but at the same time might signify a reduction in family income as wives may cease employment to devote their full-time attention to the role of mother.

As a result, family savings may be reduced and there may be dissatisfaction with the family's financial position.

4. *Full Nest II* – young married couples with youngest child six or over. At this stage the husband's income is likely to have improved and the wife may have returned to employment either full time or part time. As a result, the family's financial position has improved. Expenditure continues to be heavily influenced by the children.

5. *Full Nest III* – older married couples with dependent children. At this stage the family's overall income continues to improve because the husband's income has risen, and the wife returns to employment or enjoys a higher salary. Typically the family will replace several items of furniture and buy luxury appliances.

6. *Empty Nest I* – older married couples, no children living with them, household head in the labour force. Family income has continued to increase whilst as a result of the children having left home family expenditure has declined. Consequently, at this stage the family has its greatest level of discretionary purchasing power. Typically the couple will make home improvements, buy luxury items, and spend a high proportion of income on leisure pursuits.

7. *Empty Nest II* – older married couples, no children living at home, household head retired. Since the household head has retired there may be a noticeable reduction in family income. Retirement may have been accompanied by a change of residence, typically to a smaller dwelling near the sea or in a rural area. Expenditures become orientated more towards health products.

8. *Solitary Survivor I* – in the labour force. Since he is employed, the solitary survivor still enjoys a good income. He may move to a smaller dwelling and typically is likely to spend more money on leisure pursuits and holidays.

9. *Solitary Survivor II* – retired. The retired solitary survivor follows the same general consumption pattern as the employed solitary survivor but on a smaller scale since his income is reduced. He is likely to have special needs for attention, affection, and security.

This type of analysis is likely to be more useful to the marketer than other demographics, since it relates purchasing behaviour to needs in a far more meaningful way than a single demographic variable such as age. In the U.K. over the last decade, for example, there has been a tendency for married couples to put off having children in order to consolidate their economic position. In the light of such a social trend it could be misleading to relate consumption behaviour directly to age.

Having studied the consumption requirements of various family groups, it is important to identify the decision-maker in each family unit. For groceries it might be the housewife, for consumer durables it might be the husband, or it might be that purchasing decisions are made jointly by the family. Cunningham and Green[10] in a study of purchasing roles in the U.S. family showed that important changes had occurred during the period from 1955 to 1973. Some of their findings are illustrated in the Table 5.2.

Table 5.2
U.S. Husband-Wife Decision-Making Roles In 1955 and 1973

Decision Area	% 1955	% 1973
FOOD AND GROCERIES		
Husband usually	13	10
Wife usually	54	75
Both	33	15
AUTOMOBILE		
Husband usually	70	52
Wife usually	5	3
Both	25	45
VACATION		
Husband usually	18	7
Wife usually	12	9
Both	70	84

Such findings have important implications for both product design and for advertising. If the purchase decision is taken jointly by husband and wife then obviously it could be a great mistake to give a product, and its advertising, a masculine or feminine image.

It is also useful to distinguish between those who are decision-makers within the family unit and those who influence the decision that is taken. Furthermore, there is a distinction between buyers and users of products. It is important that the marketer identifies both the decision-maker for, and the purchaser of, his product. Both these functions may be performed by one person, by two or more separate people, or they may be joint activities. If the buyer is different from the decision-maker, point-of-sale promotions may be inappropriate and effort may be better directed to media coverage. In this sense, it must be noted that the great advantage of television advertising is that it can be aimed at the family unit gathered together and therefore can reach influencers, decision-makers, buyers, and users simultaneously.

The pattern of family decision-making can however change over time, reflecting changes in the general social environment, and it is important, therefore, to understand not only the purchasing decision roles within the family but also the general role shifts that are likely to occur.

In recent decades significant changes have taken place in roles within the family, particularly in the traditional role of women. Education and changes in social values, plus legislation, have resulted in more women being able to work and to enter managerial and professional positions. A married woman may now often have her own bank account, have a second family car, and arrange hire purchase on her own account. Women now play a more important part in family decision-making and this has necessarily led to a change in marketing strategies. Many stores, for example, are now open for late night shopping and consumer durable advertising is increasingly orientated towards women.

5.8 Life-styles

It will be apparent from the preceding sections of this chapter that social influences on the consumer are both profound and complex. Various social influences will have differing effects on individual consumers and will lead to differing styles of living based on a wide range of activities, interests, and opinions. Demographics, whilst allowing easy quantification and classification of consumers, does not provide a sufficiently broad view of consumers in the sense of explaining how their life patterns influence purchasing decisions. As a result, a method of segmenting markets according to the life-styles of consumers has been developed and over the last ten years has become increasingly accepted by marketers as a powerful aid to the understanding of consumer behaviour.

The market profiles resulting from life-style measurements are known as *psychographics* and are usually based on demographic information as well as ratings of consumers' activities, interests, and opinions (known as AIO measures). Life-style dimensions can encompass a number of factors and Plummer[11] identifies the major elements shown in Table 5.3.

Table 5.3
Major Elements of Life-Styles

Activities	Interests	Opinions	Demographics
Work	Family	Themselves	Age
Hobbies	Home	Social issues	Education
Social events	Job	Politics	Income
Vacation	Community	Business	Occupation
Entertainment	Recreation	Economics	Family size
Club membership	Fashion	Education	Dwelling
Community	Food	Products	Geography
Shopping	Media	Future	City size
Sports	Achievements	Culture	Stage in life cycle

As a result of such an analysis we can obtain 'a broader, more three-dimensional view of customers, so that one can think about them more intelligently in terms of relevant product positioning, communication, media, and promotion' (Plummer).

An example of a psychographic profile is provided by Bartos[12] reporting on a study comparing differences between four categories of women in the U.S.A. The main findings are shown in Table 5.4.

5.9 Socialization

So far in this chapter, we have examined the theoretical concepts used in studying social behaviour. However, it is important to understand the process by which the individual learns the social expectations, goals, beliefs, values, and attitudes that enable him to exist in society. This process is known as *socialization*.

Table 5.4
Psychographic Profiles

Category	Demographics	Psychographics
Stay-at-home Housewife	Older, least affluent, least educated, has fewer children at home.	Sees herself as tense, refined, low on ego and humour.
Housewife who Plans to work	Younger, more affluent, much better education, has young children at home.	Sees herself as tense, awkward, stubborn, affectionate, creative, kind, sociable, trust worthy, not egocentral.
The working Woman who says 'Its just a job'	Works in a clerical or other category, better educated than 'Stay-at-home' but less than 'Plans to Work'; income on par with 'Plans to work'	Sees herself as awkward, tense, affectionate, not very intelligent or creative
The Working Woman who Believes her Work is a Career	The most affluent, best education, slightly younger than 'Just a job' but older than, 'Plans to work'	Has a very strong self-image, is amiable, affectionate, efficient broad-minded, refined, trustworthy, sociable and creative.

Elkin[13] defines socialization as 'the process by which someone learns the ways of a given society or social group well enough so that he can function within it'. Although the term usually applies to childhood experiences, it is important to note that the process commences at birth and, because of the dynamic nature of society, necessarily continues throughout the individual's life. The process must be seen as a reciprocal one, for whilst the individual is moulded by the society of which he forms a part, he still has a capacity for innovation and direction and consequently may significantly influence and change the nature of his culture and society. Socialization therefore can be seen as having two main functions:

1. It prepares the individual for the roles he will be required to play, provides him with the necessary range of habits, beliefs, and values, the appropriate pattern of responses and perceptual modes, and the appropriate level of skills and knowledge.
2. It ensures the continuity of the culture through communicating it from one generation to the next. It must be noted, however, that although socialization allows the persistence of a culture, the culture may not continue in the same form since culture is adaptive.

An understanding of the socialization process is important to the marketer because childhood experiences have an important effect on adult behaviour and a knowledge of the process may allow the prediction of certain consumer behaviours. Again, the changes in values, attitudes, and life-styles that occur from one generation to the next can be better appreciated if the agencies and processes which bring about these changes are understood.

The main agencies of socialization are: the family, school, peer groups, and the media.

1. *The family*. The individual's first social contact is with members of the family group into which he is born. The family has probably the greatest influence in shaping future behaviour, especially since the manner of socialization tends to be authoritarian.
2. *The school*. The formal educational process transmits not only skills and knowledge but also various cultural values. The educational environment is also a social process that allows for the development of informal peer groups.
3. *Peer groups*. As the individual develops patterns of social interaction with his peers, he experiences social pressures to conform to the attitudes and beliefs common to the group. These may be in conflict with those inculcated by the family group and the extent to which he will conform to peer group influences in opposition to the family influences will depend on a number of factors, one of which is personality. The importance of peer group influence was demonstrated by the study of female students at Bennington College that was conducted by Newcomb[14] in the mid-1930s. This study showed that a young person's peers may influence his or her economic and political beliefs to such an extent that family influences become secondary.
4. *The mass media*. Exposure to the media has a considerable influence on the shaping of the individual's behaviour and can either reinforce the effects of family, school, and peer groups or can dilute them.

The socialization process continues to operate and influence the social behaviour of adults. As the adult individual experiences new situations and interacts with different social groups, his behaviour is modified. The peer group in the work situation, for example, can have a profound effect on attitudes and behaviour, as shown in Chapter 9 where we discuss the Hawthorne Studies. Again, the social behaviour of the young adult may be modified when he starts his own family. Finally, the mass media will continue to influence behaviour by demonstrating different life-styles and experiences, and through persuasive messages.

The basic factors underlying the socialization process are to be found in learning theory, as outlined in Chapter 3, but genetic factors may also play a part. The main mechanisms of socialization are summarized below:

1. *Conditioning and shaping of behaviour*. The factors of reward and punishment, reinforcement, and shaping of discrete acts of social behaviour play an important part in learning. This appears to be true for all types of social behaviour. Sex-related roles, for example, are learned. Boys tend to adopt pursuits considered to be masculine and girls tend to adopt interests considered feminine; deviations are punished by such

methods as labelling boys 'sissy' if they show any interest in 'feminine' activities such as playing with dolls. The learned nature of sex-related roles has been illustrated by the anthropologist Margaret Mead[15] who showed in a study of three different Pacific tribes that sex-related roles differed considerably between the tribes.

2. *Imitation.* A great deal of social learning takes place through observation and imitation of the observed behaviour or attitudes of others. Imitative behaviour can result from curiosity or from the observation that the model for behaviour (for example, a close friend or a well-known personality) obtains some sort of reward, either intrinsic or extrinsic, for his behaviour.

3. *Identification.* This factor, first proposed by Freud, results from a desire by the individual to become as much like the perceived ideal model as possible. For example, children try to emulate their parents and the standards of the parent then become a part of the child's personality, although this can be later modified through peer group influences.

4. *Role playing.* As mentioned earlier, social roles do not exist in isolation and are necessarily defined by their relationship to each other. To perform a role it is necessary to learn the roles which are complementary to it. The consumer role, for example, is observed and learned by a child accompanying the parent on a shopping trip. In so doing the child will observe and learn the role of salesman and will come to appreciate the expectations each role has of the other.

5. *Cognitive mediation.* This refers to the interaction between the individual's mental processes and the social environment. Cognitive mediation theories see the environment as influencing, but not controlling, the individual, since cognitive processes involve factors such as selective perception which result in behaviour that cannot be explained in terms of simple S-R theory. The individual is seen as an active gatherer of information and the degree to which he is able to do this depends on the 'stage' of cognitive development reached. Older children, for example, are thought to have more complex learning skills than younger children.

5.10 Implications for Marketing

As so much of human behaviour is shaped by social influences, it is essential that the marketer has an appreciation of their nature. For without such an understanding he cannot seek to identify potential consumers of his product, design his product to suit their needs, or ensure that his promotion efforts are appropriate to his target market.

As societies become more complex, and as incomes rise, consumer needs and tastes become increasingly diversified. It is impossible for the marketer to tailor-make his efforts to appeal to individual consumer needs and it is therefore necessary to segment the market into broad groups, each having identifiable characteristics and sharing common attitudes and behavioural norms. The concepts of sub-cultures and social groups provide a possible means for such market segmentation. It may, for example, be possible to identify a number of broad social groupings that place differing values on holidays abroad. One group may be seeking relaxation in the sun; another may be interested in absorbing local cultures; yet another may be looking for excitement and adventure. If the marketer is able to establish the existence of broad market segments of this type, he may be able to identify new product opportunities or improve his product positioning among the different sectors of the market.

Having identified his market and adjusted his product planning to suit the different needs of individual market segments, the marketer must then ensure that his promotion and distribution efforts are correctly orientated towards the consumers included within individual market segments. A travel company may, for example, identify the youth market as being particularly interested in adventure holidays such as camping, sailing, trekking, and water skiing. Its researches may also show that the youth market as a whole listens more frequently to the radio than it watches the television, and that it also tends to read more magazines than national newspapers. An appropriate promotional package may therefore include advertisements in magazines and on commercial radio.

As mentioned earlier, an understanding of cultural differences is also of vital importance when marketing products overseas. It must also be taken into account when sending employees to work abroad. Many companies find it increasingly important to prepare employees and their wives or husbands for the differences in styles of working and living they will encounter when they reach their destination. If this is not done, the employee and his family may experience 'culture shock' which may seriously impair the employee's performance at his job and may, in some cases, make it impossible to settle down.

5.11 Summary

1. Society is composed of various social groupings, each group having similar life-styles, values, attitudes, and beliefs and reacting in similar ways to environmental stimuli. Social pressures result in a conformity of behaviour within these groupings and it is important to understand the social processes involved since such an understanding can aid the formulation of product and promotional strategies.
2. Roles are organized systems of behavioural expectations, and their performance is governed by social norms, the rules of society. Roles exist independently of individuals and may be regarded as basic units for marketing analysis.
3. Status is determined by power, wealth, and occupation, and forms the basis for the patterning of a particular role. Status is ascribed or achieved.
4. A social class refers to a number of individuals with sufficiently similar status to give them the same sort of command over goods and services. In the U.K. the definition of social class is usually based on the occupation of the head of the household but this presents a number of problems. As a result, attention is increasingly focused on life-style analysis as a basis for market segmentation.
5. Culture embraces institutions, ideas, and materials. Sub-cultures result

from variations in norms and life-styles within a culture. An understanding of cultural and sub-cultural differences may help reveal market opportunities and prevent ineffective marketing.

6. Groups consist of two or more people who interact together; groups are formed because goals cannot be achieved by the individual acting alone. They may be categorized in various ways but the important aspect is that they provide a frame of reference for the individual and assert a considerable influence on his behaviour.

7. The family is probably the most important reference group and should be a main focus for the study of consumer behaviour since it is both an earning and a consuming unit. The concept of the family life cycle can be usefully applied in market segmentation. Significant changes have taken place in roles within the family unit and marketers should be aware of the threats and opportunities thus presented.

8. Life-style analysis is a method of segmenting markets based on the activities, interests, and opinions of consumers. It aims to explain how life patterns influence purchasing decisions.

9. Socialization is the process by which the individual learns to adjust to his social environment. The basis for an understanding of the process is to be found in learning theory. A knowledge of socialization may allow the prediction of certain consumer behaviours.

References

1. Chinoy, Ely. *Society* (New York: Random House, 1967).
2. Green, R.T. and Langeard, E. 'A Cross-National Comparison of Consumer Habits and Innovator Characteristics', *Journal of Marketing*, July 1975.
3. Ricks, D., Fu, M.Y.C., and Arpan, J.S. *International Business Blunders* (Columbus, Ohio: Grid Publishing, 1974).
4. Dunn, W.S. 'Effect of National Identity on Multinational Promotional Strategy in Europe', *Journal of Marketing*, October 1976.
5. *Social Trends No. 10* (London: HMSO, 1979).
6. Schein, E.H. *Organizational Psychology* (Englewood Cliffs, New Jersey: Prentice-Hall, 1970).
7. Sherif, M. 'A study of some social factors in perception', *Arch. Psych.*, 1935, 27.
8. Moreno, J.L. *Who Shall Survive?* (New York: Beacon House, 1953).
9. Engel, J.F., Blackwell, R.D. and Kollat, D.T. *Consumer Behaviour* (Hinsdale, Illinois: The Dryden Press, 1978).
10. Cunningham, I.C.M. and Green, R.T. 'Purchasing Roles in the U.S. Family, 1955 and 1973' *Journal of Marketing*, October 1974.
11. Plummer, J.T. 'The Concept and Application of Life Style Segmentation' *Journal of Marketing*, January 1974.
12. Bartos, R. 'Insight on Selling the Working Woman' *Marketing Times*, May-June 1976.
13. Elkin, F. *The Child and Society: The Process of Socialization* (New York: Random House, 1960).

14. Newcomb, T.M. *Personality and Social Change* (New York: Dryden, 1943).
15. Mead, M. *Sex and Temperament* (New York: Morrow, 1935).

Further Reading

Argyle, M. *The Psychology of Interpersonal Behaviour* (Harmondsworth: Penguin, 1967).
Gahagan, J. *Interpersonal and Group Behaviour* (London: Methuen, 1975).
Katona, G., *The Powerful Consumer* (New York: McGraw Hill 1960).

Past Examination Questions

1. What are the main characteristics of the concept of culture? To what extent do differences in cultural norms affect marketing tactics? (IM 1974)
2. Assess the impact on marketing tactics and strategies of changes in roles within the family during the last twenty years. (IM 1977)
3. 'Culture provides the norms that define the roles that make the relationships that constitute the group.' Elucidate and discuss. (IM 1978)
4. A subject is placed in a darkened room and instructed to call out the apparent direction of movement of a stationary point of light. Other people in the room (who were really collaborating with the experimenter) pretend the light is moving to the left or to the right, and the subject agrees with them. Relate this experiment to conformity and other known psychological theory, and discuss its implications for the preparation of an advertising campaign for a commercial product. (CAM 1978)
5. Why is the concept of group norms of relevance to marketeers? (IM 1979)

6. ATTITUDES AND SOCIAL BEHAVIOUR

'There is no limit to the topics about which people may have attitudes . . . It would be possible to argue persuasively that in the final analysis everything in life depends on people's attitudes;'

A.N. Oppenheim

6.1 Introduction

The attitudes held by individuals have a direct influence on their purchasing decisions and these decisions, in turn, may reinforce a particular attitude or lead to its modification. An understanding of the way in which consumer attitudes are formed, reinforced, and modified is therefore of prime importance to the marketer. If the marketer is able to identify the attitudes held by different market segments towards his product, and also to measure changes in those attitudes, he will be well placed to plan his marketing strategy. Attitude research can also provide a useful basis for the identification of new product opportunities and forecasting of changes in the pattern of purchasing behaviour.

In this chapter we examine the nature of attitudes and the way in which they affect our behaviour. We then look at a number of the techniques used for measuring attitudes and describe some of the theories that have been developed to help us explain and predict changes in attitudes and their effects on behaviour. Finally, we examine some of the major factors involved in attitude change.

6.2 The Nature of Attitudes

The concept of attitude has long been of critical importance in attempts to explain man's social behaviour. However, far more than other concepts in social science, it is an abstraction that has no one absolute and correct meaning or definition. In an examination of the literature it may be seen that there are many definitions of attitude but the most widely used is probably that of Allport[1] who defines it as 'a mental and neural state of readiness, organised through experience, exerting a directive or dynamic influence upon the individual's response to all objects and situations with which it is related'. Similarly, Krech and Crutchfield[2] define attitude as 'an enduring organisation of motivational, emotional, perceptual, and cognitive processes with respect to some aspect of the individual's world'.

98

Both these definitions, and others, state or imply the following main characteristics of attitudes:

1. Attitudes are related to some person or object that forms part of the individual's environment.
2. They form part of the way the individual perceives and reacts to his environment. They affect the way in which we extract information from the environment and as a result affect our perception of the goals for which we strive; in this sense they are motivational.
3. They are learned and are relatively enduring. They may change but usually not very rapidly.
4. They imply evaluation and feeling.

The last point has led many writers to observe that an attitude has two basic components: *beliefs*, the probability an individual attaches to given pieces of information being true; and *values*, which are determined by what society considers good or bad. This relationship has been expressed as:

$$\text{Attitude} = \text{Belief} \times \text{Value}$$

Other researchers have added a third component, intention to act, and have viewed attitudes as having three components:

1. The *cognitive* or knowledge component, which refers to belief or disbelief.
2. The *affective* or emotional component, which embodies positive or negative feelings.
3. The *conative* or behaviour-tendency component, which embodies a tendency to behave in a certain way. This does not mean that a certain behaviour *will* occur but that a certain action is *likely* to occur if the opportunity presents itself. An attitude therefore predisposes an individual to act in a certain way towards a person or object.

But when studying the concept of attitude it is also important to understand the reasons for people holding particular attitudes. Katz[3] has identified four functions that form the motivational basis for attitudes:

1. *The instrumental or adjustive function.* This directs people towards rewarding objects and away from undesirable ones. As a result, people acquire attitudes that are perceived as helpful in achieving desired goals or useful in avoiding undesired goals.
2. *The ego-defensive function.* This allows people to protect themselves from acknowledging their deficiencies. To a great extent, attitudes of negative prejudice help the individual sustain his self-concept by maintaining a sense of superiority over others.
3. *The value-expressive function.* This enables people to achieve self-expression in terms of centrally-held values. Value-expressive attitudes generate pleasure and satisfaction through expression of opinions that reflect self-concepts. Such attitudes differ from the ego-defensive attitudes which serve to obscure an individual's true nature from himself.
4. *The knowledge function.* This represents the cognitive component of attitudes which gives coherence and direction to experience. Katz argues that

knowledge is sought in order to give meaning to what would otherwise be an unorganized and chaotic universe.

From the components and functions outlined above, it can be seen that attitudes are distinguished by their multiplexity; that is, it is difficult to differentiate between the individual components and functions served by any particular attitude. Another important dimension is the degree to which attitudes are interrelated. There is certainly a tendency for attitudes to be clustered, and a similar tendency to categorize people and objects leading to the formation of stereotypes or brand images.

6.3 Stereotyping

Stereotyping is the term given to the human tendency to make over-simplifications and generalizations about people or objects based on limited experience. The classic demonstration of this phenomenon was provided by Katz and Braly[4] who asked 100 Princeton University students to assign, from a given list of 84 traits, those traits they thought more characteristic of certain groups. It was found that there was a wide measure of agreement as shown in Table 6.1.

Table 6.1
Demonstration of Stereotyping

Groups	*Traits/Characteristics*
Germans	Scientifically-minded, industrious, stolid.
Jews	Shrewd, mercenary, industrious.
Negroes	Superstitious, lazy, happy-go-lucky.
Italians	Artistic, impulsive, passionate.
English	Sportsmanlike, intelligent, conventional.
Americans	Industrious, intelligent, materialistic.
Irish	Pugnacious, quick-tempered, witty.

Although people have a unique individuality, this study showed that there is a wide belief that there are definite characteristics associated with members of any national or ethnic group.

It should not be thought, however, that stereotyping is necessarily unhealthy, for it does serve the function of simplifying the complexity of social interaction. It is not possible to relate to every new person as if he were unique, and the formation of a stereotype based on the class or category to which he belongs is inevitable until experience modifies it or shows it to be incorrect. Stereotyping can be helpful for it alleviates ambiguity and enables a fairly rapid and easy evaluation of people and objects. On the other hand, it may give too simplistic an evaluation and lead to the formation of prejudices and to discriminatory behaviour.

Most work on this topic has been undertaken in the sphere of person perception (see Chapter 7) but here we are concerned with the effect of stereotyping in determining attitudes towards products. Reierson[5] examined the question of American consumers regarding foreign products in terms of national stereotypes. He found clear evidence of stereotyping and thus established the requirement for marketers to take this phenomenon into account when evaluating export opportunities or the threat provided by imported products.

Darling and Kraft[6] in a study of the Finnish market showed that:

1. Knowledge of a product's country of origin as revealed by the 'Made in . . .' label affects consumers' attitudes towards products.
2. Knowledge of country of origin affects consumers' attitudes to other aspects of the marketing mix such as warranties and guarantees, advertising and promotional activities.
3. Knowledge of a product's country of origin affects the actual shopping and buying behaviour towards products and the levels of satisfaction obtained from the purchase of these products.

Given no differences in price, quality, or styling it was found that respondents would prefer products from countries in the following order : Finland, Sweden, West Germany, England, France, U.S.A., Japan, U.S.S.R.

Bannister and Saunders[7] in a study of U.K. consumers' attitudes towards imports examined the image of 'Made in . . .' labelled products from seven countries in terms of five attributes: reliability, value for money, appearance, availability, and workmanship. They found that substantial differences exist in these stereotyped images and whereas West Germany, the U.K., and Japan generally obtained favourable ratings on all attributes, France, Italy, and the U.S.A. usually obtained mediocre or neutral ratings; the U.S.S.R. consistently obtained poor ratings.

It is apparent from these studies that importing, if it is to be successful, must take into account the existing national stereotypes or images in the target market. Whilst Gaedeke[8] suggests that a brand name may overcome the 'Made in . . .' label in consumers' assessments of imported products, there remains a problem where the brand name is comparatively or completely unknown. In this situation the label of origin is likely to play an important role in the buying situation. It is thus important to ascertain the national stereotypes or images existing in a particular market. Whilst positive images can easily be used to advantage, it is far more difficult to overcome negative images. As Darling and Kraft[6] point out, 'The exporter . . . should pinpoint the attitudinal dimensions providing barriers to successful market entry and determine the need for, and feasibility of, corrective action. If none is possible, marketing resources might more profitably be spent in other markets'.

6.4 Attitudes and Behaviour

The previous section suggested that behaviour follows from the holding of certain attitudes. The fact, however, is that behaviour can and does determine attitudes, and at best the relationship must be seen to be interactive:

Attitudes   ⟶⟵   Behaviour

The major problem involved in attempting to predict behaviour on the basis of attitudes held is that attitudes, whilst being important, are not the sole determining factor. This will be seen more readily from the discussion on modelling in Chapter 8. Again, there are a number of variables which can affect the part played by attitudes in determining behaviour. Some of these are:

1. The strength of the attitude. The stronger the attitude, the greater the extent to which it may predict certain behaviour.
2. The existence of other attitudes. Stronger attitudes may inhibit or interfere with the behavioural expression of weaker attitudes.
3. The ability to respond to an attitude. Doob[9] argues that since attitudes are learned predispositions to respond, we must when acquiring an attitude also learn what responses to make on the basis of that attitude.
4. Situational factors, which are social environment variables. Belk[10] has identified five situational characteristics.
   (a) Physical surroundings in which the behaviour occurs.
   (b) Social surroundings, including the other people present in the situation.
   (c) Temporal perspective, including season and the time of day.
   (d) Task definition, which is the way the person perceives the task.
   (e) Antecedent states, which are temporary circumstances such as the consumers' moods or available money.

Finally, there is the problem of determining whether the opinions (the verbal expression of attitudes) that are measured in attitude scales are an appropriate reflection of what we define as attitudes. For example, the unconscious nature of many attitudes suggests there may be discrepancies between actual attitudes held and those we think we hold.

6.5 Attitude Measurement

Since attitudes are hypothetical constructs they are not directly observable and their strength and direction can only be inferred. Even so, some attempt at quantification of attitudes is necessary if we are to compare individuals as groups, and also to determine behavioural changes in individuals when they have experienced attitude change. To be able to determine the effect on attitudes of, for example, advertising and sales promotion, is obviously of vital importance to the marketer, but the measurement of the direct behavioural expression of an attitude (that is, the action arising from the holding of an attitude) is usually extremely difficult.

As a result, attitude measurement techniques concentrate on what individuals describe as being their 'feelings' towards the attitude object concerned. The most widely used approach to attitude measurement has been the attitude scale. These consist of sets of statements or words relating to an attitude item. They are usually concerned with measuring the *valence*, that is, the degree of positive or negative feeling, of the attitude. The best-known scaling techniques are described below.

6.51 The Thurstone Scale

This was derived by Thurstone and Chave[11] in 1929. The method requires the collection of as many statements as possible about the issue towards which attitudes are to be measured. These statements must be simple and unambiguous and must distinguish between the different attitudes that people may hold towards the issue. The next stage is to ask a large number of people, preferably over a hundred, to sort the statements into 11 piles, representing a scale from an extremely favourable attitude towards the issue to an extremely unfavourable attitude towards it. The judges are asked not to express their own attitudes, but to be as objective as possible in indicating the extent to which the statement is favourable or unfavourable towards the issue in question. As a result, each statement is assigned a value indicating the degree to which it represents a favourable or unfavourable attitude. A limited number of statements, possibly 20, that show good agreement among the judges and whose scale values have approximately equal intervals between them, are then chosen and form the attitude scale. Respondents are presented with these chosen statements in random order and asked to indicate those with which they agree. By checking the assigned numerical values already given to each statement chosen, a measure of the subjects' attitudes is obtained.

In examining attitudes to the Church, Thurstone and Chave produced the following scale values:

Scale Value	Statement
0.5	I feel the Church is the greatest agency for the uplift of the world.
2.4	I feel the Church is trying to adjust itself to a scientific world and deserves support.
5.2	I am neither for nor against the Church but I do not believe that Church-going will do anyone any harm.
8.0	I think the Church is petty, easily disturbed by matters of little importance.
11.0	I have nothing but contempt for the Church.

The scale values represent the degree of positive or negative attitudes to the Church, 1 being the most favourable, 11 the least favourable, and 6 being neutral. Thus, an individual agreeing with statements scoring an average of 5.2 could be described as holding an attitude slightly favourable to the Church.

The Thurstone scale has the advantage that statements are ascribed numerical values based on the agreement of judges prior to the actual use of the scale. They are based, therefore, on the social perceptions of the society in which the testing occurs. It must be realized, however, that the scale deals with equal-appearing intervals which may, or may not, be equal. Again, the use of a continuum of 11 units is arbitrary so that, for example, a score of 4 is not necessarily twice as high as a score of 2. Another problem is that the construction of the scale is cumbersome and time-consuming; and though its results have been shown to be reliable, it is no longer in wide use.

6.52 The Likert Scale

This was designed by Likert[12] in 1932 and is probably the most commonly used scaling technique. Here, each individual is asked not only if he agrees or disagrees with a statement such as 'Capital punishment is morally wrong', but is also required to indicate the extent to which he agrees by choosing one of five categories: Strongly agree; Agree; Neutral/Don't know; Disagree; and Strongly disagree.

To produce a numerical score a value is given to each category. Thus 'strongly agree' might be assigned a score of 5, 'agree' 4, and so on. The different item scores are summed to produce a total score. Obviously the item scores should have a common basis so that a high score on one item should not be neutralized by a low score on another item if the attitude is in a similar direction. Thus a high overall score can be interpreted as a positive attitude to a topic and a low overall score as a negative attitude.

It must be realized, however, that the same overall score can be obtained in many different ways and for this reason it is the pattern of responses that is far more meaningful. This does entail a more complicated analysis. Again, as with the Thurstone scale, the technique cannot produce equal intervals and, thus, a score of 4 does not represent an attitude twice that of a score of 2.

6.53 Osgood's Semantic Differential Scale

This was devised by Osgood *et al.*[13] in 1957 as part of a study of the meaning of words. It consists of a number of semantic scales based on bipolar adjectives. Respondents are asked to rate a concept in terms of a positioning between $+3$ and -3. An example is given in Table 6.2.

Table 6.2
Company A

	+3	+2	+1	0	-1	-2	-3	
Good	–	–	–	–	–	–	–	Bad
Modern	–	–	–	–	–	–	–	Old-fashioned
Fast	–	–	–	–	–	–	–	Slow
Active	–	–	–	–	–	–	–	Passive
Responsible	–	–	–	–	–	–	–	Irresponsible
Important	–	–	–	–	–	–	–	Unimportant

In this example respondents are asked to show the degree to which they feel the adjectives best describe an organization, Company A. The result can be expressed as a profile such as that given in Figure 6.1.

Profiles of this kind can be easily compared. For example, the profile of Company A can be compared with that constructed for its main competitor and the results used to form the basis of a corporate advertising campaign.

Osgood *et al.* also found that some scales tend to produce similar results. They identified three main clusters of similar scales which they labelled *Evaluation* (e.g. good – bad), *Potency* (e.g. strong – weak), and *Activity* (e.g. active – passive). These three factors account for nearly 50% of the

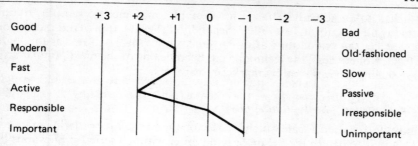

Figure 6.1 Profile of an organization derived from Osgood's Semantic Differential Scale

total 'meaning' of a concept, irrespective of the concept involved, the adjectives used, or the respondents questioned. By analysing various responses in terms of these three factors a concept can be represented in 'semantic space', as shown in Figure 6.2.

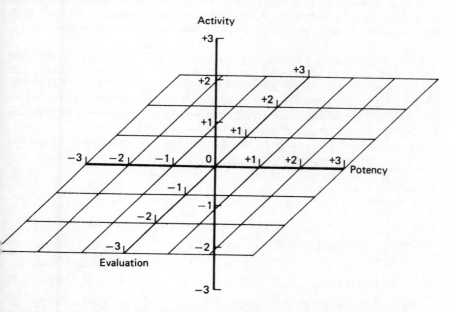

Figure 6.2 The three-dimensional matrix for mapping a concept in 'semantic space'

As with profile analysis, different three-dimensional ratings can be compared.

There are, however, many problems with the semantic differential scale, two of which may be noted here. Firstly, different semantic meanings may be attached to an adjective; 'fast', for example, may mean 50 m.p.h. to one person and 150 m.p.h. to another. Secondly, the evaluation of one dimension may affect the evaluations of other dimensions; this is known as the 'halo effect'. Nonetheless, the technique has become one of the most popular attitude scaling devices used by market researchers.

6.54 Guttman's Scalogram Analysis

Guttman[14] devised a scale which is based on the cumulative ordering of items. The aim is to determine the underlying order within a series of questions by means of obtaining dichotomous responses; that is, the respondent is required to answer 'yes' or 'no' to each question. The idea of a cumulative scale can be illustrated by reference to distance. Consider the following statements:

1. I live five miles or more from my nearest supermarket.
2. I live three miles or more from my nearest supermarket.
3. I live one mile or more from my nearest supermarket.

If a respondent answers 'yes' to the first statement, it follows that he has to answer 'yes' to statements 2 and 3. If the respondent answers 'no' to all three statements then it follows that he lives within a mile of his nearest supermarket.

This type of ordering is perfectly straightforward for statements involving items with a linear dimension. In addition to distance, such items could involve age, weight, or the number of times a particular supermarket was visited. Attitude statements, however, are not so easily ordered and to arrive at a satisfactory attitude scale usually involves a fairly complex mathematical treatment of data obtained from questionnaire surveys.

An example of a cumulative attitude scale, or scalogram, is given below:

Essential to modern family life is ownership of a:

Video recorder	yes	no					
Hi-fi system	yes	yes	no				
Colour TV	yes	yes	yes	no			
Freezer	yes	yes	yes	yes	no		
Automatic washing machine	yes	yes	yes	yes	yes	no	
Refrigerator	yes	yes	yes	yes	yes	yes	no
Attitude category	1	2	3	4	5	6	7

This scale is based on the assumption that a respondent who answers 'yes' to a video recorder would answer 'yes' to all other items; a respondent answering 'yes' to a freezer would answer 'yes' to an automatic washing machine and refrigerator, but 'no' to a colour television, hi-fi system, and video recorder. On this basis a respondent is placed in an attitude category depending on his 'crossover' point; that is the point at which he first answers 'no'. Thus, a respondent who answers 'no' to a video recorder but 'yes' to a Hi-fi system would be placed in category 2. On the basis of the category assigned to a respondent we should be able to reproduce exactly which items on the scale were covered and which were not; this is the principle of *cumulative reproducibility*.

It can, however, be readily argued that not all respondents will fall into one of these seven categories relating to ownership of consumer durables. For example, a respondent might answer 'yes' to a Hi-fi system, but 'no' to a colour television. This problem often occurs but can be allowed for in the mathematical treatment and a 90% 'fit' is considered to be more than adequate.

Scalogram analysis is a very useful technique for examining small shifts or changes in attitudes and, whilst such scales do not have equal-appearing intervals, they are generally reliable. Validity, however, depends largely on the item content, as can be ascertained from the above example. Again, the procedures involved in the construction of a scalogram are laborious and there is no guarantee that a useful scale will result. Responses must be dichotomous but this is not always possible because of the wide variety of responses that may be produced by a particular question; translating all possible responses into dichotomies involves a considerable amount of extra work.

6.55 Kelly's Repertory Grid Technique

Kelly[15] devised this technique as a means of 'mapping' the individual's 'personal constructs', their interrelationships, and changes over time. Kelly defined a construct as 'a way in which two things are alike and in the same way different from a third'. Thus, a construct is a dichotomy; it is either present or absent. In applying the test the respondent is asked to consider three objects, persons, products, etc., and to say in which way two are alike but also different from a third. The respondent can be left to supply his own constructs. Having completed this initial task further items can be introduced and the third grid built up. A grid for five brands of beer might be as shown in Table 6.3.

Table 6.3
Repertory Grid for Brands of Beer

Constructs	Brand A	Brand B	Brand C	Brand D	Brand E
Strong	x	—	x	—	—
Man's drink	x	—	x	—	—
Reasonably priced	x	x	—	—	x
Real ale	x	—	x	—	—
Good taste	x	—	x	—	x
Artificial taste	—	x	—	x	—
Good colour	x	—	x	—	—

If the same grid is applied to a number of respondents the results, when factor analysed, can be an invaluable indicator of brand positioning. Successive applications over time can be used to study changes in attitudes as a result of advertising or sales promotion.

The Repertory Grid is a very powerful tool in that it indicates individuals' subjective perceptions and has a great advantage in its flexibility since it can be used for various types of investigation.

6.6 Methodological Problems of Attitude Measurement

The requirements of any scientific technique are reliability – the ability of any given method to produce results that are consistent; and validity – the degree to which a technique measures what it is designed to measure.

The attitude scales described above have all demonstrated fairly good reliability, but difficulties arise with regard to the question of validity. Obviously, before being able to measure something we must define that something; and analysis of the literature on attitudes will reveal a number of different definitions. As stated earlier, recent writers generally agree that attitudes consist of three major components: conative, cognitive, and affective. But most of the techniques used in attitude measurement are self-report measures and what they measure is the affective component of attitudes. In other words, the attitude scale is essentially a one-dimensional measure that cannot represent the total complexity of an attitudinal system. Although there are exceptions such as the Semantic Differential which is one approach to multi-dimensional scaling, attitude scales generally assume the respondent's degree of 'like/dislike' to represent 'attitude', and this is then taken to indicate behaviour.

Despite their widespread use, attitude scales represent far too simplistic an approach to a very complex issue; and more sophisticated techniques are required. The Fishbein Model, described later, is one such approach but this also has its drawbacks and it is therefore true that a satisfactory explanation, and hence measurement, of attitude has still to emerge.

6.7 Theories of Attitudes

Attitude theories seek to explain how various attitudes are related, and how they operate to form a basis for individual behaviour. Since marketing seeks to reinforce positive attitudes and change negative attitudes to a product, it is important to be able to explain the variables influencing attitudinal structure and change. The traditional theories are based on the premise that the individual strives to maintain consistency among currently perceived attitudes and, when an inconsistency occurs, tension arises which results in pressure to return to a consistent state. The Balance, Congruity and Cognitive Dissonance theories outlined below are all consistency theories. However, recent work has emphasised the multi-dimensional nature of attitudes and compensatory theories are based on the premise that a strong attribute of an object will compensate for a weak attribute of the same object; the Fishbein Model described below is such a theory.

6.71 Balance Theory

This was developed by Heider[16, 17] who considered attitude systems as being either balanced or imbalanced. According to this theory attitudes towards persons or objects have positive or negative values, and there is a tendency for individuals to change attitudes when the attitude system becomes imbalanced as a result of attitudes not being similarly signed.

The theory is basically concerned with the situation of one person receiving information from a second person about some object. In other words, it is concerned mainly with dyadic relationships. The examples in Figure 6.3 illustrate the main tenets of the theory.

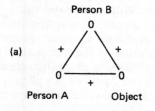

(a)

Here the system is balanced. Person A has a positive attitude to Person B. Person A has a positive attitude to the object as does Person B.

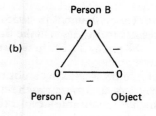

(b)

Here the system is imbalanced. Person A has a negative attitude to Person B and to the object. But Person B expresses a negative opinion of the object, agreeing with Person A and thus imbalancing the system.

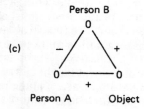

(c)

Here the system is again imbalanced. Person A has a negative attitude to Person B and a positive attitude to the object. But Person B expresses a positive opinion of the object, causing an imbalance.

Figure 6.3 Attitude change situations in terms of Balance Theory

When there is an imbalance in the attitude system it produces tension which the individual will attempt to alleviate. It may, of course, be possible to live with the tension but if not then attitude change has to occur. Change can be in two directions:

1. The attitude to the other person can change. In Figure 6.3 (b), person A might change his attitude towards person B, thus bringing about a balanced system.
2. The attitude to the object can change. In Figure 6.3(b), person A might change his attitude to the object, again bringing about a balanced system.

The theory has important implications for promotion techniques generally and for face-to-face selling in particular. For example, the techniques used by a salesman may provoke a negative attitude towards the salesman by the prospective customer. The customer may have a positive attitude to the product but this might change as a result of the negative attitude towards the salesman. It is worth noting in this context that many U.K. consumers do not appreciate the American style of aggressive selling and may react unfavourably in a manner that can be analysed in terms of this theory.

Balance theory has an advantage in that it is simple and easy to understand. But it examines the relationship in terms of positive and negative signs only and does not attempt any quantitative evaluation of the degree of attitude feeling. It is therefore difficult to predict the direction of attitude change, if any. Again, it has been criticized on the grounds of its simplicity, since consumer behaviour consists of a series of attitudinal systems and a complete analysis requires a greater degree of sophistication.

6.72 Congruity Theory

This theory was proposed by Osgood and Tannenbaum[18] in 1955. Like Balance Theory, it deals with positive and negative attitudes. Unlike Balance Theory, it attempts to provide some idea of the strengths of these attitudes through measurement.

The theory is concerned with the effect of one person taking a positive or negative position towards another person or object, and measures the evaluation of that position on a scale from $+3$ (highly favourable) to -3 (highly unfavourable), with a rating of 0 being a neutral attitude. From this base, several predictions can be made regarding the effect on an individual of another person's evaluation of an object. If *congruity* (that is, consistency of attitudes) is to be achieved, evaluation of the person and object must change by an amount equal to the discrepancy between them. The final evaluation is dependent on the discrepancy between the initial evaluation of the person and object.

Thus, if someone we like a great deal (whom we evaluate at $+3$) praises something we like a great deal (which again we evaluate at $+3$) then there is no discrepancy. On the other hand, if someone who is liked (say $+2$) says something positive about something that is not liked very much (say -2) then there is a discrepancy of 4. In this situation, there is a condition of tension which is resolved by reducing the favourable attitude toward the person and also by decreasing the unfavourable attitude toward the object that is not liked. It might be expected that the result would be that the attitude to both person and object becomes rated at 0 (neutral); that is, both have changed by 2. In the case of there being a strong attitude towards the person ($+3$) and a weaker negative attitude towards the object (-1) then the same degree of change will occur but the person might now rate $+2$ (a change of 1) and the object $+2$ (a change of 3). Strong attitudes are generally more difficult to change than are weak attitudes. These examples are illustrated in Figure 6.4.

It must be noted however that this magnitude of change does not neces-

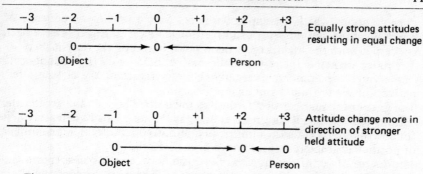

Figure 6.4 Attitude change situations in terms of Congruity Theory

sarily occur since:

1. if the individual does not believe the information, he can reject it and no change in attitudes will occur;
2. if the individual only slightly disbelieves the information, then attitude change is likely to be only slight.

The congruity principle is often used in advertising and sales promotions. Advertisers often use film stars and other celebrities to promote their products and services. For example, consider the case of David Niven promoting instant coffee. What effect could this have on a consumer's attitude towards the product? If the consumer rates David Niven at $+3$ and instant coffee at -1 then the effect could be, as mentioned above, that both become rated at $+2$. The product has gained considerably in the consumer's opinion although David Niven has become liked a little less. If, on the other hand, the consumer does not believe the message on the grounds, for example, that David Niven would not drink instant coffee, and only appears in the advertisement for financial reward, then there is likely to be no attitude change. Of course, there are other possible outcomes but these two examples serve to illustrate the type of predictions that can be made by this theory.

6.73 The Theory of Cognitive Dissonance

This theory was formulated by Festinger[19] and is based on the premise that attitudes held by an individual tend to be consistent and that the individual's actions are usually consistent with his attitudes. In taking any decision, for example to purchase a product, the individual encounters a conflict situation in which he has to weigh up the positive and negative attitudes to the various alternatives. Dissonance theory deals with inconsistencies that occur between two cognitions after a decision has been made. Thus following a decision, information about the positive features of rejected alternatives and about the negative features of the chosen alternative, can produce *dissonance*. The extent, or magnitude, of the dissonance will depend on a number of factors.

1. The more significant the decision to the individual, the greater the dissonance. Thus dissonance is likely to be strongest for the purchase of

durable goods which are expensive items with a very low frequency of purchase. Many studies (for example Ehrlich *et al.*[20], Engel[21]) have been concerned with the incidence of dissonance in motor car purchasing.
2. The more attractive the rejected alternative, the greater the dissonance.
3. The greater the number of negative characteristics of the chosen alternative, the greater the dissonance.
4. The greater the number of alternatives the individual has, the greater the dissonance. Since all alternatives will have some positive features, it follows that the greater the number of alternatives, the greater the number of positive characteristics that have been rejected.
5. The degree of *cognitive overlap* that exists between the considered alternatives. The term cognitive overlap refers to the extent to which the alternatives have similar characteristics. The greater the degree of cognitive overlap, the smaller the magnitude of dissonance.

The theory postulates that dissonance is 'psychologically uncomfortable' and the resulting tension induces the individual to attempt to reduce the dissonance and achieve more consistency or consonance between the cognitions involved. *Consonance* can be achieved in a number of ways.

1. The decision can be revoked. However this is not always possible and can be expensive. The second-hand value of a three-month-old motor car is considerably less than the purchase price when new.
2. The chosen alternative can be made more attractive by the individual giving attention only to information supporting its positive features, or by devaluing information pointing to its negative features.
3. The rejected alternatives can be made less attractive by the individual giving attention only to information illustrating their negative features, or by devaluing information pointing to their positive features.
4. The attitudes or beliefs can be changed so that they are consistent with behaviour. For example, a consumer may hold an unfavourable attitude towards a product, but a coupon offer may induce him to try it. His behaviour in trying the product is inconsistent with the attitude he holds and dissonance results. By re-evaluating the product, possibly through establishing or even imagining a cognitive overlap, and adopting a positive attitude towards it, the individual achieves consonance; that is attitudes and behaviour are now consistent.

The theory appears to have several implications for marketing:

1. Advertising must be careful not to exaggerate the positive features of a product. If a product does not live up to the consumer's expectations, as derived from advertisements, then dissonance will occur and this could be reduced through a subsequent negative evaluation of the product. This could result in unfavourable word-of-mouth communication to other members of that consumer's peer group.
2. Attitude change can be induced when attitudes held are inconsistent with behaviour. Incentives, such as free samples or coupon offers, can be used to entice consumers to try the product, the resulting dissonance provoking attitude change. This could have an impact on brand loyalty.

Mittelstaedt[22] found that the greater the post-decision dissonance after the first purchase, the greater the probability of buying that brand again. Here it must be noted that there is some evidence that small inducements are better, since large offers allow the consumer to rationalize his behaviour. Engel, Blackwell and Kollat[23], however, argue that the consumer is likely to resist dissonance and avoid the induced behaviour if that behaviour was perceived as unacceptable, and that free samples may result in the product not being given a fair trial, dissonance being of a small magnitude. As a result, it is possible that many of these incentive offers are ineffective in inducing greater market penetration.

3. Purchasers can be reinforced. Advertisements may convey the positive features of a product as a reinforcing rather than a persuasive message. However the evidence is rather inconclusive and money spent on such advertising messages may well be wasted. A better strategy is likely to be that of providing more information about the product purchased. For example, in the case of a kitchen appliance, a user's manual and a free cookbook could be packed with the product.

In conclusion it can be stated that Cognitive Dissonance is an interesting theory but one that needs to be treated with caution. The evidence is often inconclusive and studies have been criticized on the basis of their measurements of cognitive dissonance and the experimental designs employed. Whereas the theory may have important consequences for marketing, note should be taken of Aronson[24] when he states that knowledge 'of situations in which dissonance *can* occur is not always useful in determining whether dissonance *does* occur'.

6.74 Fishbein's Model

This was postulated by Fishbein[25] in 1967 and resulted in a new way of thinking about attitudes in that it drew attention to the different components of attitude. Basically the model states that an attitude towards an object is equal to the sum of the products of the belief about each attribute of the object, weighted by the evaluation of the importance of each attribute. This is stated by the following equation:

$$A_o = \sum_{i=1}^{n} B_i \, a_i$$

where:

A_o = the attitude towards abject o;
B_i = the strength of belief i about o;
a_i = the evaluation aspects of B;
n = the number of beliefs.

This implies that the evaluations of various attributes can offset one another. As a result, the analysis has been labelled a *'compensating'* model.

For example, consider the different attributes of a particular motor car. There are obviously many attributes that consumers might take into account, but for the purpose of illustrating the Fishbein model let us consider four:

speed, style, price, and prestige. First the strength or importance of each attribute is determined using a scale from 1 (high importance) to 3 (low importance). Then, an evaluation of each attribute is made using a scaling technique such as the Semantic Differential; thus 1 is a high evaluation and 7 a low evaluation. The several products are then summed to provide a total attitude score; the lower the score the more favourable the attitude. This is shown in Table 6.4.

Table 6.4
Attitude score according to Fishbein Model

Motor Car Attribute	Importance B_i	Evaluation a_i	Product $B_i a_i$
Speed	1	4	4
Style	2	5	10
Price	3	3	9
Prestige	1	1	1

$$\text{Attitude Score} = \sum_{i=1}^{4} B_i a_i = 24$$

In this example the overall attitude is quite favourable, the maximum score being 84, but the important attributes to the respondent are those of prestige and speed.

The advantage of the Fishbein model is that it indicates which attributes are of importance to the consumer in determining attitude toward the object, and the degree to which the consumer evaluates the object in terms of these different attributes. This can provide a valuable basis for determining product positioning in the market. It indicates which attributes could best be emphasised in advertising and sales promotion, and also helps to determine which product attributes might be altered in order to secure a wider market. The main problems involved with the technique concern the choice of attributes used in each investigation and also the way in which respondents interpret the 'importance' criteria in the scaling technique employed in the evaluative part of the investigation.

Fishbein also recognized the problem that certain constraints can inhibit the translation of an attitude into purchasing behaviour. Thus, an individual may have highly favourable attitudes towards various attributes of a particular motor car, but limited financial resources could result in a low tendency to purchase the car. As a result, Fishbein[26] developed a model that seeks to predict an individual's attitude towards an act; this is known as the *Extended Fishbein Model* and it describes behavioural intentions resulting from an individual's attitude towards performing a particular act and that individual's subjective perception of the norm concerning that act. The model is stated as:

$$\text{A-act} = \sum_{i=1}^{n} b_i e_i \qquad \text{where:}$$

A-act = the individual's attitude towards performing a specific act (e.g. the purchase of a motor car).

b_i = the individual's perceived belief that performing the behaviour will lead to some consequence i;

e_i = the individual's evaluation of consequence i;

n = the number of salient consequences involved.

Fishbein is saying that the attitude towards any act is a function of a particular belief or set of beliefs about the act and the strength with which these beliefs are held. This is quantified in a manner similar to that shown above for the original model.

Lutz[27] has drawn attention to three marketing strategies that can be developed as a result of the Extended Fishbein Model.

1. Change consumers' existing beliefs (b_i) through, for example, increasing advertising.
2. Change consumers' evaluation of the value of a particular consequence (e_i).
3. Introduce a new $b_i e_i$ factor.

The Fishbein Extended Model has, however, provoked quite a lot of criticism. Sampson[28] whilst giving credit to Fishbein for drawing attention to the belief and evaluation components of attitude, doubts that 'behavioural intent' is a satisfactory surrogate for behaviour. In Sampson's view, people's stated intentions and their eventual actions are usually quite different and often have no relation to their attitudes. On the other hand, the Fishbein Model when first introduced appealed greatly to many market researchers for it claimed to provide a method of relating attitudes to behaviour and this, after all, is one of the fundamental issues in market research. The model still has many disciples, and for a fuller exposition of the merits of Fishbein the reader should consult Mary Tuck's book *How Do We Choose?*

6.8 Changing Attitudes

The last section provided an appreciation of the structure of attitudes and indicated a basis for a strategy of attitude modification. Obviously, the changing of attitudes is an important function of marketing communication and it is the aim of this section to describe some of the variables that can affect the process.

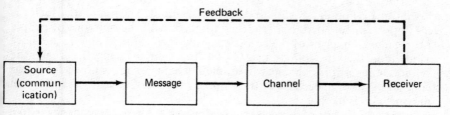

Figure 6.5 The communication process

Any communication system can be analysed in terms of four variables, as shown in Figure 6.5.

These four variables are the same irrespective of the situation. The source, for example, may be a friend talking in a pub or may be a personality in a television advertisement. Feedback may be immediate, as in a face-to-face interaction, or may be obtained by means of market research surveys. The important point to note is that each of these variables can have an effect on the extent of attitude change resulting from a particular communication. It is not intended, however, to attempt an evaluation of any particular channel of persuasive communication, for as Wilmshurst[29] points out:

> To discuss whether advertising is 'better' than public relations or personal selling is meaningless. Each method has advantages and disadvantages, and, depending on the circumstances, one may be more cost-effective than another.

In this section it is intended, therefore, to concentrate on source, message, and receiver variables in the context of planned persuasive communication situations. Whilst this might seem to exclude important influences on the individual, such as reference groups mentioned in the last chapter, it must be emphasised that the general findings outlined below hold for many different types of communication situation.

6.81 Source Factors

The two most important aspects here are the personal attributes of the communicator and the receiver's perceptions of the intentions of the communicator.

Personal Attributes. A vital factor is the amount of prestige that a communicator commands. Prestige here refers to the receiver's perception of the expertise of the communicator and the degree of respect involved. Hovland and Weiss[30] showed that communications attributed to high-prestige sources produced greater attitude modification than those attributed to low-prestige sources. The reason for this appears to be that people are prepared to consider more carefully an expert's views, but the expertise has to be established before the communication is made, otherwise the same degree of attention will not be given to it.

The extent to which someone who has a great deal of prestige in one area can transfer that prestige and influence attitude change in another unrelated area is an open question. Thus, a racing driver promoting a particular motor car will be perceived as talking as an expert, but in promoting a brand of margarine he may be perceived as being any other famous personality who is associating his popularity with that particular brand. The popularity factor is very important for there is a tendency to agree with the opinions of people who are liked. In terms of the consistency theories outlined above, the more an individual likes the communicator of a discrepant message, the greater the likelihood that attitude change will result. This can be a more powerful factor than that of prestige because of the tendency for individuals to identify with someone who is liked.

Allied to this factor of liking is that of similarity. There is a tendency to like people who are similar in terms of economic and ethnic background and such people can influence us more than people who are different. This appears to be the product of a tendency to regard similar people as perceiving things in a similar way to our own, due to a perceived common background and value system. This can be explained in terms of balance theory: if A is similar to B on many dimensions, but differs on one issue, then an imbalance occurs. The resulting tension can be resolved either by changing all the things on which there is agreement, or by changing the attitude on the issue which causes the tension. Obviously in this case we would expect the attitude toward the issue producing tension to be changed.

Intentions. Generally the more disinterested the source appears to be in a particular issue, the more that source is trusted. If the communicator is perceived as setting out to change attitudes then he is already suspect and the message tends to lose effectiveness. On the other hand, any characteristic of the source that implies expertise or honesty tends to increase the effectiveness of the message, even if the source has low prestige. For example, Walster *et al.*[31] showed that a low prestige and highly doubtful source, a convicted criminal, can have a considerable amount of influence when he argues in favour of a position that would hurt rather than benefit him, in this case harsher criminal punishment.

An interesting phenomenon that has been observed regarding the effectiveness of a source has been termed the 'Sleeper Effect'. Whilst the impact of the source is strongest immediately after exposure to the message, it appears to be less important some time later. Kelman and Hovland[32] showed that the immediate effect of a positive (that is competent, well-informed) source is greater than that of a negative (that is biased, uninformed) source. After a few weeks and when the subjects were not reminded of the source of the message, the effect of the positive source had declined while that of the negative source had increased. When the subjects were reminded of the positive or negative nature of the source, the original effect recurred.

This study indicates that individuals tend to forget the source of a message more rapidly than the content. The source effect may disappear over time whilst the message effect remains relatively constant. The immediate result was a product of the perceived trustworthiness of the negative source. However, when the actual source became no longer spontaneously associated with the message, the source effect declined, the positive effect no longer helping the message and the negative effect no longer damaging it. This illustrates the difference between getting a message through and getting people to accept it. It would appear that people hear a message and assimilate its contents irrespective of how they feel about the source.

6.82 Message Factors

Although there are a number of message variables that can be identified it must be appreciated that their effectiveness is related to both source factors and receiver factors.

1. *Amount of discrepancy.* It is apparent from the discussion so far that the greater the discrepancy between message content and an already held attitude, the greater the required attitude change. Whilst it may often be easier

to change an attitude than to reject the source, there seems to be a threshold after which the discrepancy is so extreme that it becomes difficult to resolve, and rejection becomes the main mode of resolution. The threshold level is, however, affected by the prestige of the source: the higher the level of prestige, the greater the threshold level.

2. *One-sided and two-sided messages.* The approach in which both sides of an argument are stated is usually more effective than when only one side of the argument is presented. This is related to the perceived intentions of the source: a two-sided presentation appears less like an attempt to manipulate attitudes than does a one-sided statement. But the characteristics of the target audience have an effect; a two-sided message directed at a poorly-informed, relatively unintelligent audience could confuse and result in a weakening of an already held attitude.

3. *Repetition of the message.* A message that contains new information on a topic is likely to be more effective than one which repeats previously communicated information. On the other hand, repetition aids human learning and can be important. As was shown in Chapter 3, information is moved from short term memory into long term memory through repetition, enhancing cognitive rehearsal. It appears that there is again a threshold level after which a message suffers habituation, or wear-out, and not only loses effectiveness but also may alienate the audience. Generally, messages that contain only one item of information, or are humorous, tend to wear out quickly. This can be overcome by varying the number of messages, for example, by use of a series of advertisements, or by each message having several items of information. The important principle seems to be that of being able to introduce factors that extend the learning process.

4. *Fear arousal.* The effectiveness of appeals to fear in persuasive communication has been a controversial matter with a number of different studies resulting in different conclusions. In Chapter 2 it was mentioned that a consumer's motivation can affect his perception of messages involving fear appeals and we shall now examine this topic further.

The original work in this area was that of Janis and Feshbach[33] in 1953. They found that those subjects who had received the most fear-arousing message had the least change in attitude, whilst those who had received moderate messages changed significantly in the intended direction. It was concluded that fear arousal reduced compliance as a result of the inhibitory effects of anxiety. Subsequently some studies supported this finding, but many others found that the greater the fear aroused, the stronger was the attitude change and the effect on behaviour. An analysis by Higbee[34] of the various studies concluded that the weight of evidence supported the positive effect of fear as a persuasive appeal.

In attempting to reconcile the contradictory results of the different studies one has to consider the various methodological issues involved. Such factors include the importance to the subject of the fear topic involved, the initial anxiety regarding the fear topic, and even the subjects' personalities. Janis[35] has suggested that the relationship between fear and attitude change depends on the level of fear involved. At low levels fear arousal produces greater attitude change but there is a threshold after which fear becomes so intense as to trigger defence mechanisms against the message. McGuire[36] emphasises the need to take account of subjects' initial concern with a topic as a factor in determining the effect of a fear-arousing message. Given a high initial concern, a fear-arousing message may overwhelm the subject with anxiety, thus producing a reduction in the effectiveness of the appeal.

6.83 Receiver Factors

In Chapter 2 it was shown how perceptual processes can produce a distortion of sensory data. In relation to persuasive messages, it must be emphasised that every individual will categorize and interpret various messages in the light of his previous experiences. It must be remembered that each individual is unique in terms of a wealth of experience and, by and large, receiver factors are what may be termed personality attributes. Although personality is the subject of the next chapter it is useful at this stage to identify the following receiver factors.

1. *Self-esteem*. This refers to the individual's feelings of adequacy and self-worth (See Chapter 7). People who have low self-esteem tend to be more easily persuaded than those who have high self-esteem.
2. *Intelligence*. Hovland, Janis and Kelley[37] point out that:
   (a) people with high intelligence will tend to be more influenced than those with low intelligence when exposed to persuasive messages that rely primarily on impressive logical arguments;
   (b) people with high intelligence will tend to be less influenced than those with low intelligence when exposed to persuasive messages that rely on unsupported generalities or false, illogical, and irrelevant arguments.
3. *Sex differences*. Several studies have indicated that women are more persuasible than men. This is, however, a sex-typed role function rather than a genetic factor. Generally, women occupy the more submissive and dependent roles in society and, as a result, tend to be conditioned to respond to persuasive messages. It should be noted that this situation is rapidly changing as the pattern of traditional roles in society changes.

6.9 Implications for Marketing

Although there are considerable methodological problems connected with both the definition and the measurement of attitudes, existing knowledge, albeit limited, can be successfully applied in marketing.

It has been seen that the attitudes held by consumers influence the way they perceive a particular product and this, in turn, affects buying decisions. Attitude research can therefore be a useful tool in the identification of market segments, and can provide a basis on which the marketer can devise a marketing strategy appropriate to individual target markets.

The theories of attitudes presented in this chapter suggest a number of basic strategies that could be applied by the marketer.

1. He could try to modify those attitudes that strongly influence the purchase of a particular product class, so as to bring consumer attitudes in line with his company's offerings. For example, British Rail's advertising campaign 'Let the train take the strain' drew attention to the convenience and relaxation of a train journey compared with a similar journey by car.

2. He could try to change the consumer's choice criteria by adding to the product characteristics already established as being important to the consumer. Examples include adding a mouthwash to toothpaste, a fabric softener to washing powder, and 'coolness' to a cigarette. This strategy is frequently employed with products at the 'maturity stage'.

3. Alternatively, if a brand is rated higher than competing brands for a particular product attribute the marketer may seek to change consumers' perceptions of the importance of this particular attribute in relation to other product characteristics. For example, a motor car manufacturer may draw attention to a special rust-proofing treatment, or a washing machine manufacturer to a 'no tangle' washing action.

4. Another strategy would be to attempt to bring consumers' perceptions of a particular brand in line with their image of the 'ideal' brand. This might be achieved by drawing consumers' attention to two or three key product features which attitude research has identified as being most important to the consumer in his evaluation of competing products. Ideally, the product attributes being promoted should be those for which the brand has a relative advantage, as otherwise post-purchase dissonance could arise leading to the formation of a negative attitude towards the particular brand.

5. A final strategy which, like 4 above, also involves changing consumers' brand perception sets, would be to attempt to change consumers' perceptions of competing brands. For example, Avis's 'We try harder' campaign drew consumers' attention to the fact that the biggest is not always the best.

Each of the strategies mentioned above involves the development of consumers' attitudes about a product in such a way that their perceptions of a particular brand are likely to be favourable. As was noted earlier, however, the communication processes that influence attitude formation are affected by source, message, and receiver variables. Although the marketer can exercise no control over variables inherent in the receiver, he can influence both the source and message variables.

A company can enhance its source credibility by building a sound corporate reputation. This would involve producing reliable products; providing good after sales service; giving sound warranties and guarantees; using friendly and helpful staff; and acting in a socially responsible manner. Such a reputation may take many years to build and may need reinforcement periodically by a corporate advertising campaign.

A company's choice of retailers for his product is also important since retailers act as important sources of information at the local level. Unknown brands may sell more easily through well-respected department stores or speciality shops than through other outlets that have a reputation for neither reliability nor expertise.

Source credibility can also be enhanced by the choice of media through which a product is promoted. Specialist magazines that have established a reputation for expertise can be particularly credible sources of product information; such magazines include *Ideal Home, Yachting World*, and *Practical Gardening*.

6.10 Summary

1. Attitudes are hypothetical constructs that may be distinguished by their multiplexity. They may be viewed as having three main components — cognative, affective, and conative.
2. An attitude predisposes an individual to behave in a certain way towards a person or object but the relationship between attitudes and behaviour is interactive. Attitude is not the sole determining factor in behaviour.
3. Attitudes tend to be clustered and interrelated. The tendency to categorize people and objects leads to the formation of stereotypes.
4. Attitude measurement techniques usually concentrate on determining the affective component of attitude. The best known techniques are the Thurstone Scale, Likert Scale, Osgood's Semantic Differential Scale, Guttman's Scalogram Analysis, and Kelly's Repertory Grid. Whilst showing good reliability, the question of their validity is open to doubt. Although more sophisticated techniques, such as the Fishbein Model, attempt to account for the complexity of attitude systems, a satisfactory technique for the measurement of attitudes has yet to emerge.
5. Attitude theories attempt to explain how various attitudes are related and how they operate to form a basis for behaviour. Most theories are based on the premise that the individual strives to maintain consistency among currently perceived attitudes, and are hence labelled consistency theories. The best known of these are the balance, congruity, and cognitive dissonance theories. More recent theories, such as that of Fishbein, are based on the premise that a strong attribute of an object will compensate for a weak attribute of the same object and are thus labelled 'compensatory' theories.
6. Attitude modification or change is an important function of marketing communication. The important variables in any communication process are source, message, channel, and receiver.
7. The important source factors are personal attributes and the intentions of the source as perceived by the receiver. The message factors of interest are discrepancy, one- and two-sided messages, repetition, and fear arousal. Receiver factors that should be noted are self-esteem, intelligence, and sex differences.
8. A knowledge of attitudes is important to successful marketing. Attitude research can be a useful tool in the identification of market segments and can provide a basis for marketing strategy appropriate to individual target markets.

References

1. Allport, G.W. 'The Historial Background of Modern Social Psychology', *Handbook of Social Psychology*, G. Lindzey, ed. (Reading, Massachusetts: Addison-Wesley, 1954).
2. Krech, D & Crutchfield, R.S. *Theory and Problems of Social Psychology* (New York: McGraw-Hill, 1948).
3. Katz, D. 'The Functional Approach to the Study of Attitudes', *Public Opinion Quarterly*, 1960, 25.
4. Katz, D. & Braly, K. 'Racial Stereotypes of One Hundred College Students'. *J. Abnorm. Soc. Psychol.*, 1933, 28.
5. Reierson, C. 'Are Foreign Products seen as National Stereotypes?', *Journal of Retailing*, 1966, 40.
6. Darling, J.R. & Kraft, F.B. 'A Competitive Profile of Products and Associated Marketing Practices of Selected European and Non-European Countries', *European Journal of Marketing*, 1977, 11.
7. Bannister J.P. & Saunders, J.A. 'U.K. Consumers' Attitudes towards Imports: The Measurement of National Stereotype Image', *European Journal of Marketing*, 1978, 12.
8. Gaedeke, R. 'Consumer Attitudes toward Products "made in" Developing Countries', *Journal of Retailing*, 1973, 49.
9. Doob, L.W. 'The Behaviour of Attitudes', *Psychological Review*, 1947, 54.
10. Belk, R.W. 'Situational Variables and Consumer Behaviour' *Journal of Consumer Research,* 1975, 2.
11. Thurstone, L.L. & Chave, E.J. *The Measurement of Attitudes* (Chicago: University of Chicago Press, 1929).
12. Likert, R. 'A Technique for the Measurement of Attitudes', *Archives of Psychology*, 1932, 140.
13. Osgood, C.E., Suci, G.J. & Tannenbaum, P.H. *The Measurement of Meaning* (Urbana, Illinois: University of Illinois Press, 1957).
14. Guttman, L. 'The Basis for Scalogram Analysis', *Measurement and Prediction*, S.A. Stouffer, ed. (Princeton, New Jersey: Princeton University Press, 1950).
15. Kelly, G.A. *The Psychology of Personal Constructs* (New York: W.W. Norton, 1955).
16. Heider, F. 'Attitudes and Cognitive Organization', *Journ. Psychology*, 1946, 21.
17. Heider, F. *The Psychology of Interpersonal Relations* (New York: Wiley, 1958).
18. Osgood, C.E. & Tannenbaum, P.H. 'The Principle of Congruity in the Prediction of Attitude Change', *Psychol. Review*, 1955, 62.
19. Festinger, L. *A Theory of Cognitive Dissonance* (New York: Harper & Row, 1957).
20. Ehrlich, D., Guttman, I. Schonback, P.M and Mills, J. 'Post Decision Exposure to Relevant Information', *Journ. Abnormal and Social Psych.*, 1957, 54.
21. Engel, J.F. 'Are Automobile Purchasers Dissonant Consumers?' *Journ. Marketing*, 1963, 27.

22. Mittelstaedt, R. 'A Dissonance Approach to Repeat Purchasing Behaviour', *Journ. Marketing Research*, 1969, 6.
23. Engel, J.F., Blackwell, R.D. and Kollat, D.T. *Consumer Behaviour* (Hinsdale, Illinois: Dryden Press, 1978).
24. Aronson, E. 'Dissonance Theory: Progress and Problems', *Theories of Cognitive Consistency*, Abelson *et al*, eds. (Chicago: Rand McNally, 1968).
25. Fishbein, M. 'Attitude and Prediction of Behaviour', *Attitude Theory and Measurement* M. Fishbein, ed. (New York: Wiley, 1967).
26. Fishbein, M. 'Attitude, Attitude Change, and Behaviour: A Theoretical Overview'. *Attitude Research Bridges the Atlantic*, P. Levine, ed. (Chicago: American Marketing Association, 1975).
27. Lutz, R.J. 'Changing Brand Attitudes through Modification of Cognitive Structure', *Journ. of Consumer Research*, 1975.
28. Sampson, P. 'The Technical Revolution of the 1970's – Will it Happen in the 1980's', *Journ. MRS*, 1980, 22.
29. Wilmshurst, J. *The Fundamentals and Practice of Marketing* (London: Heinemann, 1978).
30. Hovland, C. and Weiss, W. 'The Influence of Source Credibility on Communication Effectiveness', *Public Opinion Quarterly*, 1954, 15.
31. Walster, E., Aronson, E. and Abrahams, D. 'On Increasing the Persuasiveness of a Low Prestige Communicator', *Journ. Expt. Social Psych.* 1966, 2.
32. Kelman, H. and Hovland, C. ' "Reinstatement" of the Communicator in Delayed Measurement of Opinion Change', *Journ. Abnorm. Social Psych.*, 1953, 48.
33. Janis, I.L., and Feshbach, S. 'Effects of Fear Arousing Communication', *Journ. Abnormal & Social Psych.* 1953, 48.
34. Higbee, K. 'Fifteen Years of Fear Arousal: Research on Threat Appeals: 1953–1968', *Psych Bulletin*, 1969, 72.
35. Janis, I.L. 'Effects of Fear Arousal on Attitude Change: Recent Developments in Theory and Experimental Research', *Advances in Experimental Social Psychology Vol. 3.* L. Berkowitz, ed. (New York: Academic Press, 1967).
36. McGuire, W.J. 'Attitudes and Opinions', *Annual Review of Psychology Vol. 17,* P.R. Farnsworth, ed. (Palo Alto, California: Annual Reviews, 1966).
37. Hovland, C.I., Janis, I.L. and Kelley, H.H. *Communication and Persuasion* (New Haven, Conn.: Yale University Press, 1953).

Further Reading

Oppenheim, A.N. *Questionnaire Design and Attitude Measurement* (London: Heinemann, 1966).
Reich, B. and Adcock, C. *Values, Attitudes and Behaviour Change* (London: Methuen, 1976).
Tuck, M. *How Do We Choose?* (London: Methuen, 1976).

Past Examination Questions

1. 'It is extremely doubtful whether attitudes can be located, identified and defined sufficiently closely to warrant the importance currently assigned to them by much market research practice'. Give reasons for agreeing or disagreeing with this statement. (IM 1975)
2. Is an attitude towards a product a function of usage or is usage of a product a function of attitude? (IM 1976)
3. Why do individuals' attitudes change? (IM 1977)
4. Examine the effectiveness of any one attitude scaling technique as a method of attitude measurement. (IM 1978)
5. What are attitudes? To what extent does a knowledge of attitudes enable us to predict action? What else might affect a consumer's buying behaviour? (CAM 1979)
6. In an experiment, university students were asked to rate three fictitious national groups along with thirty-two other known ethnic groups. Most students showed no hesitation in assigning unfavourable traits to the fictitious groups. Relate this finding to psychological and sociological concepts that you know, and discuss its relevance to marketing. (CAM 1979)

7. THE INDIVIDUAL WITHIN SOCIETY

'A continuing awareness of the existence and force of individual characteristics will help any propagandist to avoid the trap of seeing his audience as a lump of humanity instead of as separate, distinct individuals.'

Abelson

7.1 Introduction

In the previous two chapters we have examined some of the social processes that affect the individual. The essential point is that all interaction is a two-way process involving at least two individuals, each having unique characteristics, who function at an individual level within society whilst, at the same time, contributing to the functioning of that society. The unique characteristics of an individual make up his 'personality' and this is partly determined by biological factors and partly by the socialization process; although to what extent it is determined by the social environment is impossible to say. This has led writers such as Allport[1] to characterize personality as an 'open system' involving a mutual transaction between the individual and his environment. Hollander[2] has proposed the schematic representation of personality shown in Figure 7.1.

According to Hollander, the *psychological core* is the central feature of personality. It embodies the individual's pyschological states, such as his attitudes and beliefs, his past experiences, and his self-concept. The latter is important because it is a factor determining the extent to which the individual will be susceptible to social influence.

Typical responses refer to such things as characteristic activity levels and sense of humour, which are associated with learned modes of adjustment. The way the individual typically behaves depends on his perception of present circumstances and is based, as was shown in Chapter 2, on previous experiences. From this behaviour we may infer certain things about the psychological core.

Role related behaviour, as was shown in Chapter 5, depends on the social context in which the individual finds himself at a point in time. It forms a basis for a dynamic aspect in personality functioning.

Hollander has used wavy lines in his schematic representation to separate these sets of variables in order to emphasise the two-way flow process. Thus, the psychological core affects certain typical responses which in turn affect the core. Roles are affected by typical responses and the core, in terms of its store of past experiences, may be affected by role performance (see Figure

125

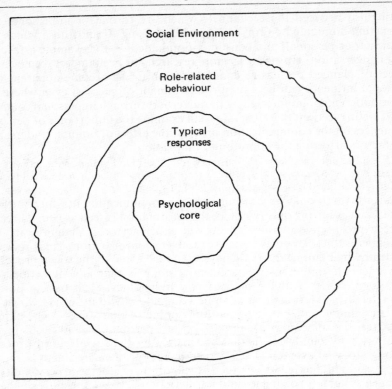

Figure 7.1 The personality within the social environment
Source: Hollander. E.P. *Principles and Methods of Social Psychology*, 3rd edn.
(Oxford: Oxford University Press, 1976. By permission)

5.1). Thus, a dominant role such as that of physician has a pervasive effect on the total personality because of the totality and persistence of the role itself.

This kind of analysis does much to explain the mechanism of interaction and its effects on the individual. In the last chapter we discussed some of the factors that can affect the communication process. It was shown that a number of personal attributes in both the communicator and receiver can affect a communication situation. In this chapter it is intended to explain further the communication process, taking into account personal influence effects, the typical responses and role related behaviour of Hollander's model, and to explain the importance of the concept of personality as a 'whole' or *Gestalt*.

7.2 Communication and Personal Influence

In the last chapter it was indicated that the effect of particular communication channels would depend on the circumstances involved. We can broadly distinguish between those channels which are formal or impersonal and marketing-dominated – for example, advertising – and those which are informal, or personal, and consumer-dominated – for example a face-to-face conversation. However, as more research has been undertaken into the effect of planned persuasive communication it has become apparent that personal influence can be a major determinant of success, even where the information is communicated by the advertiser through impersonal channels only. In this section, therefore, we shall examine the importance of personal influences on the communication process, the effect of opinion leaders, and the factors affecting the adoption of innovation.

7.21 The One-step Flow of Communication

This is the traditional view of impersonal communication in which the process is seen as having only one step; the information is seen as being directed at each prospective consumer who will either act on it or ignore it. The consumer is thus viewed as a passive receiver of information. This process is illustrated by Figure 7.2.

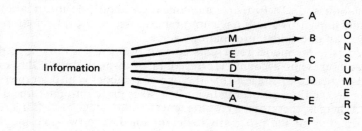

Figure 7.2 The one-step flow of communication

By varying the choice of media, the theme, and the copy, the advertiser can appeal to different market segments. This seems fairly obvious and straightforward and, indeed, much advertising strategy is based on this view. But it is a model that has been increasingly criticized for its oversimplification. Numerous problems arise, including the extent to which the information actually reaches the target audience and the fact that it does not take into account the effect of personal influence. With regard to the latter point, it must be appreciated that communication is not merely the transmission of information to an audience, but involves the transmission of information among members of that audience. Consequently researchers have looked for a more comprehensive explanation, one result being the two-step flow model.

7.22 The Two-step Flow of Communication

This model suggests that information flows via the media to *influencers*, or *opinion leaders*, to whom other members of the audience look for information and evaluation. Through interpersonal networks these influencers not only reach members of the target audience who may not have been exposed to the information, but may also reinforce the impact of the information on those who have. The process is illustrated by Figure 7.3.

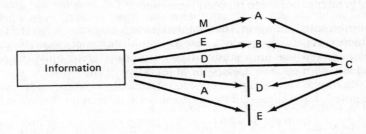

Figure 7.3 The two-step flow of communication

In Figure 7.3, C is an opinion leader. A and B have been exposed to the information and C's further communication about the information reinforces its impact. D and E have not been exposed to the information and C thus acts as an original information source.

Obviously this model represents an improvement on the one-step idea, because it takes into account the effect of interpersonal contact. But, even so, there is evidence to suggest that the two-step model is also an oversimplification as the flow of information often takes place through three or more stages. There is, therefore, a requirement for multi-stage models if a realistic understanding of the process is to be obtained. The two-step model has, nonetheless, been useful in drawing attention to the importance of opinion leaders and the part they play in personal influence.

7.23 *Opinion Leaders*

Opinion leaders are individuals who are able, in a particular situation, to exert personal influence. Generally they do not exert absolute leadership but they are looked to by others for advice and information. As is demonstrated by the two-step model, they are important to the marketer because of the way they informally and subtly influence the behaviour of others towards products and services.

Although a great deal of research has been undertaken to determine the characteristics of opinion leaders, the results tend to be inconclusive. The following profile, which is by no means exact, can be deduced from various studies.

Opinion leaders tend to:

1. be of the same social class as non-leaders, but may enjoy a higher social status within that class[3]. This is understandable because people interact mainly with those of similar interests and background;
2. be more gregarious than non-leaders[4] and more self-confident[5];

3. be more orientated to innovations than non-leaders[6];
4. adhere more closely to group norms than non-leaders[7];
5. have greater interest and knowledge of the area of influence than do non-leaders[4];
6. have greater exposure to relevant mass media[8].

It must be noted, however, that opinion leaders may have a limited sphere of influence regarding product categories. Montgomery and Silk[9], for example, showed that in a study of seven product areas only 3% of the respondents were opinion leaders for at least five of the items.

The situational variables giving rise to influence by opinion leaders should also be noted. Katz[7] suggested that influence will depend on the following:

1. *Who one is.* Individuals who personify group values may be able to exert influence;
2. *What one knows.* Individuals who are knowledgeable about a subject are likely to be influential, at least in regard to that subject;
3. *Where one is located.* That is, whom one knows within the group and outside the group.

Certainly, the degree to which an individual seeks to be influenced will depend on the extent of his own knowledge about a topic, on the amount of perceived risk involved (for example, the higher the cost of an item the greater the amount of perceived risk), on his particular position in the reference group, and on personality factors (for example, whether the person feels insecure or easily persuasible).

Whilst the concept of opinion leaders is very interesting, its usefulness as a basis for marketing strategy is somewhat limited. The main difficulty lies in being able to identify influencers. This might be achieved through sociometric techniques, described in Chapter 5. This would, however, be a laborious and expensive exercise in consumer markets, especially when it is remembered that opinion leadership is unlikely to be the same for different product categories and that certain categories are unaffected by personal influence. Nonetheless, Myers and Reynolds[10] suggest that the following approaches might usefully be employed:

1. analysis of mailing lists drawn up from coupon replies (opinion leaders have greater exposure to mass media);
2. additional questions on interaction/influence in consumer surveys;
3. analysis of common interest organization membership (Lazarsfeld *et al.*[11] showed that members of certain types of organizations, such as women's clubs, are likely to be opinion leaders);
4. comparison of subscription mailing lists. Since opinion leaders are more likely to use mass media than non-leaders, such a comparison might reveal the individuals who receive several publications and who may therefore be opinion leaders.

Once influencers have been identified the appropriate information can be directed towards them; resulting, hopefully, in the advertiser gaining a number of extra and unpaid salesmen.

From the above comments it is clear that the social network of individuals and their resulting communication patterns are of considerable importance in consumer decisions. One area in particular where this process is of vital concern must be new product development, especially when one considers the vast number of product failures (generally estimated at over 90% of all new product launches). The adoption and diffusion of innovations has therefore attracted a great deal of research and it is relevant to the above discussion to examine some of the findings of this work.

7.24 The Adoption and Diffusion of Innovation

An *innovation* may be defined as 'any idea or product perceived by the potential innovator to be new' (Rogers[3]). Thus an innovation may be a modification of an existing product or may be a radically different product that requires an alteration in existing behaviour patterns. *Adoption* is the process by which the individual becomes committed to the continued use or repurchase of an innovation. Rogers[3] identified the following stages in the adoption process:

1. *Awareness*. The innovation is known to exist but the consumer has little information and no well-founded attitudes about it.
2. *Interest*. The consumer becomes aware that the innovation may be useful or solve some problem.
3. *Evaluation*. The consumer develops a favourable or unfavourable attitude towards the innovation and reaches a decision about whether or not to try it.
4. *Trial*. The consumer tests the product but, if possible, only in a limited way.
5. *Adoption*. The innovation is accepted or rejected. If accepted the consumer becomes committed to continued purchase or use of the innovation.

Of course, the process may be terminated at any of these stages and the innovation will not be adopted. At the awareness stage, for example, selective perception may act against the innovation. The influence of interaction and peer group pressure can therefore be of paramount importance in securing successful adoption, although it does not appear that word of mouth communication is most important in the final stages of the process. Another significant factor is that the time span of the process will vary for different consumers; for some the process is fairly rapid, while for others it proceeds more slowly.

The length of time involved will depend on the way in which the innovation is perceived by consumers. Product characteristics, real or otherwise, are therefore very important. Rogers and Shoemaker[12] identify the following characteristics of products as those which appear to influence the speed and extent of adoption:

1. *Relative advantage*. The degree to which an innovation is perceived as being superior to preceding or competing products. Products with greater relative advantage will be adopted more rapidly.

2. *Compatibility*. The degree to which an innovation is consistent with existing consumer values. Products that are not compatible with consumer norms will take longer to be adopted.
3. *Complexity*. The extent to which the innovation is difficult to understand and to use. The more complex the item the longer the adoption process.
4. *Trialability*. The extent to which an item may be sampled. If sampling is not possible, adoption will be slower.
5. *Observability*. The extent to which a product is visible in social situations. Products that are highly visible will be communicated most rapidly to other adopters.

The process of adoption in aggregate form over time is known as *diffusion*. Since diffusion is a group process it follows that research should concentrate on the pattern of social networks and the social structure of communication rather than on the individual. This research has indicated that diffusion follows a normal distribution over time and that adopters can be classified on the basis of time taken for adoption. Rogers[3] has identified five categories of adopters, members of each group adopting an innovation at approximately the same time.

1. *Innovators* (2.5% of a market) are the first to adopt an innovation. They are usually quite venturesome and eager to experiment with new ideas. They usually have more discretionary purchasing power than other categories and can therefore afford to take the material and social risks that may be attached to the use of an innovation.
2. *Early adopters* (13.5% of a market) are the second group to adopt an innovation. They are respected by others, have the highest proportion of opinion leaders and are therefore very important in speeding the diffusion process. They are younger than later adopters and above average in education. They observe the behaviour of innovators and adopt the innovation when it appears successful. They take more publications than later adopters, but not as many as innovators and have the greatest contact with salespeople.
3. *The early majority* (34% of a market) may take more time before adopting an innovation and are usually followers. They are slightly above average in education, age, social status, and income. They rely fairly heavily on informal sources of information and take fewer publications than do the first two categories.
4. *The late majority* (34% of a market) are sceptical of new ideas and may adopt largely as a result of social pressure or economic factors. They are above average in age and below average in education, social status, and income. They exhibit little opinion leadership, take few publications, and rely heavily on informal sources of information and influence.
5. *Laggards* (16% of a market) are tradition-bound and are suspicious of new ideas. The length of the adoption process for this group is quite long and by the time they finally adopt an innovation it may already have been superseded. They have the least education, the lowest social status, and income, and are the oldest of the adopter categories. They possess virtually no opinion leadership and take few publications.

As stated above, the diffusion process reveals a normal distribution which can be illustrated as shown in Figure 7.4.

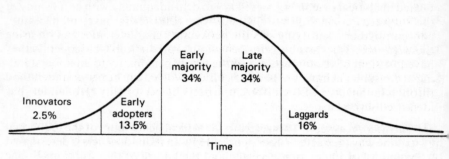

Figure 7.4 Distribution of the diffusion process

The identification of these categories suggests various market strategies depending on the stage reached in the diffusion process. At the innovation stage, for example, advertising appeals should emphasise the excitement of trying a revolutionary idea and should be aimed at relatively young people with high social status, education, and income. Again, at the early majority stage it should be stressed that adopters, especially the relevant opinion leaders, have already adopted the innovation. Such strategies can be extremely productive but the concept, like that of the product life cycle, suffers one very practical problem: that is, the identification of the stage of the diffusion process in operation at a given point in time. The innovation stage is obvious, but differentiating between the early adopter and the early majority stages may be difficult and, as a result, a particular promotional activity may be totally ineffective.

Although there are other models that seek to explain and predict the diffusion process we have concentrated our discussion on the model proposed by Rogers. It must be noted that this model has been criticized in terms of its methodology and validity. Nonetheless, the Rogers model is easily understood and has perhaps been the most influential in focusing attention on the diffusion process.

7.3 Personality

The preceding discussion has demonstrated the importance of social influence in the communication process. We have, however, identified few personality dimensions affecting the process, even though from Hollander's model, discussed in the introduction, it is apparent that personality is a vital factor determining the outcome of any social interaction situation. Whilst we can describe opinion leaders as being gregarious and self-confident, and laggards as being tradition-bound, we do not have any real understanding of the personality dimensions that will determine a particular pattern of behaviour.

The problem is that personality is a complex topic, encompassing a number of variables, and researchers do not have the theoretical base, or the sophisticated analytical machinery, necessary to deal adequately with a full study of the subject. Personality has a *Gestalt* but researchers have, of necessity, concentrated on identifying specific personality characteristics and on using these characteristics as a basis for behavioural prediction. Consequently they have lost sight of the importance of the whole personality to an understanding of consumer behaviour. The difficulties involved can be better understood through an analysis of the different aspects of personality. Hollander[2] has identified several aspects.

1. *The external aspect*. This refers to the typical behaviours of the individual and the way they affect other people. How an individual acts is determined by the social interaction involved and the nature of the situation. In one situation the individual might be assertive, but in another he might be submissive.
2. *The internal aspect*. This is the psychological core, relating to the psychological states which determine the individual's disposition towards his environment. These states include values and attitudes which, as we saw in the previous chapter, can only be inferred from behaviour.
3. *The dynamic aspect*. This allows the individual to adapt to the demands of a changed environment. Individuals are continuously experiencing different situations and this can result in altered behaviour patterns as, through the learning process, the individual makes the appropriate social adjustments.
4. *The consistent aspect*. This refers to the stable cognitive processes that generate a characteristic style. It is based on the premise that individuals have a characteristic mode of reacting to the environment.

As can be seen, there are a vast number of variables that must be taken into account in order to produce a comprehensive view of a total personality. Research has concentrated on identifying consistencies in character, but situational variables are very important. A person who in one situation might be described as 'generous' might be described as being 'mean' in another. The identification of personality characteristics which hold in a variety of situations is therefore very difficult. For example, it is known that certain people are susceptible to social influence, but Linton[13] showed that there does not appear to be any general susceptibility to persuasion which characterizes some people but not others. Another problem is that we can only infer personality characteristics from observed behaviour, or from personality tests, since we cannot directly observe a person's underlying needs, thought, or feelings.

Much of our knowledge about personality comes from the field of clinical psychology and many testing techniques have been developed as a means of identifying behavioural disorders. As a result, such tests are not easily, if at all, adaptable for use in studying consumer behaviour. Personality dimensions measured by these tests, such as extroversion or introversion, may be useful to an understanding of specific behaviours, but are not necessarily relevant to an understanding of everyday purchasing behaviour.

Nonetheless, tests such as the Edwards Personal Preference Schedule and the Minnesota Multi-Phase Personality Inventory have been used in consumer research studies. It is not very surprising to find that research has been unable to identify strong associations between personality characteristics and consumer behaviour. In fact, Kassarjian[14], in reviewing a large number of studies investigating the relationship between personality and various aspects of consumer behaviour, could only conclude that the results were at best 'equivocal'.

Allied to this is the problem of the theoretical frameworks within which personality research has been undertaken. Existing theories have attempted to explain, rather than predict, how individuals interact with their environment. But if personality *per se* is to be a valuable concept in marketing, it must be possible to make predictions of behaviour based on a knowledge of an individual's personality characteristics.

7.4 Theories of Personality

Whilst existing theories have offered little predictive value they have provided some explanation of personality as a factor in consumer behaviour. The following analysis of three such theories will, it is hoped, illustrate further the problem areas discussed so far, as well as demonstrating some of the ways in which marketing has sought to benefit from the limited amount of relevant knowledge available.

7.41 Freudian Theory

One of the first and certainly the most influential accounts of personality was that provided by Sigmund Freud[15]. His views, with their emphasis on the prevalence of sexuality in all aspects of our mental processes or minds, quickly caught the popular imagination and many of the terms used in his theory of psychoanalysis have passed into common usage. Although many of Freud's views have been severely attacked by later writers, his work still has a profound influence on the study of personality.

Freud believed that all human actions are the inevitable result of antecedent conditions. Whilst the individual apparently exhibits behaviour resulting from a freedom of choice, in fact his behaviour is merely the mechanistic expression of his heredity and his previous environment. Although this deterministic approach seems, at first glance, to be able to offer much to a study of consumer behaviour, it must be appreciated that Freud regarded psychoanalysis not as a predictive science but rather as a postdictive science; in other words, it looks back and unearths the causes that produced a particular event, rather than attempting to predict future events.

There has been a great deal written about Freudian analysis and Freud's original work has been revised and refined both by Freud himself and by others, especially after Freud's death. As a result there has often been some confusion regarding which aspects of the theory are in fact attributable to Freud. However, it is not intended here to provide a full assessment of psychoanalysis, but merely to outline the main tenets of the theory and to indicate its relevance to marketing practice.

In this sense, Freud's most important contribution was to demonstrate that people are motivated by both conscious and unconscious forces. According to Freud, the mind can be compared with an iceberg, with only a small part of it revealed, and is composed of three interacting and conflicting forces:

1. *The id* which is the source of psychic energy. It operates on the pleasure principle and seeks immediate gratification for biological and instinctual needs such as sex and aggression. It operates at a subjective and unconscious level and, as a result, is not fully capable of dealing with reality.
2. *The ego* which enables the individual to maintain a balance between the external environment and the impulses of the id. It operates on the reality principle and is capable of postponing the release of tension until it can be effectively directed at coping with the external environment. As a result of the social learning process it develops the individual's abilities to interact with his environment.
3. *The superego* which equates with the concept of *conscience*. It defines what is morally right and influences the individual to strive for perfection rather than pleasure or reality and, in this sense, serves as an ethical constraint on behaviour.

It must be emphasised, however, that the id, ego and superego are merely concepts. They are names given to psychological processes and do not have a separate identity or any corresponding physical structure within the brain. These three processes have different goals and, as a result, there is always some degree of conflict which acts to produce personality.

When this conflict becomes intense, anxiety develops and if this becomes too great for the ego to handle the situation is dealt with by the ego through unconscious processes called *defence mechanisms*, the most important of which are:

1. *Repression*, where unacceptable feelings are repressed into the unconscious and as a result distort the individual's reactions to the environment.
2. *Sublimation*, where the individual is able to satisfy otherwise unacceptable motives through socially acceptable outlets. For example, by becoming a soldier an individual may be able to satisfy a desire to kill.
3. *Projection*, where an individual, who is unable to accept his own feelings, may project these feelings onto others and see them in others but not in himself.

Of course, all these processes operate mainly at the unconscious level and are unknown both to the individual involved and to those with whom he interacts. The unconscious stirrings of these forces, however, manifest themselves in dreams, responses to ambiguous stimuli, and 'slips of the tongue'. These, according to Freud, are meaningful and can be interpreted by the trained observer.

Freud also proposed a theory of socialization, whereby an individual is said to pass through a number of stages during the first few years of life, and which determine the adult personality. These stages are sequential and at each stage the child experiences sexual pleasure through a different zone of the body. Each stage involves a crisis which must be resolved, otherwise the individual becomes 'fixated' at that stage. These stages were termed *oral*, *anal*, *phallic*, and *genital* and are important because of the personality typing resulting from possible fixation at different stages. For example, at the anal stage the child's primary pleasure comes from relieving anal tensions and the crisis to be resolved is that of toilet training. The child must learn to postpone the pleasure of relieving himself in order to please his parents. If toilet training is very strict then the child may hold back the faeces and become constipated. This behaviour gives rise to what is termed the 'anal retentive' personality type and in adulthood exhibits such characteristics as obstinacy, stinginess, and excessive neatness. The opposite is the 'anal expulsive' type which in adulthood exhibits characteristics such as disorderliness and destructiveness.

Many of the basic premises of Freudian psychology are open to question and have drawn vicious criticism, particularly from the Behaviourist school. Eysenck[16], for example, has dismissed Freudian theory as 'surmise, conjecture, and interpretation'. Certainly it is extremely difficult to generalize about overall consumer behaviour on the basis of Freudian analysis. Even so, the vital factors that the marketer must consider are that products and advertisements appeal to unconscious as well as conscious motives, and that the symbolism inherent in product and advertising design, especially if it contains sexual implications, can have an effect opposite to that intended. For example, if an advert is sexually explicit it could offend the superego and therefore lose impact.

The main problem, however, is that of being able to make use of the personality typologies of Freudian theory, even if one accepts their validity. Since personality is determined by unconscious processes it can only be ascertained through various assessment methods that include face-to-face analysis and projective techniques. Obviously this kind of research is expensive and time-consuming, and whilst it offers nothing as a quantitative segmentation tool, it has been widely used as a framework for motivational research.

7.42 Trait Theory

This is a quantitative approach which looks at personality as being composed of a number of predispositional attributes or traits. Such traits may be honesty, aggressiveness, sociability, or any of the other eighteen-thousand-plus adjectives to be found in an English dictionary. The object of the trait approach is to identify, through such methods as factor analysis (a complex statistical technique which enables a large number of variables to be reduced to a smaller number of independent variables), the important attributes in personality, and to study their organization and effect on behaviour. The main assumptions underlying the approach are summarized below:

1. A particular trait, for example honesty, is common to many individuals, although its strength will vary in absolute terms between individuals. Thus, one individual may have a high degree of honesty, whilst another may have a fairly low degree of honesty. Every individual can be described

in terms of a number of traits, each differing in degree of magnitude. As a result of these differences, no two individuals are exactly alike.

2. Traits are relatively stable and enduring and have a fairly universal effect on behaviour, irrespective of situational variables.
3. Traits can, therefore, be inferred from consistencies perceived in the behaviour of individuals and can be used as a basis for predicting behaviour.

The best-known work in this area is that of Cattell[17] who suggests that, by factor analysing all traits making up personality, one can develop a mathematical equation to predict a person's behaviour in a given situation. Cattell, through various methods of investigation, has identified sixteen factors which he believes are the basic traits underlying personality. Each factor is represented as a dimension; the two names in each representing the extremities of the dimension's continuum. The sixteen traits are:

A	Reserved − Outgoing
B	Less intelligent − More intelligent
C	Affected by feelings − Emotionally stable
E	Humble − Assertive
F	Serious − Happy-go-lucky
G	Expedient − Conscientious
H	Restrained − Venturesome
I	Tough-minded − Tender-minded
L	Trusting − Suspicious
M	Practical − Imaginative
N	Forthright − Shrewd
O	Self-assured − Apprehensive
Q_1	Conservative − Experimenting
Q_2	Group-dependent − Self-sufficient
Q_3	Uncontrolled − Controlled
Q_4	Relaxed − Tense

Each individual can be represented in terms of these dimensions and, as a result, a personality profile for each individual can be developed. The main problem, of course, is that of measuring points on the continuum of each dimension, and to perform this task Cattell developed the 16PF test (Sixteen Personality Factor Questionnaire).

But the personality variables identified often depend on the research method employed. Self-ratings, or ratings of one person by another, and the type of factor analysis used, can all produce differing results. Other personality researchers have identified far fewer basic factors than those of Cattell. Eysenck[18], for example, has concentrated on only two dimensions: introversion − extroversion, and stability − instability.

Despite these basic differences in identifying particular factors, it has long been thought that traits could usefully form a basis for market segmentation, and trait theory has been used more in consumer research than any other personality concept. However, apart from some success in contributing to the development of psychographic profiles, the results have been somewhat disappointing. The classic study was conducted by Evans[19], who used the

Edwards Personal Preference Schedule to determine personality differences between users of Ford and Chevrolet motor cars. He found that measurable personality differences were of little value as a prediction of ownership. Subsequent studies on a variety of products have also failed to produce any meaningful results. This does not mean that the trait approach should be dismissed as a marketing aid for, as mentioned above, it has been shown to be of some value in psychographics research. However, in assessing the theory *per se*, account must be taken of many problems, some of which are listed below.

1. Traits are inferred from behaviour and thus to use them to explain behaviour is not very meaningful. For example, we may describe an individual who always backs down in an argument as being submissive. Can we then say that he refuses to stand his ground because he is submissive?
2. The interaction of various traits results in the *Gestalt* of a unique personality which is different from the sum of the traits which are, after all, merely aspects of the total personality.
3. Situational variables are important in determining given behaviour. Indeed, research indicates that it is the interaction between individual differences and situational variables that is important. Social factors such as role-playing can dramatically affect an outcome. For example, in a situation where he is meeting with his superior, a man may be a submissive subordinate, but in a situation where he is meeting with his own staff he may become an assertive superior.

7.43 Self-concept Theory

Both psychoanalysis and trait theory attempt to analyse personality in terms of categories assigned or developed by the researcher. But how an individual perceives himself, and others, may differ considerably from the way in which a researcher may categorize that individual. Self-concept theory is an attempt to resolve this discrepancy by explaining and predicting behaviour through an understanding of how the individual perceives himself and his environment.

The theory centres around the concept of 'self' which Newcomb[20] defines as 'the individual as perceived by that individual in a socially determined frame of reference'. This perceived self influences the person's perceptions of both his environment and his behaviour. As was demonstrated in Chapter 2, perception is influenced by many factors and the self provides an important subjective input to the process. Thus, an individual with a strong, positive self-concept views his environment quite differently from an individual whose self-concept is weak. Again the self-concept does not necessarily reflect reality since an individual who is regarded as successful by others may perceive himself as a failure. Of importance, therefore, is the 'ideal self' which is a concept relating to the kind of person the individual would like to be. The closer the ideal self to the real self, then the more fulfilled and happy will be the individual. A large discrepancy between the two will result in an unhappy dissatisfied individual.

Self-concept develops in a number of ways, but of importance are the level of aspiration of the individual, and his own self-perception compared with his perception of others. Once developed, self-concept is reinforced by the process of selective perception. Perceptions that are incompatible with a self-image pose a threat and are either rejected or modified to comply with the existing image. This produces behaviour which is aimed at maintaining and enhancing an internally consistent self-image. Resulting behaviour patterns, therefore, tend to have a consistency that may not always be apparent to others. The important factor is that, given his social frame of reference and the information available to him, the individual reacts in a way that is consistent with his self-image.

This theory has important implications for marketing for if individuals seek to maintain and enhance their self-concepts, they are likely to purchase those goods and services that enable them to satisfy this objective. This provides the opportunity to use self-image profiles, which can be constructed through cognitive mapping techniques (see Chapter 3), as a market segmentation tool. Marketing strategy can then aim at matching brand images with conscious self-concepts.

The evidence provided by many studies using self-concept has been most encouraging and, in general, shows that consumers do prefer brands which relate to their self-perceptions and to their subjective images of brands. In one of the first studies Birdwell[21] investigated the relationship between self-concept and the purchase behaviour of motor car owners. Using a random sample, owners were asked to evaluate themselves, their own car, and eight other models. He found that owners' self-perceptions were more highly congruent with their perception of their own car than with their perceptions of other cars. In another study of car owners, Grubb and Hupp[22] found that, while owners perceived other owners of the same model of car to have similar self-concepts to themselves, they perceived the self-concepts of owners of competing models to be significantly different. It should be noted that this study was concerned with the stereotyped images of car owners and the results suggest not only that there is awareness of stereotyping on the part of consumers, but also that this affects purchase decisions. Studies in product categories other than motor cars have found similar results. Landon[23], for example, investigated the relationship between consumers' self-images, ideal self-images, and product images in nineteen product categories, ranging from country club membership to coffee, beer, and wine. He found that consumer preference was positively related to either self-image or ideal self-image.

Although the work in this field holds much promise, there are a number of contentious issues regarding both the nature of the theory itself and the methodology of many of the studies. The following points should be noted:

1. There is a lack of agreement about the specific meaning of 'self'. The very subjective nature of the concept means that definition, and hence measurement, becomes difficult.
2. The theory concentrates on, and emphasises, conscious processes, and does not therefore give a great deal of importance to subconscious processes. Self theorists maintain, however, that the perception of the environment as available to the consciousness of the individual plays a

predominant role in the determination of his behaviour.
3. Investigations in this field have used techniques such as the Osgood Semantic Differential which, as noted in the last chapter, has its own methodological problems.
4. Whilst studies have indicated that self-image is related to product image, it does not necessarily follow that purchase behaviour will result from a particular brand preference. Economic considerations and environmental influences may act as moderating variables that inhibit the translation of preferences into purchases.

7.5 Person Perception

The discussion of self-theory has focused attention on the importance of perceptual processes regarding other people and objects. We continually make judgements about other people, not only to help us evaluate our own self-concepts, but also to use as a basis for predicting their behaviour in certain situations. The social environment demands that the individual has increasingly to rely on other people for his continued well-being, and it is vital therefore that he has some idea of how they will react in given situations. The judgements formed of other people determine the extent to which close ties or friendships will develop; the individual relies on friends to maintain and bolster his self-image, to provide a social framework, and to help with difficulties. The judgements made about salesmen, and hence the organizations they represent, by prospective customers in the face-to-face selling situation play an important part in determining whether a particular sales pitch will be successful. On the formal level, on the basis of an interview, judgements are made about the future of an individual in a job function. It is therefore important to have an understanding of the subjective factors affecting the social interaction process, and it is the aim of this section to examine some of these factors and the problems that can arise. The specific problem of the formal interview is dealt with in Chapter 9, but many of the factors mentioned here are of relevance and should be noted when reading that section.

As we saw in Chapter 2, the term 'perception' implies the use of direct sensory information. In the social context this is not, however, entirely the case. The evaluations, opinions, and impressions that are formed of other people involve subjective judgements and inferences that go beyond the direct sensory input which characterizes the perception process. Often a judgement of another person is based not on direct observation but on statements about him by third parties or on prior knowledge of his status or achievements. As a result, there are a great number of variables affecting the person judgement process, but each can be classified under one of the following broad headings:

1. Variables within the judge (the perceiver).
2. Variables within the person being judged (the receiver).
3. Variables appertaining to the judgement situation.

We shall look briefly at these broad categories of variable and then examine some of the reasons why error occurs in person judgements. It must, however, be emphasised that assesssment of accuracy in person perception has raised some very difficult methodological problems and much research is still required before any valid conclusions can be drawn.

7.51 Variables Relating to the Perceiver

There is no simple relationship between perceiver characteristics and how other people are perceived. The mode of perceiving and describing others can vary from simple dimensions, such as outward appearance, to complex traits, depending on the level of sophistication, intelligence, and complexity of the perceiver. Less sophisticated and complex perceivers are likely to base judgements on factors such as body build, facial features, and mannerisms. Certainly, it is difficult to form judgements of people who are more complex than ourselves. The self-image of the perceiver is also important, for people are likely to attribute to friends similar characteristics to those they attribute to themselves.

7.52 Variables Relating to the Receiver

A great deal of work has been undertaken in this area and some of the cues which are used in forming judgements are stated below.

1. *Appearance and body build*. It has been suggested that personality characteristics may be arrived at through a process of direct inference from the nature of the body structure. Appearance in terms of personal grooming and clothing style is widely used as being indicative of underlying character.
2. *Nonverbal cues*. These include expressive movements and gestures. For example, a person who waves his arms about whilst speaking may be judged to be emotional.
3. *Voice qualities*. These have been shown to be adequate cues in the judgement of social class. Personality characteristics may also be inferred from stereotypes associated with particular voice qualities.
4. *Information presented by the receiver about himself*. Obviously, the greater the amount of information the receiver presents about his attitudes, beliefs, opinions, education, and interests, the greater the opportunity the perceiver has to form a judgement.
5. *Indirect evidence*. As mentioned above, judgements are often formed on the basis of information about a person from third parties.

7.53 Variables Relating to the judging situation

The main influences are role related behaviours. In different situations people will be expected to play different roles and this affects communication patterns and personal styles. At a social gathering, for example, communication and dress may be informal and this will lead to different judgements from those made in more formal situations where roles may be better defined. For this reason, many companies when recruiting senior staff will not restrict the recruitment procedure to formal situations, but may invite candidates to lunch or dinner.

7.54 Errors in Person Perception

Just as there are many variables in the judging process, there are many reasons why assigned characteristics may be inappropriate or mistaken. While it is not possible to provide a comprehensive listing, the following will give some indication of the reasons why mistakes are made:

1. *The 'halo' effect.* This is the tendency to organize perceptions of other people around an evaluative factor. A positive evaluative factor will lead to positive characteristics being generally attributed to that person. For example, if a perceiver regards tact as an important characteristic, then a person displaying this attribute may be perceived as being shrewd, intelligent, and analytical, despite there being no evidence for these other attributes.
2. *The logical error.* This refers to the idea that perceivers generally have a relatively fixed set of biases in judging others. Without being aware of it, the perceiver has his own personality 'theory' and this 'theory' influences his judgements. For example, a perceiver may believe that the characteristics of aggression, forcefulness, and dynamism always occur together. Thus, if someone is aggressive he must also be perceived as being forceful and dynamic.
3. *Stereotyping.* This, as we saw in Chapter 6, involves the placement of an individual in a firm category and attributing to him all the characteristics that are associated with that category. As was shown, this has the effect of putting a straitjacket on other judgements.
4. *Appearance and body build.* There are many ill-founded relationships that are thought to be true. For example, body height is often used as a guide to intelligence and people wearing spectacles are often perceived as being more intelligent than people not wearing spectacles.

7.6 Implications for Marketing

In this chapter we have been concerned with the individual, his personality, and the influence he may exert on the purchasing behaviour of others.

As has been indicated, there is still much work to be undertaken in the area of personality, the results of existing studies being often inconclusive and even contradictory. This means that care must be taken in applying the results of personality research to planned persuasive communications.

Nonetheless, psychoanalysis theory has formed the basis for some advertising campaigns, typically where sexual, aggressive, or fantasy themes are employed. For example, in the promotion of a men's cologne, an explicit sexual theme may be evoked through packaging and advertising with the intention of stimulating the id. The product is, however, made acceptable to the superego by incorporating in the advertising a later image of the man with his wife and family. The ego, which dictates purchase behaviour, is therefore satisfied as the id has been stimulated and the superego placated. While there is no doubt that this type of advertising can be successful, this does not in itself mean that psychoanalysis theory has validity, since an equally possible rationale for this type of strategy could be found in the need to obtain cognitive consistency between the sexual drive and socially prescribed behavioural norms.

Despite its limitations, self-concept theory has been employed fairly widely in marketing and has been used in market segmentation, product promotion, and product development. If it is possible to identify homogeneous sets of self-image profiles this can be helpful in the design of promotional campaigns, particularly for products which are purchased for personal consumption and have ego-involvement and social visibility, for example cars, clothing, cosmetics, and home furnishing. It could also help in the identification of new product opportunities if it can be established that for certain self-image profiles there is no matching product profile.

Trait theory, despite its apparent relevance to an understanding of consumer behaviour, has so far proved disappointingly unsuccessful in both explaining and predicting behaviour. It has nonetheless been of some value in psychographics as a means of 'humanizing' consumer profiles.

It is well established that certain individuals exert a positive influence on the opinion formation of others. Personality theory, however, has so far been unable to provide us with any real assistance in the identification of these individuals, even though it seems probable that such individuals share common personality traits. We are therefore forced to use other techniques, such as sociometry or evaluation of past purchase records and coupon replies, to identify opinion leaders. This is likely to prove time-consuming and expensive, particularly as it seems clear that opinion leaders are very rarely active in more than a small number of product areas. For this reason, it may be easier, and less costly, to create or simulate opinion leadership in promotional campaigns.

Opinion leaders may be created, for example, by providing certain well-placed individuals with the opportunity of purchasing a product on preferential terms if they agree to demonstrate it to their friends. Such an approach is sometimes employed in the case of home improvements. Another frequently used approach is to get well-known personalities or experts in a particular field to sponsor a product. This approach is used extensively by manufacturers of sporting goods. Party plan selling, such as jewellery and Tupperware parties, is another way of creating opinion leadership as the hostess is placed in the position of bringing the product to the attention of her friends.

Opinion leadership may also be simulated in advertising by the use of product testimonials which convey a favourable opinion of the product. Such advertising may show a person recommending a product to a friend or street corner interviews of 'average' individuals. Care must be taken in such promotional campaigns that the testimonials appear to be spontaneous and disinterested and for this reason nonprofessional actors may be used. In other cases, testimonials may be solicited from well-known personalities with expertise in a field closely related to the product.

Even if it is not possible to identify opinion leaders for a particular product, a company may be able to stimulate their activities by encouraging discussion about the product. This may be helped by a particularly distinctive, amusing, or topical advertising campaign. In-store demonstrations and magazine articles about a product may also aid the flow of information to opinion leaders.

In this connection it is appropriate to consider the role of public relations as a means of stimulating the activities of opinion leaders. Television personalities and newspaper and magazine columnists may be important leaders of opinion in their own right. They also exert control over the flow of information through the media. It is therefore important that there is close integration between the marketing and public relations functions to ensure that, as far as possible, a product's positive features get maximum media exposure and that adverse comment is minimized. A sound public relations effort can be particularly important to the launch of a new product. In the case of a ne w model of car, for example, favourable comment in national and technical press may be an important prerequisite of success.

7.7 Summary

1. Society may be viewed as a series of interactions between individuals. The set of unique characteristics, or 'personality', of each individual is a vital factor determining the outcome of any social interaction.
2. Traditional views of the communication process, as represented by the one-step model, ignored the interpersonal aspect of impersonal communication. The search for more comprehensive explanations has led to the two-step model; this takes into account the effect of influencers, or opinion leaders. Even so, there is evidence to support more sophisticated models.
3. Opinion leaders are individuals who are able, in particular situations, to exert personal influence. There is, however, a problem in the identification of such individuals and the usefulness of the concept to marketing is consequently somewhat limited. Nonetheless, there are a number of marketing strategies that are suggested by the existence of opinion leaders.
4. Personal influence is of importance to the adoption and diffusion of innovations. Adoption is the process by which the individual becomes committed to the continued use or repurchase of an innovation. Diffusion refers to the aggregate of adoption. Several models have been proposed to explain the adoption process, the best known being that of Rogers.
5. Personality is a complex topic that encompasses a number of variables. We can identify the external, internal, dynamic, and consistent aspects of personality but researchers have concentrated on identifying consistencies in character.
6. Some major theories of personality of relevance to marketing are psychoanalysis, trait theory, and self-concept theory. All have implications for marketing but their methodological limitations must be recognized. The most serious problem is that we lack the sophisticated analysis required to account for the *Gestalt* of personality.

7. Person perception is the term given to the process by which we form judgements about other people. There are many variables affecting this process but all may be classed under one of three headings: perceiver variables; receiver variables; and situational variables. A knowledge of how these variables affect interpersonal situations and the errors that can occur is important and has implications for face-to-face selling situations and recruitment situations.

References

1. Allport, G.W. 'The Open System in Personality Theory', *Journ. Abnorm. Social Psych*, 1960, 61.
2. Hollander, E.P. *Principles and Methods of Social Psychology* (New York: Oxford University Press, 1976).
3. Rogers, E.M. *Diffusion of Innovations* (New York: Free Press, 1962).
4. Summers, J.O. 'The Identity of Women's Clothing Fashion Opinion Leaders', *Journ. Marketing Research*, 1970, 7.
5. Reynolds, F.D. and Darden, W.R. 'Mutually Adaptive Effects of Interpersonal Communication', *Journ. Marketing Research*, 1971, 8.
6. Summers, J.O. and King, C.W. 'Interpersonal Communication and New Product Attitudes' *Marketing Involvement in Society and the Economy*, P.R. MacDonald, ed. (Chicago: American Marketing Association, 1969).
7. Katz, E. 'The two-step flow of Communication: An Up-to-date Report on an Hypothesis', *Public Opinion Quarterly*, 1957, 21.
8. Mason, R. 'The Use of Information Sources by Influentials in the Adoption Process', *Public Opinion Quarterly*, 1963, 27.
9. Montgomery, D.B. and Silk, A.J. 'Patterns of Overlap in Opinion Leadership and Interest for Selected Categories of Purchasing Activity', P.R. MacDonald, op.cit.
10. Myers, J.H. and Reynolds, W.H. *Consumer Behaviour and Marketing Management* (Boston: Houghton Mifflin, 1967).
11. Lazarsfeld, P.F., Berelson, B.R. and Grudlet, H. *The People's Choice* (New York: Columbia University Press, 1948).
12. Rogers, E.M. and Shoemaker, E.F. *Communication of Innovations* (New York: Free Press, 1971).
13. Linton, H.B. 'Dependence on External Influence: Correlates in Perception, Attitudes and Judgement', *Journ. Abnorm & Social Psych*. 1955, 51.
14. Kassarjian, H.H. 'Personality and Consumer Behaviour: A Review', *Journal of Marketing Research*, 1968, 5.
15. There are numerous works on Freudian theory. The most comprehensive is probably *The Pelican Freud Library*, Angela Richards, ed. (Harmondsworth: Penguin).
16. Eysenck, H.J. *Sense and Nonsense in Psychology* (Harmondsworth: Penguin, 1958).
17. Cattell, R.B. *The Scientific Analysis of Personality* (Chicago: Aldine, 1966).

18. Eysenck, H.J. *Fact and Fiction in Pyschology* (Harmondsworth: Penguin, 1965).
19. Evans, F.B. 'Psychological and Objective Factors in the Prediction of Brand Choice', *Journal of Business*, 1959, 32.
20. Newcomb, T.M. *Social Psychology* (New York: Holt, Rinehart, and Winston, 1950).
21. Birdwell, A.E. 'Influence of Image Congruence on Consumer Choice', *Reflections on progress in Marketing*, G. South, ed. (Chicago: American Marketing Association, 1965).
22. Grubb, E.L. and Hupp, G. 'Perception of Self, Generalized Stereotypes, and Brand Selection', *Journ. of Marketing Research*, 1968, 5.
23. Landon, E.L. 'Self Concept, Ideal Self Concept, and Consumer Purchase Intentions', *Journ. of Consumer Research*, 1974, 1.

Further Reading

Cattell, R.B. *The Scientific Analysis of Personality* (Harmondsworth: Penguin, 1965).
Peck, D. and Whitlow, D. *Approaches to Personality Theory* (London: Methuen, 1975).

Past Examination Questions

1. What factors determine how we perceive another person? (IM 1974)
2. Show how the market for a specific product or service can be segmented in terms of personality factors. (IM 1977)
3. What do we mean by 'opinion leaders' or 'opinion formers'? In what way might such people be of interest to a company intending to market a new type of domestic appliance? (CAM 1979)
4. What is an opinion leader? How do opinion leaders differ from those that they influence? (IM 1979)

8. MODELLING CONSUMER BEHAVIOUR

'Every decision maker possesses a model of consumer behaviour. That is to say, each person has at least some idea of the things that should be studied.'

Engel, Blackwell and Kollat

8.1 Introduction

Marketers are frequently called upon to describe consumer behaviour, to explain it, and sometimes to predict it. The description of consumer behaviour poses no real problems for the marketer since market research techniques have become an established part of his tools of trade. The explanation and prediction of consumer behaviour does, however, create a number of problems, not least being our far from complete understanding of human behaviour. In earlier chapters we have described some of the ways in which an experimental approach can aid our understanding of consumer behaviour and we have also discussed the contribution made by motivational research techniques. However, both these approaches concentrate on only a few of the variables involved in consumers' decision-making processes and they can therefore provide only a partial solution to the problem of explaining and predicting consumer behaviour.

As will be clear from the preceding chapters, consumer behaviour is extremely complex and is a function of both personal and situational variables. Personal variables include the consumer's motives, attitudes, beliefs, and past experiences; while situational variables will include advertising and other promotional activities, product distribution, competition between suppliers, and word-of-mouth communications. Furthermore, these variables interrelate in a complex and dynamic manner.

Given the complexity of consumer behaviour it is not surprising that until recently much of the work in this area was of a piecemeal nature. In recent years, however, technology has become available, through the computer, which enables a number of variables to be studied together and their interactions to be examined. It has also been found that it is possible to simplify consumer behaviour into its principal components and that, in practice, a relatively small number of variables account for the vast bulk of consumer behaviour. This has become known as the *modelling approach* and it has been used with some degree of success as a method of explaining and predicting behaviour.

In this chapter we examine the nature of the modelling approach and the characteristics of models, and describe some of the ways in which they have been applied in marketing.

8.2 The Nature of the Modelling Approach

A model is a simplified representation of a real phenomenon. It may be internalized; it may be verbal — e.g. 'Consumption is a function of income' it may be expressed algebraically — e.g. 'C = f (Y)'; or it may be represented pictorially, as in the case of a map. In whatever form a model is expressed, its key purpose is to simplify by including only those aspects of a real phenomenon that are of interest to the model builder. Thus it is possible for there to be a number of totally different models of the same phenomenon. Looking in any geographical atlas the reader will find various representations of the British Isles: some will be topographical, some will be climatic, and other will be geological. Each will concentrate on one aspect of the islands and the whole will be represented in two-dimensional form.

All marketers, in collecting, analysing, and interpreting data, use model of some form. They may be intuitive, or based partly on fact and partly on past experience. Most commonly they will be internalized and therefore no capable of being used by others. For this reason it is almost impossible to test their validity in a scientifically accepted manner.

In this chapter we are concerned with the use of models as a basis for the systematic study of consumer behaviour. We are interested in understanding the decision processes involved and must therefore concentrate on the relationships between the variables that affect the decision process. If model are to be of practical assistance in the study of consumer behaviour, they must be capable of scientific evaluation and this means that all assumption must be explicitly stated. Models of consumer behaviour can be expressed verbally or algebraically, but in most cases they take the form of elaborate flow charts.

Models fulfil two main purposes. First, they assist in the development of theories of consumer behaviour and, second, they aid understanding of the complex relationships involved. By simplifying consumer behaviour into it principal components and by identifying the relationships between variables a model serves as a frame of reference that can be used to direct research Models provide a framework within which research findings can be integrated and gaps in knowledge more easily identified. The researcher is presented with a simple representation of the relevant variables and this aids understanding and the development of theories regarding their precise nature and the linkages involved. By clearly delineating the variables involved in consumer decision-making and their interrelationships, models can produce a unified view of behavioural processes. This framework can be used to explain behaviour and its underlying causes and to predict how consumers would react to a given situation.

8.3 Model Characteristics

In 1973 the British Market Research Society established a Study Group concerned with modelling. One of its first tasks was to agree on a set of descriptions that would enable the classification and evaluation of different models. The following eleven descriptions were agreed[1].

1. *Micro- or macro-.* In a micro-model each individual or unit in the market or data base is represented and processed at the individual level. The output may or may not be a resultant of the aggregation of individual data. In a macro-model the total market is considered as a whole and the model's output is a global market response.

2. *Data-based or theory-based.* Data-based models are the logical outcome of the process of data analysis used. Theory-based models are developed through the application of reason and have their basis in theories adopted from the behavioural sciences.

3. *Low, medium, or high level models.* This relates to simplicity or lack of it. At the lowest level simple models can be devised that require few variables but they inevitably have certain limitations because of their narrow coverage. They are better regarded as sub-models or component parts of some larger, more comprehensive model. At the other extreme there are 'grand' models that seek to orchestrate all relevant market variables and represent the full range of marketing stimuli. The medium category lies somewhere between the two.

4. *Descriptive (historical or current), diagnostic, or predictive.* Here the distinction is made between models that describe market behaviour, those that seek to explain or diagnose why consumers behave as they do, and those that set out to predict how consumers will behave under specified circumstances.

5. *Behavioural or statistical.* In behavioural models reference is made to underlying assumptions about how the individual behaves. They seek to relate the total process of consumer responses to a given stimulus. With the statistical model there are no implicit assumptions about how or why consumers behave as they do. The internal parameters are hypothesised as a function of the analytical procedures employed.

6. *Generalized or ad hoc.* Here a distinction is made between models that are intended to be, or can be, applied to a wide range of markets and those that are developed in the context of, and for use in, one market only.

7. *Functional or intellectual.* The functional model represents the actual function of the object; it is meant to have real world application. The intellectual model need not be rooted in practicability.

8. *Static or dynamic.* The static model represents a particular system at a given point in time and cannot take account of time effects. The dynamic model is able to represent systems over time. It can take account of changing values of parameters and even changes in basic relationships between parameters over time.

9. *Qualitative or quantitative.* In the case of qualitative models no explicit variables are measured. In the case of quantitative models they are. A quantitative model is therefore more likely to be helpful in predicting behaviour as it should provide an indication of the weighting of importance that should be given to individual variables.

10. *Algebraic, sequential/net, or topological.* In algebraic models summation or other manipulation is independent of the order of the variables. With sequential or net models the order of the variables is explicitly taken into account by the model. Topological models are based upon field theory concepts involving space and geometry, forces, and motion. They are *Gestalt* models; that is they are concerned with the total situation.
11. *Successful or unsuccessful.* These concepts are indefinable. What constitutes success or lack of it will differ among different people. Nonetheless it was felt to be a useful criterion.

Models vary widely according to their purpose and function and it is therefore not possible to be dogmatic about the attributes of a 'good' model. It is, however, possible to point to general criteria that the modeller should bear in mind when constructing his model. These are:

1. *Simplicity.* Whether the model is of high or low level, it should seek to break down complex behaviour patterns into simple, easily understandable components.
2. *Factual basis.* A model should be consistent with the facts as far as they are known.
3. *Logic.* To be plausible a model must make sense and be internally consistent.
4. *Originality.* If a model is to advance knowledge it should be original, either in its basic construction or in the way in which it links together previously separate areas of knowledge.
5. *Explanatory power.* A model should seek to explain how, and why, specified behaviour takes place.
6. *Prediction.* A model should aid the prediction of a consumer's reaction to a given stimulus.
7. *Heuristic power.* This refers to a model's capacity to suggest new areas of research.
8. *Validity.* If a model is to have validity it should be verifiable. This means that it should be possible, at least in theory, to test the relationships proposed between variables.

It would be unrealistic to expect a model of consumer behaviour to meet all these criteria as our knowledge of human behaviour is far from complete and we still lack the techniques to evaluate adequately the relationships postulated in the individual models. Nonetheless, the above list should serve as a guide to the reader when evaluating the models of consumer behaviour outlined later in this chapter.

8.4 Classes of Variables

In order to apply modelling techniques to a phenomenon as complex as consumer behaviour it is first necessary to identify the principal categories of variables that influence the decision-taking of individuals. These are: internal, external, past experience, present environment, and future expectations.

1. *Internal variables* include basic physiological needs, such as hunger and thirst; and the psychological structure of the individual, including processes such as perception, motivation, learning, attitude formation, values, and beliefs.
2. *External variables* are those factors present in the external environment that affect the individual's psychological condition and therefore his behaviour. External variables may arise from past experience, the present environment, and future expectations.
3. *Past experience* in the form of prior learning and attitude formation can be helpful in understanding and reacting to a present situation. The individual may, or may not, be consciously aware of the influence of his earlier experiences.
4. *The present environment* has immediate relevance to a particular buying situation and includes physical factors such as the proximity of various stores, available transport, and the weather; economic factors such as the price of alternative products; the individual's current financial situation, and the state of the economy; and social variables, such as the opinions and experiences of reference groups, and the individual's social class and culture. Variables also affecting the present environment will be the market activities of rival firms, such as advertising, in-store promotions, and other media communications.
5. *Future expectations* including job prospects, health, the economic outlook, and possible changes in family circumstances can affect present buying decisions, particularly where goods such as consumer durables are concerned.

In grouping these variables into five categories we have obtained a simple model of consumer behaviour which can be represented pictorially as shown in Figure 8.1. It should, however, be obvious to the reader that this simple model takes no account of the relative influence of the individual categories of variable in a particular buying situation. It tells us nothing of the variables included within each of the categories or of the way in which they interact. Nonetheless it provides us with a frame of reference for more complex model building.

Having identified the categories of variable that exert an influence on consumer decision-taking, it is necessary to examine the causal relationships involved. This leads to a second way of grouping variables; that is, into stimulus variables, response variables, and intervening variables.

1. *Stimulus variables* act as inputs to consumers' behaviour and arise mainly through the individual's external environment. They include environmental factors, such as products, advertisements, and other media information; and social factors such as relatives, peer groups, and other reference groups. Stimulus variables can also arise internally through physiological needs such as hunger, thirst, warmth, and cold.
2. *Response variables* are the observable reactions of individuals to stimulus variables. They may include discussions with salesmen regarding products; changes in voice, tone and gesture; and physical acts such as product purchase. In all cases the response is overt and this means that it is

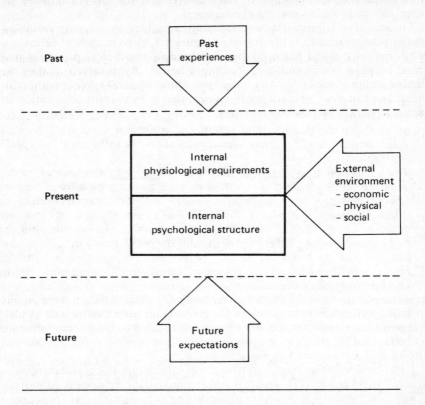

Figure 8.1 Categories of variables influencing the individual

either directly observable or capable of being measured.
3. *Intervening variables* are so called because they intervene between stimuli and overt responses. They include the way in which we perceive our environment, our motives, attitudes, and beliefs. These variables are internal to the individual and for this reason are not observable and cannot be directly measured.

The existence of intervening variables suggests that stimuli do not affect responses directly but that behaviour is in some way modified by them. The fact that these variables are internal to the individual also means that we cannot expect all individuals to react in the same way to a given stimulus variable and that an individual's reactions may change over time.

As intervening variables are not observable we can only make inferences about their role and likely structure by observing the relationship between stimulus and overt response. This is no easy undertaking given the multitude of variables involved. By their very nature, intervening variables are largely the invention or construction of the observer and for this reason they are often referred to as *hypothetical constructs*.

The causal relationship between stimulus variables, intervening variables, and response variables is illustrated in Figure 8.2. Such models of behaviour are commonly called *black box models* because the mental processes that stand between inputs and outputs cannot be directly observed – they are hidden within a black box. Any judgement about what takes place within this black box can only be made by *inference*; that is by careful observation of inputs and their associated responses.

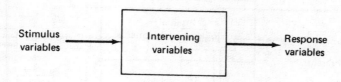

Figure 8.2 Black Box model

Another frequently drawn distinction is that between endogenous and exogenous variables. *Endogenous variables* are those which have a clearly specified effect on behaviour and are therefore included in the model. *Exogenous variables*, on the other hand, are thought to have some influence on behaviour but their precise role in the decision-making process is not well known and is therefore left unspecified.

It has been seen that models can be classified in a number of different ways depending on the level of analysis and the analytical techniques employed. When looking at the application of modelling to marketing it is appropriate to consider the level of analysis employed; that is, the classes of variables the model takes into account. For this reason we shall consider models of consumer behaviour under three broad headings: black box models; personal variable models; and comprehensive models. Black box models take no account of the mental processes involved in decision-taking and internal variables are therefore ignored. Personal variable models, by comparison, are primarily concerned with internal psychological variables and take no account of external environmental variables. Comprehensive models aim to include all categories of variables that have an influence on consumer behaviour.

8.5 Black Box Models

Black box models treat the individual and his physiological and psychological make-up as an inpenetrable black box. They are concerned with the external environmental influences on behaviour and in the context of consumer behaviour may more properly be called *market models*. Market models may be of assistance in market research, particularly where new markets are involved, as they establish a framework for study.

Markets can be described in a number of ways. Figure 8.3 shows a simple model of the market for consumer goods and identifies the interactions between the producer, its competitors, distributors, retailers, and consumers. The producer is affected by the actions of its competitors and the government; distributors are affected by the sales and marketing efforts of their suppliers and by the needs of retailers; retailers are influenced by their distributors, producers, and the needs of consumers; and, at the end of the system, consumers are affected by the marketing activities of producers and retailers and by the actions of other consumers.

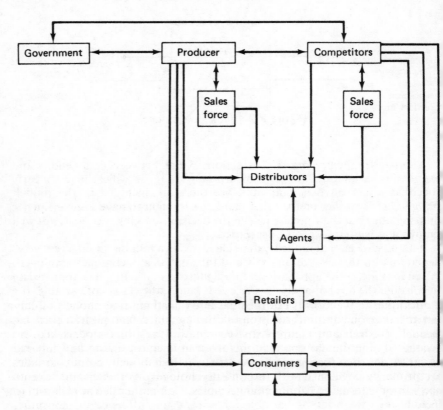

Figure 8.3 The market — a simple model

Source: Palmer, J. and Sampson, P. 'Setting Advertising Appropriations: A Science for "Imitating" Consumer Behaviour', Gold Medal Paper The Thomson Medals and Awards for Advertising Research 1972 (London: The Thomson Organization Ltd., 1973. By permission of the authors).

Another way of looking at the market is to examine the decision environment facing the consumer. Here the consumer is the focal point of the model, as shown in Figure 8.4, and the relationships between the factors influencing a consumer's decision environment are not explored. The main influences on the consumer are identified as: the alternative brands known to the consumer; the advertising communications of producers and retailers; other promotional activities; availability; price; the social environment, including the views of family and friends; and the perceived opportunities for using the product.

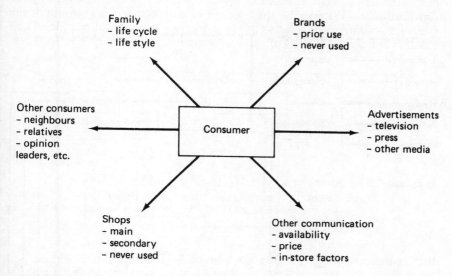

Figure 8.4 The consumer's decision environment
Source: *see* Figure 8.3

Both the above models examine the external stimulus variables that have an influence on consumer decision-taking. The third example of a black box model, illustrated in Figure 8.5 shows the buying process conceived as a system of inputs and outputs. Stimulus variables and the ways in which they are transmitted to the consumer are shown on the left, while output variables, in the form of the consumer's responses, are shown on the right. In the centre stands the consumer, whose cognitive processes are hidden within a black box.

Black box models can be useful to the marketer because they concentrate on the external influences on behaviour on which marketing strategy can exert an influence. By evaluating the relative importance of stimulus variables, the marketing strategist will be in a stronger position to determine the action needed to influence consumer behaviour in favour of his particular product. For example, research on consumer purchasing behaviour regarding colour television sets may show that the consumer is not in a position to evaluate alternative brands in terms of their technical sophistication. A model of television purchasing may therefore reveal that consumers are particularly influenced by the level of after sales service and by advertising

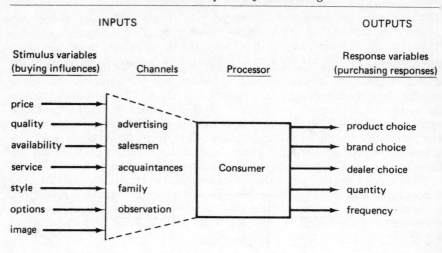

Figure 8.5 The buying process − inputs and outputs

Source: Kotler, P. 'Behavioural Models for Analysing Buyers', *Journal of Marketing* Vol. 29 No. 4, pp. 37−45 1965. (By kind permission of the American Marketing Association)

that reassures them regarding the product's technical sophistication and reliability. By comparison, a model depicting household furniture purchasing may show the consumer to be able to judge reliably the relative quality of alternative brands. Style and colour may then have a far more important influence on buying decisions.

8.6 Personal Variable Models

Personal variable models take account of personal variables like beliefs, attitudes, and buying intentions, but exclude external and environmental variables that may affect behaviour. Typically, they are relatively simple, or low level, models involving only a few variables. They are often used as submodels of more complex models. The following sections describe some of the personal variable models in common use.

8.61 Linear Additive Models

Linear additive models are based on the assumption that individual consumers rate objects on the basis of a number of perceived attributes or beliefs and that an individual's attitude towards a particular object is the sum of these scored beliefs or attribute ratings. The overall score may be obtained by straight addition, weighted addition, or, alternatively, by straight averaging or weighted averaging. An example of a linear additive model is the Fishbein model which, as the reader will recall from Chapter 6, can be expressed algebraically as:

$$A_o = \sum_{i=1}^{n} B_i a_i$$

Linear additive models, such as Fishbein's, can provide the marketer with useful information on the product attributes that are significant in determining the consumer's attitude towards a product. They can also provide data on the consumer's evaluation of the product according to those attributes. Such information may be helpful in product development and in the planning of promotional campaigns. Care must, however, be taken in selecting the product attributes to be studied and it is clearly preferable if the consumer uses only those attributes which he considers to be relevant.

Such models may be helpful in describing and explaining aspects of consumer behaviour, but they have so far proved to be inadequate as predictors of behaviour. A problem is the absence of any satisfactory independent measure of 'behavioural intent' that could be correlated with the attitude scores obtained from linear additive models.

8.62 Threshold Model

The threshold model is based on the premise that brand choice decisions are made by a form of sorting process, where brands are accepted or rejected because they possess, or do not possess, certain required levels of each relevant product attribute. This implies that, for each product attribute there is a threshold level of acceptability. Brands are accepted on the basis of a particular product characteristic if they are rated above the threshold, but are rejected if they fall below. Thus a product may be assessed for each product attribute as, for example, having: enough of . . . . or not enough of . . . .; or the right amount of . . . . or too much of . . . .

This type of model has proved to be particularly successful in handling price, since a product may be rated highly on all attributes but price and is rejected because it is too expensive. The threshold model has been used with some success in higher level models as a method of choice prediction.

8.63 Trade-off Model

The trade-off model is based on the assumption that, when faced with a series of choices between different amounts of a number of attributes, consumers will trade a reduction in one attribute for an increase in another. In this way they reach a compromise between their 'ideal' product and the most satisfactory available alternative. This behaviour is termed 'satisficing'.

The trade-off concept has its origins in the theory of utility used in economics. It assumes that consumers' purchasing intentions are the sum of the 'utilities', or value, ascribed to certain products. In marketing, the theory has been used to explain why one brand may be preferred to another brand. The consumer is assumed to place a certain utility on each product attribute and will choose the particular brand that provides him with the highest overall utility.

For example, a consumer choosing a deep freezer may be faced with a trade-off between cubic capacity and price, a greater cubic capacity involving a higher price. By asking him to rank in order of preference a number of alternative combinations of price and cubic capacity it is possible to obtain a measure of the consumer's utility for the different price levels and cubic capacities examined. The utilities so obtained provide a useful measure of the importance the consumer attaches to specific product attributes. When correlated with demographic variables, such as income, this information can be helpful in the planning of product ranges.

The trade-off model appears to work best for specific rather than image-related variables. A limitation is, however, that interactions between variables are ignored. Nonetheless, research using this model has suggested that it is a very powerful low level model that could have much to offer as a sub-model in higher level information processing models.

8.7 Comprehensive Models

Comprehensive models take both personal and environmental variables into account. They include the so-called 'grand' models such as those put forward by Howard and Sheth; Engel, Kollat, and Blackwell; and Nicosia. Also included under this heading are information processing models.

8.71 The Howard-Sheth Model

The Howard-Sheth model[2] of buyer behaviour is based on a model originally conceived by John Howard which has been revised and refined with the assistance of Jagdish Sheth. It is essentially an S-O-R model (see Chapter 3) where input stimuli consist of information obtained from the social and commercial environment, and output responses are buyer behaviour, including attitudes and motivational sets. In the Howard-Sheth model the intervening variables comprise 'hypothetical constructs' and exogenous variables. Hypothetical constructs in this model are essentially concerned with perception and learning. The exogenous variables are external to the model but are nonetheless important in predicting perception and learning. They include factors such as the importance of the purchase to the consumer, personality traits,

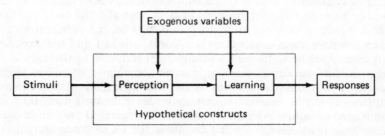

Figure 8.6 The Howard-Sheth model of buyer behaviour – simplified version

social class, culture, financial status, and the social and organizational setting. In its simplest form the model can be represented by Figure 8.6.

Input stimuli may take various forms and may be either social or commercial. Social inputs arise from the buyer's social environment: his family, reference groups, and social class. Commercial inputs include price, product quality, distinctiveness, service, and availability. These commercial inputs may be *significative*, that is actual attributes of the brands the consumer confronts, or *symbolic*, that is the product attributes generated by the symbolic communications of producers through advertising and other promotional activities.

Output responses are clearly defined in the Howard-Sheth model and comprise five sequential stages: attention; brand comprehension; attitude; intention; purchase. The relationship between the output stages is illustrated in Figure 8.7; solid lines represent the sequence of behaviour, while broken lines show feedback effects.

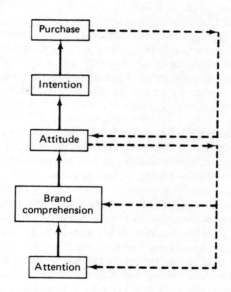

Figure 8.7 Output stages of the Howard-Sheth model

If, for example, we consider the process of buying a hi-fi system, a person's first response will be to become aware of the need for a hi-fi system and he may perhaps be attracted by a shop window display – *attention*. His next move will be to find out as much as he can about the different systems available on the market – *brand comprehension*. From the information gathered he will form an *attitude* about hi-fi systems in general and the available brands. This attitude will provide the basis for formulating *intentions* to purchase that may subsequently lead to actual *purchase*.

Having purchased a hi-fi system, the feedback effects come into play. The consumer's experience with the hi-fi system purchased will influence his subsequent attitude towards hi-fi systems and the brand purchased. This experience may lead him to revise his comprehension of different brands and he may attend to hi-fi systems in a more informed way than previously. His future buying behaviour will also be conditioned by his initial experience. If he is satisfied with the system purchased he may be encouraged to buy that particular brand again. If, however, there were shortcomings with the system purchased he may evaluate other brands in the light of the experience gained with the initial purchase.

The output responses of the Howard-Sheth model are one of its distinctive features. Unlike many other models, purchase is not the only response but the ultimate of five output stages, at any one of which a consumer may stop. But, even if the consumer does not actually purchase a product, the formation of an attitude towards the product and the brands available will influence any subsequent buying behaviour.

With regard to the intervening variables in this model, it will be seen from Figure 8.8 that the hypothetical constructs are of two types – perceptual and learning. The perceptual constructs are attention, stimulus ambiguity, and search; and the learning constructs are motives, choice criteria, brand comprehension, attitude, intention, confidence, and satisfaction. It will be noted that some of the hypothetical constructs have the same names as the output stages. This may be somewhat confusing to the reader but arises because the hypothetical constructs are not observable; that is, it is not possible to see an attitude or brand comprehension. It is, however, possible to measure an attitude, within clearly defined limits, by use of an attitude scale; and brand comprehension by means of a questionnaire survey. It is the measurement of attitude and brand comprehension that is included in the output stages. The more abstract real phenomena are included in the hypothetical constructs.

The relationship between the hypothetical constructs can again be illustrated by the person contemplating the purchase of a hi-fi system. First, the consumer notices an advertisement for a hi-fi system – the stimulus. But, not knowing much about such systems, he is unable to judge whether a particular system will meet his requirements – *stimulus ambiguity*. He therefore finds out more about the different systems available by buying specialist magazines, visiting shops, and questioning salesmen – *overt search*. The consumer reads the magazines and listens to the salesmen – *attention*. The information received as a result of overt search (more stimuli) may lead him to seek further information – overt search again. Not all the information obtained will be remembered and some may become distorted and confused in the process of perception – *perceptual bias*. The consumer may remember more about one product than another because it is in a price range he can afford – exogenous variable.

The next stage is the formation of an attitude. This will depend both on *choice criteria* and on *brand comprehension*. Choice criteria will be affected by the consumer's motives for purchasing a hi-fi system. Is it required to enhance the consumer's status and impress his friends (exogenous variable)? Is it required for popular or classical recordings, for domestic or other use?

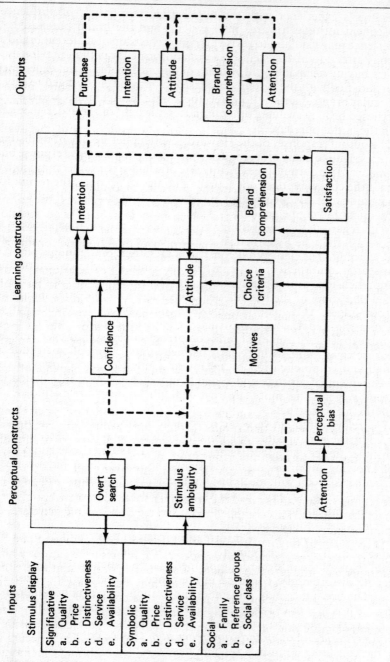

Figure 8.8 The Howard-Sheth model

Source: Howard, J.A. and Sheth, J.N. *The Theory of Buyer Behaviour* (New York: John Wiley & Sons Inc., 1969. By permission).

What equipment is to be linked into the system? If the choice criteria are not known then the consumer may have to engage in extensive problem-solving activity. If the choice criteria are known, but alternative brands have not been evaluated in terms of these criteria, then limited problem-solving activity will ensue. Where the consumer knows both the choice criteria to be used and how the different brands relate to these criteria, routinized response behaviour will occur. This type of response might be expected with repeat purchases of convenience products such as washing powder and baked beans. Thus, in order to form an attitude about a particular product and the available brands, the consumer embarks on a learning process that involves problem-solving behaviour. The extent of this problem-solving behaviour will depend on the consumer's knowledge of the features of alternative systems and the criteria he should use to evaluate the alternatives available.

Having once established an attitude towards hi-fi systems, the consumer may, depending on the extent to which he is certain in his evaluation of the competing brands (*confidence*) decide whether he intends to purchase a particular brand (intention). Having formed an intention the consumer may then go to a shop and buy the chosen system (output, purchase).

The Howard-Sheth model is essentially a model of consumers' rational choice decisions. It assumes a degree of rationality on the part of the consumer to the extent that decisions are rational within the limits of the consumer's perceptual, learning, and information-processing capabilities. The consumer is not assumed to consider all the various alternatives but rather forms an evoked set (see Chapter 2) of brands meeting the criteria necessary to be deemed satisfactory alternatives. For this reason, the model is particularly suited to brand choice decisions but is less capable of dealing with decisions between two different product alternatives; for example, buying a new car or a bigger house.

The model concentrates on the way in which information is perceived and the adaptive behaviour that results through the learning process. Implicit to the model is the assumption that the consumer will always try to simplify his buying decision through the acquisition of more information and through gaining experience. The model does not, however, fall into the trap of assuming that behaviour takes place in a vacuum. Thus a change in the exogenous variables may lead the consumer to consider new brands or alter his choice criteria. This complicates his buying decision and generates a new round of simplifying activity.

Three types of buying situation are distinguished by Howard and Sheth. The first category, *extended problem-solving*, relates to situations where the consumer has little prior knowledge of alternative brands and where the risk associated with the decision is high. This may be the case for high-priced, one-off purchase decisions. In such cases, the consumer is likely to spend time collecting and assimilating information about alternative brands, gradually simplifying his choice until he makes his purchase decision. The second category of buying decision, *limited problem-solving*, occurs where the consumer has some prior knowledge of alternative brands but has not yet established a strong brand preference. He engages in limited problem-solving behaviour, collecting comparative information on the brands he is actively considering in order to clarify his buying decision. The final category of consumer buying identified by Howard and Sheth is termed *routinized response behaviour*. It occurs where sufficient past experience has been obtained on alternative brands for the consumer to have developed strong loyalty towards one or two brands. These brands form the consumer's evoked set and he is unlikely to consider other brands unless in exceptional circumstances, such as in the case of a change in an exogenous variable. There is therefore very little likelihood that new learning will take place and the consumer's perceptual bias in favour of the preferred brand will reduce the possibility of another brand being considered seriously.

The Howard-Sheth model has attracted a great deal of interest, not least because it embraces the principal determinants of behaviour; perception; communication; learning; attitudes. It does, however, suffer from a number of shortcomings and these stem mainly from the fact that a number of the variables and the relationships between them are not well defined. The distinctions between the endogenous variables and the exogenous variables, for example, are not sharp, and empirical evidence has suggested that some of the exogenous variables have as much influence on the outcome as some of the endogenous variables. The model has evolved considerably since it originally appeared in 1969 and empirical evaluation is continuing. The fact that the model is continually being modified does not in any way detract from its significance as an important contribution towards understanding consumer behaviour.

8.72 The Engel, Kollat and Blackwell Model

This model of consumer behaviour bears similarity to the Howard-Sheth model, which is not surprising since they are similar in scope and intent. Both models concentrate on learning processes but they differ in the ways they treat the processing of information and the role of post-choice experience.

It will be seen from Figure 8.9 that the Engel, Kollat and Blackwell model[3] includes five groups of variables which are not dissimilar from the basic components of the Howard-Sheth model. These are: information input; information processing; product-brand evaluations; general motivating influences; internalized environmental influences. These variables interrelate and are linked together through five sequential decision process stages: problem recognition; information search; alternative evaluation; choice; outcomes.

Problem recognition occurs either through external or internal stimuli. External stimuli affect the consumer's awareness of information or experience about a product; for example, an expensive car repair may cause the consumer to consider the replacement of his present car. Internal stimuli include primary motives such as feeling thirsty. Once a problem has been identified, the consumer undertakes an *information search*. Initially this will involve an unconscious review of information, stored internally in memory, concerning attitudes and beliefs towards possible alternatives. Such a review may reveal strong brand preferences and routine purchase may result. If, however, insufficient information is available from this internal search then

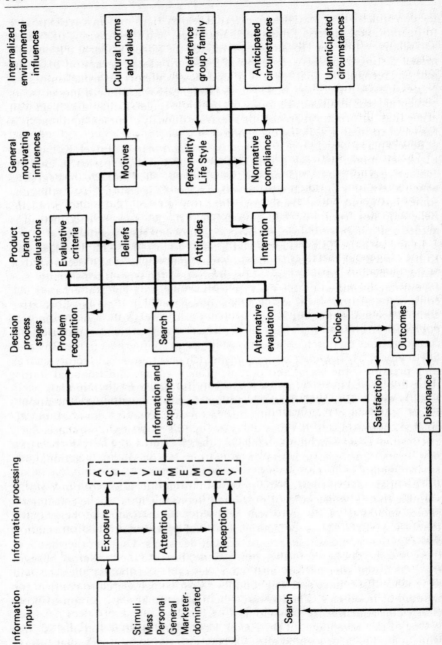

Figure 8.9 The Engel, Kollat and Blackwell model

Source: Engel, J.F., Blackwell, R.D., and Kollat, D.T. *Consumer Behaviour*, 3rd edn. (Hinsdale, Ill.: Dryden Press, 1978). By permission of Holt Rinehart and Winston.

the consumer will embark on an external search. This may involve exposure to promotional material, mass media sources, and the opinions of friends and relatives. Like the Howard-Sheth model, the Engel, Kollat and Blackwell model distinguishes between exposure, attention, and reception of information, recognizing that there is a tendency to distort information during processing. A difference, however, is that the Howard-Sheth model treats perceptual bias as an endogenous variable while Engel, Kollat, and Blackwell argue that 'information processing is extraordinarily complex' and that 'it is far wiser to treat it as being exogenous'.

Beliefs play a central role in *alternative evaluation* in the Engel, Kollat, and Blackwell model and are a function of information, experience, and the evaluative criteria by which products are judged. They indicate the degree to which alternative brands are perceived to possess the characteristics the consumer has identified as being important to the resolution of his problem. Beliefs do not feature in the Howard-Sheth model but reference instead is made to stored information, satisfaction, and exogenous variables.

In line with the Fishbein Extended Model (discussed in Chapter 6), Engel, Kollat, and Blackwell see attitudes as a function of beliefs; attitude towards a brand being defined as 'a learned predisposition to respond consistently in a favourable or unfavourable manner with respect to a given alternative'. A consumer's attitudes will influence his purchase intentions, but normative compliance and anticipated circumstances also play a role here. *Normative compliance* refers to the effect of perceived social influences and life-style considerations on purchase intentions; it has no counterpart in the Howard-Sheth model. *Anticipated circumstances* include a number of factors such as time pressures, the social and organizational setting, and financial status; these are treated as exogenous variables in the Howard-Sheth model.

Although *choice* will normally follow formulated purchase intentions, Engel, Kollat, and Blackwell introduce a variable to take account of unanticipated circumstances that may delay or become a barrier to purchase. Such circumstances may include a change in financial status, the introduction of a new brand onto the market, or alteration in social, organizational, or environmental influences.

The final stage of the decision process in this model is that of *outcomes*, a variable that takes account of post-choice consequences. If the consumer's choice is found to be consistent with his expectations and beliefs, the purchase will result in satisfaction. This will contribute to his information and experience and will affect subsequent decisions. On the other hand, if there is some doubt about the choice made, because the consumer believes that unchosen alternatives also have desirable attributes, then he will experience dissonance and will conduct a post-choice search to confirm the wisdom of his choice. The Howard-Sheth model takes no account of post-choice consequences for behaviour.

One of the advantages of the Engel, Kollat, and Blackwell model is that, while including a large number of variables that influence consumer behaviour, the model is relatively easy to understand. Additionally it takes account of the range of buying decisions, from routine purchase to one-off purchase, and this contributes greatly to its flexibility. However, like the Howard-Sheth model there is a lack of clarity regarding the precise role of some of the variables and the way in which they interrelate. The role of environmental variables, for example, is noted but the way they affect behaviour is not well defined. Motives, although included in the model, are not discussed in any detail and their precise role is not specified. The model has also been criticized for the mechanistic way it treats the decision-making process and, in particular, for the over-precise distinction drawn between information processing and product brand evaluation. Nonetheless, the model has attracted a great deal of interest because of the way it has successfully integrated the findings of research into individual aspects of consumer behaviour.

8.73 The Nicosia Model

Unlike most other models of consumer behaviour, Nicosia's model[4] of consumer decision processes explicitly includes the selling firm. Central to the model is the circular relationship between the firm and the consumer. The firm affects the consumer through its advertising and promotional communications and, in turn, the behaviour of the consumer affects the firm. The consumer's buying experience also affects his or her behaviour in the future.

It will be seen from Figure 8.10 that the Nicosia model is divided into four fields:

1. Field One consists of two sub-fields: the firm's attributes and the consumer's attributes. The communication flow between the two sub-fields involves all the processes normally associated with the encoding and decoding of information; including selective exposure, perception, and retention. It also takes account of environmental and social influences present at the time of the communication. If the communication is compatible with the consumer's existing belief systems and is pertinent to an established need, then it is likely to be successful and will lead to the formation of a positive attitude on the part of the consumer.
2. In Field Two the favourable attitude to the communications of the firm encourages the consumer to engage in problem-solving activity involving search and the evaluation of alternatives.
3. Field Three assumes that the action undertaken in Field Two motivates the consumer to a decision whether or not to purchase and that he acts accordingly.
4. Field Four is concerned with post-decision feedback effects both to the firm and to the consumer. Whatever the consumer's action (purchase or non-purchase) it will exert an influence on the attributes of both the firm and the consumer and will thereby affect their future behaviour.

The interactions between these four fields may occur simultaneously or in sequence. The process may also be initiated at any of the stages; that is, it may be initiated by the firm, by the consumer, by a purchase experience, or by a failure to purchase.

The four fields described above are the central components of the Nicosia model and each is further elaborated by additional sub-systems to produce a

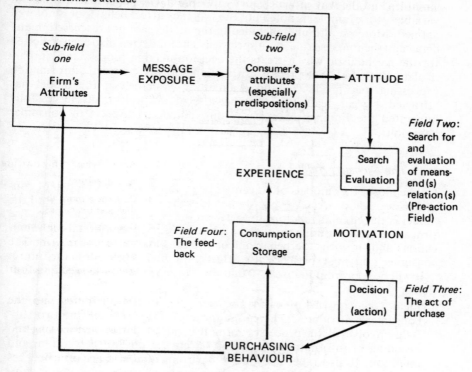

Figure 8.10 The Nicosia model — a summary flow chart

Source: Nicosia, F.M. *Consumer Decision Processes: Marketing and Advertising Implications* (by kind permission of the author).

complex and sophisticated model. One of the strengths of the Nicosia model is that it does not consider the individual consumer in isolation, but views consumer behaviour as an overall process involving both the consumer and the firm. The circular information flow means that the actions of one party influence the actions of the other and, in turn, their future behaviour. In this way behaviour is seen as an adaptive process. Also, unlike other models, consumer behaviour is seen here as a decision process rather than the end result of a decision process. The model, for example, recognizes that actual behaviour is not a direct result of the formation of an attitude but that other steps intervene.

Although the model has undergone some successful empirical investigation and testing, it is in many ways a descriptive model rather than an explanatory or predictive model. The linkages in the model show flows rather than causation. Further information is needed regarding the way the attributes of the firm and the consumer function if the model is to provide an adequate explanation of behaviour. It is nonetheless an important and interesting model that offers scope for further development.

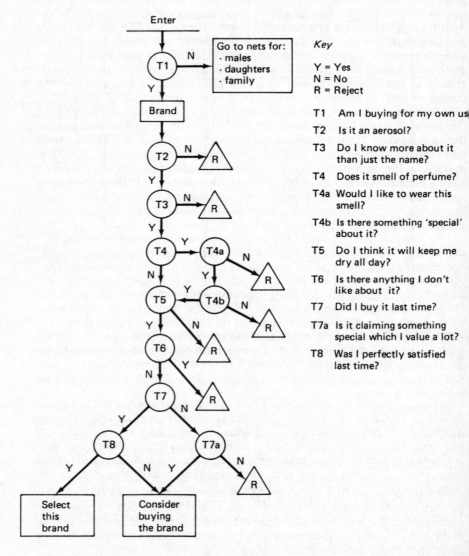

Figure 8.11 An individual's decision net for the purchase of a deodorant

Source: Palmer, J. and Faivre, J.P. 'The information processing theory of consumer behaviour'. *European Research*, 1973, 1. (by permission of ESOMAR)

8.74 Information Processing Models

Information processing theory is based on the premise that behaviour takes place after people think, make decisions, and solve problems. Consumers are not passive receivers of information, but they select and organize information; rejecting some and retaining some. They determine the value of a product in relation to their needs and these needs will depend on the consumer's personal motives and environmental factors. The information processing approach to modelling consumer behaviour aims to reproduce as closely as possible the manner in which information is processed by the consumer and, in doing so, aims to predict the behavioural outcome.

Information processing models involve the use of decision nets which take the form of a tree of tests that sort and classify information until a final decision is taken. Each test relates to a specific attribute of the input variable and classifies the attribute into one of a number of categories. The tests making up the decision net may be relatively simple, such as 'Does the brand have a pleasant smell?', or more complex, for example, 'Is there something special about this brand?'. One test may exit into a number of further tests, but in practice, for the sake of simplicity, only two exits are normally used. Figure 8.11 gives an example of a typical decison net.

The decision net shown involves a consumer's decision to purchase a deodorant. It is constructed by asking the subject to verbalize the thought processes and actions involved in the decision to purchase a particular brand. A transcript is prepared and this is converted into a sequence of Yes/No questions. In the diagram the questions the consumer asks himself are designated 'T'. The reader should find it fairly easy to work through the net, with the aid of the Key, and see how the consumer is thought to make his decision.

The decision net, once constructed, can be written as a computer program that can be used to simulate consumer decision-taking, when supplied with data on consumers' need requirements, brand perceptions, and associations. Subjects are processed through the decision net individually and an aggregate prediction is obtained.

Information processing models can make use of linear additivity, threshold, and trade-off analysis, as appropriate, to deal with the choices facing the consumer at each test in the net. They are therefore not subject to the limitations of other models which are based on a theory, or theories, that provide only partial explanations of consumer purchasing behaviour. Information processing models can provide useful descriptive and diagnostic information on existing situations. They can also be used to process new information, although some modification may be needed to particular variables. In this way new outcomes can be predicted, for example revised market shares. Higher level modelling can also be achieved by introducing additional variables such as advertising and distribution patterns.

8.8 Summary

1. Models are simplified representations of reality and provide us with a

means of identifying relevant variables and specifying their relationships in an attempt to explain consumer behaviour. They enable us to look at the processes involved as a whole and to identify gaps in our knowledge. Modelling can therefore be a valuable tool in identifying new areas of research. It can also provide us with techniques for tackling problems not readily suggested by conventional market research and experimental methods.

2. Models vary widely according to the problems they seek to answer, the level of analysis they employ, and the analytical techniques involved. There is not, nor could there be, given our present state of knowledge, a 'best' or 'correct' model of consumer behaviour. A 'good' model should, however, be simple to understand, factually based, logically consistent, original, explanatory, predictive, have heuristic power, and be capable of validation.

3. None of the models reviewed in this chapter fully meet these criteria, but this does not invalidate them; each have their strengths and weaknesses. The so-called 'grand' models, the Howard-Sheth, the Engel, Kollat, and Blackwell, and the Nicosia, each have significant heuristic value but are rather cumbersome and difficult to use for practical purposes. On the other hand, black box models, personal variable models, and information processing techniques, though less sophisticated than the 'grand' models, provide practical, but basic, tools of marketing analysis.

References

1. Sampson, P. 'Consumer Behaviour Prediction and the Modelling Approach', *Esomar Congress Proceedings*, 1974.
2. Howard, J.A. and Sheth, J.N. *The Theory of Buyer Behaviour* (New York: Wiley, 1969).
3. Engel, J.F., Blackwell, R.D. and Kollat, D.T. *Consumer Behaviour* (Hinsdale Ill: Dryden Press, 1978).
4. Nicosia, F.M. *Consumer Decision Processes* (Englewood Cliffs, N.J.: Prentice-Hall, 1966).

Past Examination Questions

1. Discuss the view that behavioural modelling saves marketing from becoming an unwieldy mass of scattered facts. (IM 1975)
2. 'Models are the key to the development of consumer behaviour theories'. Discuss. (IM 1976)
3. Describe how the Howard-Sheth model attempts to explain the relationship between the various factors underlying buying behaviour. (IM 1976)
4. What role can the modelling approach play in developing a better foundation for marketing? (IM 1977)
5. Compare and contrast the Howard-Sheth model of buying behaviour with that of Engel, Kollat and Blackwell. (IM 1978)

9. BEHAVIOURAL ASPECTS OF THE ORGANIZATION

'. . . you never expected justice from a company, did you?
They have neither a soul to lose, nor a body to kick.'

Rev. Sydney Smith (1771–1845)

9.1 Introduction

Marketing takes place primarily within an organizational framework, and the marketer has the role of harnessing the capabilities of the organization he represents to ensure that the products produced and sold both are acceptable in the market place and generate a profitable return for the organization. The marketer therefore needs to know how formal organizations operate, how best they should organize the people they employ, how information and ideas are disseminated by organizations, and how they should equip themselves to cope with changes in the market environment.

An organization is more than a formalized system of roles; it is a complex interrelationship between formal and informal norms and attitudes. As companies become larger and their functions more differentiated, it becomes more difficult to distinguish between the formal and informal systems operating within the organization. Lines of communication also lengthen, bringing problems for management in integrating the various parts of the organization into a meaningful whole with clearly defined motivations and goals.

In this chapter we examine the characteristics of organizations and discuss the principal theoretical approaches to their study. We then examine methods of co-ordination and communication within the organization, as these behavioural aspects of the organization are clearly of prime importance to the effective implementation of a marketing philosophy. Behavioural influences affecting the organization's ability to cope with change in its internal and external environment are also discussed. Finally we look at some of the special features of industrial buyer behaviour; that is the marketing of products where the purchaser is another organization.

Behavioural factors influencing the individual's relationship with the organization, and in particular the motivation of employees, are discussed in Chapter 10.

171

9.2 Characteristics of an Organization

We all spend a great deal of our lives as members of organizations, be they companies, government departments, local authorities, schools, hospitals, or clubs. They differ widely in structure, form, and purpose, yet possess certain common characteristics which are identified in the following definition given by Schein[1].

> An organization is the rational coordination of the activities of a number of people for the achievement of some common explicit purpose or goal, through division of labor and function, and through a hierarchy of authority and responsibility.

From this definition it can be seen that organizations have in common the following attributes:

1. *Co-ordination of effort.* Organizations are established because the individual alone has not the time or resources to satisfy all his needs. By combining the resources of a number of people, the organization seeks to provide more than would be achieved by the individual efforts of its members acting alone. To be effective in this objective there has to be some means of co-ordinating the contributions of those involved to ensure that no conflict or unnecessary duplication of effort arises.
2. *Common goals or purpose.* It is essential that an organization has commonly agreed, or mutually recognized, goals or purpose. If no such agreement existed, the organization would quickly disintegrate or fragment as it would be impossible to co-ordinate the efforts of all participants. In addition to providing a common bond, goals can also serve as a means of evaluation; that is, the effectiveness of the organization can be measured by the extent to which goals are attained.
3. *Division of labour.* Organizations are able to achieve more than the sum of the individual efforts of their members through the division of labour. Each individual is allocated a function that is necessary for the attainment of the agreed goal and the resulting specialization benefits the organization as a whole. Ideally, individuals should be presented with tasks for which they have innate talent or expertise. This is not always possible and some form of training is usually required. Depending on the nature and size of the organization, it may not be possible for each identified function to be fulfilled by one person and in this case a sub-organization may be formed. For example, in a large company the sales function may be too much for one man to handle and a sales department is therefore formed. This becomes a mini-organization within the organization itself; individual tasks are allotted in a further division of labour.
4. *Hierarchy of authority and responsibility.* If there is to be effective co-ordination of effort to ensure that each of the functions identified in the division of labour are performed properly, in the interests of the organization as a whole, then there has to be some form of hierarchy of authority. Also, in order that this authority can be exercised, areas of responsibility must be defined. In most organizations authority and responsibility are defined by a hierarchy of ranks and positions which are

generally defined according to the functions identified in the division of labour. Responsibility is given for the performance of certain tasks and the authority to ensure that these tasks are carried out properly is usually delegated to those that carry the responsibility. This may not always be the case and the divergence of authority and responsibility can often be the source of organizational problems.

5. *Gestalt*. While an organization cannot exist without people, it can exist without particular individuals. In effect, an organization is a hierarchy of prescribed roles, each having designated responsibility and authority. It is independent of the particular people who fulfil these roles and can continue in being even if there is a 100% turnover in membership. The organization is, therefore, more than the sum of the individuals of which it is comprised; it has a *Gestalt* – an identity of its own. This attribute is recognized by Schein's definition which refers to the co-ordination of activities rather than to the co-ordination of people.

These factors do not mean that individuals have no impact on the organization. Roles can be redefined and the people who comprise the organization are generally instrumental in generating any change that may take place in the organizational structure. An organization is an adaptive body, which evolves in response to changes in its internal and external environment. Although some people would like to think otherwise, few organizations would crumble with the loss of one individual. An organization may, however, suffer a setback, or change, in response to the loss of an individual in a position of significant authority and responsibility.

9.3 Theoretical Approaches to Organizations

Given the complexity of organizations and their varied nature, it is not surprising that organizational theorists have approached the study of organizations from different viewpoints and have reflected in their theories ideas and attitudes prevalent at their time of writing. It is not possible here to review all the theories that have been proposed, but rather it is intended to discuss the three principal approaches : classical; human-relations; and the systems approach.

9.31 Classical Theory

Towards the end of the last century, with the further developments of the Industrial Revolution and the greater emphasis on factory production, there arose a need to establish principles for the organization of people at work. Drawing on their experience of military and civil organizations, and their belief in the division of labour and scientific method, early writers set out to draw up the ideal structure for a formal organization and to establish general principles of good management. They were particularly concerned with the need to clarify authority and responsibility.

Max Weber (1864–1920)[2], a sociologist, wrote a number of papers on organizational structure, authority, and control which formed the basis of what has become known as the classical approach. He identified three bases of authority: traditional, charisma, and bureaucracy. Traditional leadership, as the name implies, involves such things as the authority of a monarch, where authority is assumed because that is the way in which things are done. Charismatic leadership, on the other hand, depends on the personal magnetism of the leader; there are certain individuals who can obtain the consent of others through personal qualities which encourage trust and belief. Neither of these bases of authority was suitable, in Weber's view, for formal organizations. He believed that organizations should adopt a bureaucratic style of leadership. By this he did not mean the red-tape and inefficiency we now associate with this word, but rather that authority should be delegated on the basis of rationally defined criteria, such as expertise, and legally defined qualifications.

Weber's concept of the ideal design of an organization was one where rules and regulations are explicit and where jobs are well designed and carry with them the authority to ensure that the job can be successfully completed. He considered that authority should be based on technical qualifications, competence, and expertise and that there should be a distinct separation between ownership and control to ensure that decision-taking is rational and objective. Implicit in Weber's concept of bureaucratic authority is a hierarchical structure in which each position carries with it rights and responsibilities, and where lines of communication run vertically rather than horizontally.

Henry Fayol (1841 – 1925)[3], a French industrialist, while sharing many of the views held by Weber, concentrated less on the ideal structure of an organization and was more concerned with identifying, from experience, those factors present in successful organizations. He identified five functions of management which still appear today in most textbooks on the subject; these were: planning, organization, command, co-ordination, and control. He also suggested a number of administrative principles relating to the allocation of authority and the chain of command. Like Weber, Fayol believed that centralization was important to the successful operation of organizations but he took a less dogmatic view and recognized that this should not be at the expense of initiative and *esprit de corps*. Although he did not develop his ideas further, Fayol was among the first to recognize the importance of the human element in organizations and the need for teamwork and the maintenance of interpersonal relationships.

The concept of 'rational economic man' developed by F.W. Taylor[4] in the United States is a further example of the classical approach, and is based on the concept of division of labour and standardization of working methods. Taylor took the view that man, being part of a mechanized system, should, in that capacity, be regarded as machine-like. He felt that a great deal of inefficiency in industry resulted when workers were allowed to decide how a task should be accomplished. He believed that the planning of each task should be separated from the doing of it and, whilst the actual performance of the task could be entrusted to the workers themselves, the planning was a complex activity that should be undertaken by people trained in the application of special techniques such as analysis and work design. Therefore, in order to increase productivity and efficiency as much as possible, work had to be put on a scientifically organized basis. The co-operation of the worker was to be gained through appeals to 'rational economic man', since Taylor firmly believed that money was the prime motivator and that man would do that which provided him with the greatest economic gain. To achieve this aim it would be necessary to have workers who were:

1. selected for their appropriate personal characteristics (e.g. physically strong if the work involved strenuous physical effort);
2. trained in the necessary skills and the most efficient methods of performing the work;
3. provided with a work environment which allowed them to function properly (e.g. by providing the minimum of distraction);
4. adequately motivated by the prospect of financial reward.

Unlike most of the other classical theorists, Taylor employed research to support his theory. Taylor's methods are illustrated by the frequently told story of his work with a Pennsylvania Dutchman called Schmidt, who was one of a gang of 75 labourers loading pig-iron into railway trucks. On average, each man loaded $12\frac{1}{2}$ tons per day but Taylor calculated that a really efficient worker could load between 47 and 48 tons per day. Taylor chose Schmidt to help him test his belief because the latter was strong, industrious and thrifty with his wages. With the promise of more money for more work Schmidt did exactly what Taylor told him to do and by the end of the day had loaded $47\frac{1}{2}$ tons. For the three years Schmidt was under observation he continued to load this quantity and received sixty per cent more wages than formerly.

'Taylorism', as his method came to be known, was fairly widely adopted and his work, together with that of Frank and Lillian Gilbreth, formed the basis of modern work study techniques. It should be noted, however, that Taylor thought that his methods would benefit, not exploit, the worker since techniques which increased the economic efficiency of the organization must make it more successful and this would in turn result in the well-being of its employees and the reduction of conflict between employees and management.

Although the classical writers made a valuable contribution to the study of organizational structures, their approach has important limitations. The preoccupation with standardization does not aid understanding of the reasons why organizations differ and how they cope with change. Apart from Taylor, little attention is given to the individuals who make the organization work, and Taylor concentrated solely on the individual employee in isolation from his social environment. There was little appreciation of the social significance of work and the importance of the interactions between employees and among different parts of the organization.

9.32 Human-Relations Approach

The human-relations approach to organizations stemmed largely from the work of Elton Mayo[5] in the 1920s. In a series of experiments conducted at the Hawthorne plant of the Western Electric Company in Chicago from 1927 to

1932, Mayo discovered that the way in which people work is affected not only by the economic incentives they are offered, but also by social influences inherent in the work situation[6]. These experiments are important because they show, for the first time, the interrelationship of the various problems in the working environment and were the first real attempt to examine factors impinging on a job that are not part of the job itself. Many of the findings seem hardly surprising now, nearly fifty years later, since so much further research has subsequently been published; but, at the time, the results were revolutionary and controversial, especially as the views of Taylor and other classical theorists had such prominence.

These studies are also important because of the scientific approach adopted and, although the various experimental designs used have been subjected to criticism, they did represent a considerable advancement in the investigation of the variables affecting human relationships and behaviour at work. Also, it was explained in Chapter 1 that many scientific advances have been made through the experimenter testing for a certain relationship, but obtaining a result that could not be explained in terms of the variables examined; the search for explanation therefore leading to further discovery. This is what happened in the Hawthorne plant experiments and it was fortunate that the management of the plant were as anxious as the investigating team to determine the factors leading to job satisfaction and hence increased productivity. Because of their importance these experiments are discussed in some detail below.

Experiments on illumination. The work that started the series was an attempt to measure the relationship between the level of illumination in the factory and the production output. Conducted by a team led by C.E. Snow, it followed in the Taylor tradition and the objective was to ascertain the optimum lighting condition for given levels of productivity. The experiment employed a classic design, the independent variable (illumination) being altered and the effect on the dependent variable (production) being measured. The expected result occurred: namely, production increased as the amount of illumination increased, but it became apparent that the increase in illumination was not the sole cause. It was decided to investigate further and, this time, the experimental method became more sophisticated and a control group was used. Two groups, comparable in terms of numbers, experience, and average production, were selected but for the control group there was no increase in illumination. Also, to avoid the impact of any competitive spirit, the two groups were placed in different buildings. Both groups, however, increased production appreciably and as the experiment had not shown a direct relationship between illumination and production, it was thought worthwhile to study the reverse situation and ascertain the effect of less illumination. The surprising result was that, despite insufficient illumination, the experimental group maintained their previous efficiency and it was therefore apparent that factors other than illumination were responsible. It was at this stage that Elton Mayo and his team, joined the research effort and the Relay Assembly Test Room Experiment began.

The Relay Assembly Test Room Experiment. This involved five female elay assembly operators being chosen to work in a special room whilst being observed by a member of Mayo's team. The experiment was divided into thirteen test periods, each one seeing a change in a variable such as rest pauses, introduction of a five day week (six day working had been usual), and provision of free lunch. In each test period production was recorded, as were temperature and humidity (i.e. all possible variables were examined). Each test period saw a higher relay output than the previous one and, in questioning the operators, it became clear that the main reason for this was the change in attitude brought about largely by freedom from the rigid supervision that was in force in the rest of the factory. This easing of supervision allowed the operators to talk more freely to each other and a group cohesiveness began to develop with the result that morale increased. They were allowed to set their own work pace and, as a result, no longer worked as individuals but developed a team spirit, working towards common goals and, for example, helping each other with the work. Other reasons for the production increase were attributed by the operators to the novelty of the situation, the interest they had in the experiment, and the attention they received in the test room. These latter factors are what became known as the 'Hawthorne effect'.

The experiment had included, as one of the variables, a change in the method of payment and, in order to isolate this variable, another experiment, the 'Second Relay Assembly Test Room Experiment', was conducted with a similar group of relay assembly operators. This time only the payment method, and not any of the environmental variables, was altered. Production by this second group also increased but not to the level achieved by the first group. As a result, it could be concluded that, although the wage incentive factor did have an effect, the other variables were far more important.

Thus, the experiment indicated a change in employee attitudes and interpersonal relations, and as the operators' attitudes towards each other, their work, and the company improved, so their output increased. In other words, there appeared to be a direct relationship between morale and output.

Naturally, given these findings, the company was interested in improving morale and Mayo's team was now asked to find out about this factor amongst the workforce; a task that was undertaken by means of interviewing individually over 20,000 employees.

The interviewing programme. The success of this programme depended on gaining the trust of the workforce if meaningful results were to be obtained. Thus, from the start, the employees were informed of the purpose of the interviews and how the results would be used. They were told, for example, that remedial action would be taken if there were substantial complaints about working conditions. In addition, the interviews were kept strictly confidential; no names or employee numbers were recorded, and anything an individual employee said that could identify him was deleted from the interview report.

The data thus obtained were found to be extremely useful, since they not only provided a list of complaints about specific environmental factors which could be investigated, but also made available, for the first time, information on a large scale about employee attitudes and opinions. It was further found,

as in the previous studies, that the employees benefited from the mere proces
of being interviewed. The company was seen to be taking an interest in it
employees and this in itself contributed to raising morale.

As with the earlier studies, however, this part of the research left man
questions unanswered. Employees, for example, seemed to react differentl
to similar working environments, for some expressed satisfaction with thing
which other employees considered unsatisfactory. In other words, employee
seemed to be reacting to situations on the basis of previous social condi
tioning. Again, the results seemed to indicate that factors such as wages
hours of work, and physical conditions should not be viewed as bein
important in themselves but should be seen as contributing to social values
Thus, these factors could only be understood through the acquisition o
information about the individual employee's position, or status, in the imme
diate working group of which he formed a part. The interview programm
had indicated that social groups within each department could exercis
considerable control over the work behaviour of its members, even to th
extent of restricting output. Since little was known about these informa
groups it was decided to take the study a stage further and obtain informatio
about the formation of, and interaction within, these groups.

The Bank Wiring Observation Room Experiment. This experiment con
sisted of observing fourteen men engaged in the wiring of telephone switch
boards (banks). The experiment was different from that of the Relay Room
since the object was to observe exactly how the men behaved in a norma
working environment. Thus, apart from having the men work in a separat
room from the rest of the department, no environmental variables, fo
example lighting or heating, were changed, and the conditions were designe
to be as close as possible to the wiring department's ordinary workin,
conditions. The role of the experimenters was restricted to observing wha
actually went on and to interviewing the men outside the room about suc
things as their thoughts, feelings and values. Although this was an unnatura
situation for the men, after about three weeks they began to relax and behav
more or less as they did in their regular working place. In other words, the
had become habituated to the experimental situation.

The results of this part of the study showed that the men had evolved into
group that had its own informal leaders and definite norms. For example
one norm defined what constituted a day's work. Although efficiency expert
had determined that two and a half banks could be completed in a day, th
group had decided to produce only two banks despite a wage incentive plan
instituted by management to promote efficiency. Group pressure was exerte
on those who exceeded or fell below the group standard. Those who did no
produce enough were called 'chislers' whilst those who exceeded it were nick
named 'slaves', 'speed-kings', or 'rate busters' and were occasionally
'binged' (physical punishment consisting of a very hard blow on the uppe
arm). In other words, this social organization served to protect the grour
both by exacting internal control through the maintenance of norms and by
providing external protection through a steady rate of production.

More than anything else, the Hawthorne studies are remembered fo
revealing the importance of the informal groups existing within the organi-

ation. These groups develop their own social hierarchies and norms, and can exert such pressure on their individual members that there can be a stronger response to the norms of the informal group than to the wishes of management. These findings challenged the basic philosophy of the classical approach and showed that managers should not only be concerned with formal structures, but must also take account of informal relationships between groups of employees. They also suggested that horizontal relationships can be as important as the organization's vertical authority structure.

Since the Hawthorne studies, a great deal of research has been undertaken to develop further our understanding of the importance of informal groups in the work situation. It is, however, difficult to identify any clear conclusions from the many and varied studies that have been made, because our understanding of human behaviour is far from complete. There is little doubt that the role of the individual in the organization is far more complex than the classical writers' concept of 'rational economic man'. In many respects the informal structure can exert as much influence on an organization's success as can its formal structure, if not more. Indeed, one only needs to look at the effectiveness of 'working to rule' as a form of industrial action to see that this is often the case. Much work has been undertaken to identify the influence of social factors on individual performance and the results of this research are discussed in Chapter 10.

The human-relations approach has focused attention on the social factors at work within the organization but it has yet to provide a recipe for success. Most companies over the last fifty years have recognized the need to maintain and improve the morale of their employees, and have introduced welfare and benefit schemes with this in view. However, despite significant improvements in working conditions, the hoped-for increases in morale and productivity have proved elusive. This has led other researchers to examine more closely the factors that differentiate organizations in order to discover whether this approach can provide any useful answers.

9.33 The Systems Approach

The underlying basis of the systems approach is that the whole is greater than the sum of the parts; that is, a *Gestalt* evolves. Systems theorists argue that it is inappropriate to examine individual parts of the organizations, but rather one should look at the relationships, both formal and informal, between and among the sub-systems within the organization. Thus, while the classical theorists emphasised the formal structure of the organization, and the human-relations school focused attention on social relationships, systems theory suggests that it is important to consider the interaction between the parts of the organization and the relationship between the organization and its external environment. Also, unlike the classical and human-relations approaches, which respectively take a negative and a positive view towards the role of the individual in the organization, the systems approach takes an essentially neutral position. It is argued that the basis for an effective organization is not the positive or negative attitude of humans but the correct match between the individual and his environment.

The systems approach starts from the premise that any system is composed of a number of interconnected parts, but that the system itself can only be explained as a totality. In addition, systems have boundaries which separate them from their environment. If the system's boundaries are rigid and impenetrable then there will be very little interaction between it and the environment. Such a system is termed a *closed system*. On the other hand, if the system has permeable boundaries then there will be much closer ties between it and the external environment. Such a system is termed an *open system*. In an open system, inputs are received from the external environment and are processed by the system, the result of this activity being an output to the external environment. Systems theorists take the view that a completely closed system is doomed to fail since there is no interaction with the outside environment and tensions will build up inside the system, leading to disorder and failure. To survive, a system must be in equilibrium with its environment. This means that its relationship with the external environment must be such as to enable a balance between inputs and outputs.

In applying a systems approach to organizations it is necessary to identify the component parts of the organization, to see how they relate to one another, and to examine the nature of the relationship between the organization and its external environment. This type of analysis, systems theorists argue, will provide the basic data from which it should be possible to take a view on the appropriate structure for a particular organization. There is, for the systems theorist, no magical blueprint that will ensure an organization's success. The effectiveness of an organization is instead seen to be contingent on the correct match between an organization's internal structure and its operating environment. For this reason systems theories are sometimes called *contingency theories*.

Empirical evidence supports the view that there is no ideal generalized structure for organizations. Porter and Lawler[7] examined the relationship between organizational structure on one hand and job attitudes and job performance on the other, and found little correlation between the two. In some cases tall hierarchical structures performed well, in others flat, decentralized structures were more effective (see Figure 9.1). Similarly, both small spans of control (where each manager controls or has reporting to him a small number of individuals) and large spans of control (where each manager controls a large number of subordinates) were shown to work successfully in certain situations.

Analyses of this type led researchers to look more closely at the relationship between organizational structure and the nature of the tasks performed by the organization. Joan Woodward[8], for example, found a number of differences between the organizational structures adopted by different categories of industrial firms. She noticed that in process industries, where manufacturing is undertaken in long production runs and labour costs are low, management structures tended to be tall and involve a number of management levels. Decisions were generally taken by a committee of senior managers rather than unilaterally by the chief executive. This situation contrasted with unit or small-batch production firms, where products are custom made and labour costs are high. In this case, management structures

Flat decentralized structure   Tall hierarchical structure

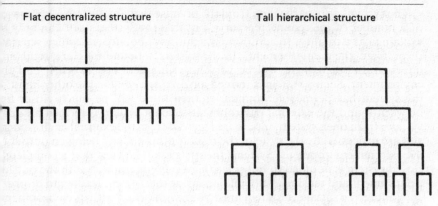

Figure 9.1 Structures of organizations

ended to be flat with large spans of control. She found that the ratio of management personnel to non-management personnel was 1:23 in unit production industries and 1:8 in process industries.

In another study, Burns and Stalker[9] identified a relationship between organizational structure and the predictability of the business environment within which the organization operated. They found that companies with more rigid hierarchical structures were less able to cope with a changing environment than those companies with more flexible management structures involving greater horizontal communication. Companies having a clearly defined hierarchical management structure were termed *mechanistic* while those with more flexible structures and less clearly defined authority systems were termed *organic*.

The findings of Burns and Stalker were supported in a later study by Lawrence and Lorsch[10] who were also interested in defining the correct match between the organization and its environment. They analysed companies facing a static predictable environment and companies facing a changing unpredictable environment, and found that the more unpredictable the environment facing an organization, the greater the need for a differentiated structure. By this they meant a heterogeneous organization with different departments having different goals and objectives, different working methods, and different types of people. They did, however, note the need for some form of integration between the diverse parts of the organization to ensure effective communication and co-ordination. This could take the form of communication flowcharts, and committees or individuals charged with the task of ensuring adequate liaison.

The systems approach, as mentioned earlier, is not confined only to the organization as a whole, but can also be applied to individual parts of the organization and to the way in which jobs are defined. For a department within an organization the external environment may be different departments within the organization, external suppliers, or customers. The nature of the demands placed on the department by these outside influences will, to a

large extent, determine the appropriate structure for the department. If th
demands are known and predictable and the tasks involved are routine, it wi
be easier, and usually more effective, to implement a structure involving clos
supervision and control. If, however, the nature of the tasks performed is le
well defined, and outside influences are less predictable, then the structure c
the department needs to be more flexible, with greater decentralization c
responsibilities and less hierarchical control.

Research has shown that the position of a department within the organ
zation is of importance and that jobs located wholly within one system a
less likely to be stressful than jobs located at the boundaries between system
This is of relevance to the marketer since marketing and sales function
lie on the interface between the organization and its external environment. I
these areas, contacts with outside bodies (such as customers, distributor
or advertising agents) are usually as important as contacts within th
organization. Care must therefore be taken in these areas to ensure tha
potential conflicts between the organization and these outside influences ar
minimized.

A great deal of research has been undertaken on the role conflict and rol
ambiguity experienced by field salesmen. Role conflict, a topic discussed i
Chapter 5, occurs when the salesman is faced with incompatible demands b
his company and his customers; and a large number of studies have show
that this can lead to anxiety, low job satisfaction, and physical stress. Simila
effects have been reported for role ambiguity where the salesman is unclea
about how he should perform his job. Despite these findings, it is not yet clea
how these effects can be minimized by changes in organizational structur
and supervisory style. Unlike Kahn *et al.*[11], who found that organization
structure and supervisory style were important in determining the consistenc
of role demands on workers located wholly within the organizational system
Walker *et al.*[12] found that these factors had little influence on the role confli
perceived by salesmen. Walker *et al.* also found that organizational structur
had little influence on role ambiguity, although close supervision an
involvement in the formulation of performance standards could, to som
extent, reduce the amount of ambiguity perceived. They noted, however, tha
experienced salesmen perceive significantly less role conflict and rol
ambiguity than those with less experience, and concluded that training coul
play a part in influencing salesmen's perceptions of their jobs and their abilit
to cope with, or resolve, the conflicts that may arise.

Although systems theorists take a neutral position with respect to huma
motivation, assuming that human beings are adaptable and will adjust t
different types of organizational structure, they have nonetheless addresse
the question of wages. Lupton[13], for example, has produced a model in whic
wages and fringe benefits occupy a positive role in maintaining an equilib
rium between internal and external pressures. They regulate the supply an
demand for labour, and play an important part in satisfying workers' jo
expectations while getting them to accept the demands the job will impose o
them. In the case of the salesman, often facing a conflict between interna
and external pressures, it is important that careful consideration is given t
the form of the remuneration package, particularly fringe benefits such a

company cars and permitted expenses, as this can do much to reduce perceived status conflicts in dealings with outside clients.

9.4 Effective Co-ordination and Communication

An organization is a collection of groups both formal and informal. Formal groups may be permanent features of the organization, such as its different departments and the senior management team, or temporary features, for example a committee or project group set up for a particular purpose. Informal groups are those arising between employees and, as mentioned earlier, tend to be formed to meet individual's emotional and social needs. Formal and informal groups may exist as distinct entities or may overlap. It is not uncommon, for instance, for members of the same department within an organization to develop strong friendship and emotional ties and for them to act together as an informal group. Equally, informal links, such as those established between managers of the same firm at the local golf club, may serve a formal function in so far as they provide a channel for the communication of information and ideas between different parts of the organization.

Effective co-ordination and communication within an organization will, to a large extent, depend on the positive interaction between the different groups existing within the organization, so that productivity is enhanced without damaging the effectiveness of any individual group. A particular problem is, however, that as individual groups become committed to their own goals and norms they are likely to see other groups as rivals and enter into competition with them. Thus, an informal group of production workers may begin to see their foreman as an enemy, particularly if he prevents communication between the group members. This may lead to a reduction in productivity and to a deterioration in labour relations. Another form of rivalry would be between different departments within the organization, for example between sales and production. A limited amount of competition of this type might be helpful to the organization as it could provide a stimulant to effort. If taken too far, however, it could lead to a breakdown of communication and be very damaging to the organizational effectiveness. Each department would blame the other for poor performance and there would be a reluctance to exchange information and solve common problems.

Sherif[14] and other researchers have shown that groups in competition tend to develop a positive stereotype of themselves and a negative stereotype of their rivals. They perceive only the positive side of their own groups and the negative side of the rival groups. This distortion of perception hinders communication since, when members of different groups are forced to interact, they may only listen to the advocate of their own group and selectively attend to representatives of the other group. They perceive only those parts of the opposing argument which reinforce their negative stereotype of the other group.

If inter-group conflict is to be minimized then the organizational structure must allow frequent interaction between groups and allow maximum communication of ideas and information. This might involve rotation between groups of different tasks performed within the organization. Such an approach may be possible for some clerical or manual jobs where little formal training is required. Where this approach is not possible, communication may be enhanced by co-ordinating committees. Such committees may not be immediately successful as it will take time for the committee to begin to work as a group rather than as a collection of individuals.

Emphasis must also be placed on organizational effectiveness rather than on group effectiveness. This might require changes in bonus systems so that the rewards of individual groups of workers are related less to the performance of their particular group, but more towards their contribution to the organization's overall performance.

The negative effects of inter-group conflict may also be reduced by finding common goals for the competing groups. This might involve the identification of a common enemy, such as a competing firm, so that the groups' efforts are channelled in the same direction rather than against one another. Alternatively, the competing groups could be set a joint goal. For example, a potential conflict between marketing and production might be avoided if the two departments were asked to work together on the development of a new product which must find a ready market while being cheap to produce.

If efforts such as these fail to prevent a conflict situation arising, then the only way in which the situation might be remedied is through a formal negotiating procedure or through additional training. Training might involve role play when a member of each group is asked to act as an advocate for the other.

In this section, stress has been laid on effective communication patterns. But what is the most effective communication pattern for a particular organization? This will depend on a number of factors, not least being the authority structure of the organization. Where this is hierarchical, there may be no difficulty in obtaining a vertical flow of information, but difficulties may arise in obtaining a horizontal flow of information. Also, the vertical flow of ideas within the organization may be restrained because of authority relationships and a feeling on the part of the subordinate that it is not his job to suggest ways in which his or another person's job could be performed. Management may therefore have to find other ways of encouraging a flow of new ideas, perhaps through suggestion boxes or awards for cost saving ideas.

Research by Leavitt[15] and Shaw[16] with small groups suggests that the choice of communication pattern should depend on the nature of the task being performed. Both researchers found that for simple problems, centralized communication networks are the most efficient while for complex problems decentralized networks are better. In Figure 9.2 a number of different types of communication networks are illustrated. The wheel is the most highly centralized, with one group member being more closely connected to the rest of the group than any other member. Both the circle and the all-channel networks are decentralized, although there is less interconnection between group members in the case of the circle. Intermediate systems are the 'Y' network and the chain.

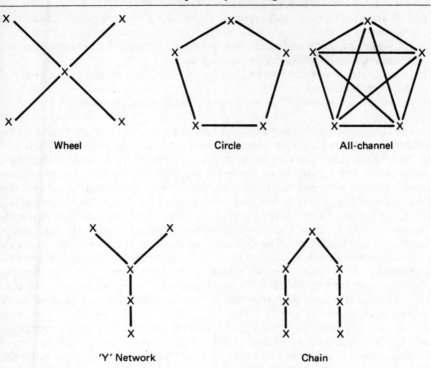

Figure 9.2 Communication networks

9.5 Organizational Change

As mentioned earlier, organizations are not static entities but evolve in response to changes in both the external and internal environment. Changes in the external environment facing an organization may take a number of forms. They may involve technical innovations which make it possible to develop new products, implement new methods of manufacture, or introduce new management aids such as the computer. Alternatively there may be a change in the market environment arising from changes in consumer tastes, government regulations, or competitive pressures. Internal stimulants to change may be an increase in the size of the organization, diversification into new areas of business, or changes in the background, training, and occupation of those employed. Changes in cultural values and social norms can also affect both the environment within which the organization operates and the attitudes and expectations of those employed by the organization.

Schein[1] identifies four conditions which appear to be necessary if the organization is to be able to cope effectively with change.

1. The ability to absorb and disseminate information in a reliable and valid manner.
2. Internal flexibility and creativity in order to make the changes that are demanded by the information obtained.
3. Integration and commitment to the successful attainment of the goals of the organization.
4. An internal climate of support and freedom from threat.

The first of Schein's conditions is of obvious importance since the organization that does not identify changes in market and supply conditions will fail to respond to these changes and will cease to be competitive. It is therefore important to the organization's survival that it maintains effective communication with its external environment. Here, the role of departments on the boundary of the organization (marketing, sales, and purchasing) is particularly important. These departments, through their regular contacts with customers and suppliers, are in a position to collect a great deal of information on market trends. The information received from these sources may not, however, be comprehensive and many companies recognize the need to supplement these sources of information by market research. There must also be a mechanism for identifying changes in the internal environment. This may be facilitated by management–employee committees or other such consultative bodies.

There is little point in collecting this information, however, if the organization's internal communication network does not ensure that the information obtained is received by those parts of the organization who will have to take any action required. As noted earlier, effective communication within the organization depends to an important extent on organizational structure and the extent to which it is appropriate to the organization's activities. It also depends on the effective use of the groups formed within the organization. Equally important is the form in which the information is presented. This must be readily understandable to all who may need to use it. It must be clearly and intelligibly presented and free from unnecessary jargon.

If an organization is rigidly geared to established procedures relating to the way in which jobs should be performed, there is likely to be resistance to change because change will require a re-evaluation of the norms and attitudes established by the various sub-parts of the organization. Schein's second condition for successful coping with change therefore highlights the need for internal flexibility and creativity. This, as mentioned earlier, is more likely to be achieved with a decentralized structure, involving a high degree of horizontal communication, than with a centralized structure. It can also be encouraged by training and management development schemes.

Training also has a role to play in the third of Schein's conditions, namely integration and commitment to the goals of the organization. But it is first necessary to set organizational goals and this is the task of senior management. Management may impose goals on the organization or establish them after consultation with employees. Whatever method is used, it is important that the goals identified are understandable to those employed within the organization. There must also be some way of establishing whether the goals set have been achieved. This may be done through identifying a number of sub-goals or objectives to be met by the various sub-parts of the organization. Such an approach is termed *management by objectives.*

In his final condition for coping with change, Schein stresses the need for an internal climate of support and freedom from threat. This is clearly important since change inevitably disturbs existing methods of working and the interpersonal relationships built up within and between individual groups of workers. If a group of workers feels threatened by change there is a danger that they will see management as an enemy and will develop group objectives in conflict with the organization's goals. They might positively resist change and thereby make it difficult for the organization to achieve its objectives.

If the organization is to engender a climate of support and freedom from threat, it must have clearly defined systems of authority and responsibility so as to avoid unnecessary conflicts and to maintain effective communication. These systems should not, however, be so rigid that they stifle initiative, creativity, and flair. The organization must also take into account the social and psychological needs of its employees in all its activities; in its policy for recruitment and selection, in its training programme, in its remuneration package, and in the way management interprets the psychological contract between the organization and its employees. These aspects of the individual's relationship with the organization are discussed in further detail in Chapter 10.

It is important that all individuals affected by a change are made aware of the need for that change. Research[17] suggests that they should be encouraged, as far as possible, to participate in decisions on how change should be implemented. This has obvious logic since the people in the sub-systems affected by change are usually in a better position than senior management to appreciate the effects various alternative strategies might have on informal group structures.

Where fundamental change involving an upheaval in management structure is required, senior management might encounter difficulty in persuading middle and junior management of the need for change because of understandable concern about the effect the change will have on career progression. In such cases, senior management have found it useful to bring in outside consultants. Such consultants, because of their prestige and independence, may be better able to convince all parts of the organization of the need for change since their recommendations may be seen as unbiased and in the best interests of the organization as a whole.

9.6 Organizational Buyer Behaviour

The topic of organizational buyer behaviour is of relevance to discussion in this chapter since it serves to illustrate a number of behavioural influences at work within the organization. It is also an important topic in its own right in a book on behavioural aspects of marketing, since an extremely large number of firms are in the business of selling their products, not to ultimate consumers, but to other companies.

It is helpful to discuss the various behavioural influences on industrial buyer behaviour by reference to a framework suggested by a workshop organized by the American Marketing Association[18]. This indicates that there are four main influences on organizational buying decisions: influences within the purchasing department; interdepartmental influences; intra-firm influences; and inter-firm influences. These various influences are illustrated in Figure 9.3.

DEPARTMENTAL INFLUENCES

	Within purchasing department	Between departments
Intra-firm influences	*Cell 1* – Intra-departmental, intra-organizational influences THE PURCHASING AGENT – social factors – price/cost factors – supply continuity – risk avoidance	*Cell 2* – Inter-departmental, intra-organizational influences THE BUYING CENTRE – organizational structure – power/conflict processes – gatekeeper role
Inter-firm influences	*Cell 3* – Intra-departmental, inter-organizational influences PROFESSIONALISM – word-of-mouth communication – trade shows, professional journals – supplier/purchase reciprocity	*Cell 4* – Inter-departmental, inter-organizational influences ORGANIZATIONAL ENVIRONMENT – technological change – nature of suppliers – co-operative buying

(ORGANIZATIONAL INFLUENCES)

Figure 9.3 Influences on organizational buyer behaviour

Cell 1 involves factors relating to the purchase agent and includes social factors; price and cost factors; supply continuity; and risk avoidance.

1. *Social factors* concern the influence that a purchase agent's friendships with suppliers exert on his activities, and the extent that his personal relationships with others within the organization influence the buying process. Available evidence suggests that purchase agents' personal relationships with vendors significantly affect their decisions, although for understandable reasons this is rarely admitted.
2. *Price and cost factors.* Research evidence relating to the significance of price and cost factors in a purchase agent's decisions, although somewhat contradictory, suggests that their influence varies according to the type of product being purchased and the background of the purchase agent. A purchase agent with an accountancy background is more likely to be influenced by cost factors than a purchase agent with an engineering background.

3. *Supply continuity*. Generally, the smaller the number of suppliers the greater will be the importance attached to supply continuity.
4. *Risk avoidance* is frequently mentioned as one of the key factors influencing individual buying decisions. Purchase agents may try to reduce risk by investigating the financial strength of possible suppliers and their industrial relations history. Past experiences, the reputation of the supplying company, and social factors such as trust, are also means by which perceived risk may be minimized.

Cell 2 relates to the individuals within the organization that participate in the buying process; this is sometimes referred to as the 'buying centre'. Of interest here are the departments involved in the buying process and the influences each exert on the decision made. The composition of the buying centre will largely depend on the structure of the organization and the degree to which the purchasing department takes independent decisions or merely implements decisions taken elsewhere. If several departments are involved in the decision process, conflicts of interest may arise which need to be resolved. The way in which they are resolved will vary according to the nature of the decision, but will also depend on the influence exerted by each individual involved in the buying centre. A key role will be that of 'gatekeeper'; that is the person who collects and filters information about alternative brands or suppliers to the other members of the buying centre.

Cell 3 concerns the environmental influences on purchase agents and includes the increasing professionalism of the purchasing function which has brought with it greater contact between purchasing agents of different companies, and a growth of specialist publications and trade shows. This is a feature peculiar to the organizational buying process. It permits the purchase agent to obtain the views of other purchase agents and he can use this information, together with that obtained from suppliers, as an input to the decision-making process. Trade journals and exhibitions are also important sources of information. It is necessary, from the point of view of the supplier, that advertising communications in such media are appropriate to the individual in the buying centre who is likely to receive the advertising communication. For instance, it would be appropriate when advertising in journals that are read by purchase agents to stress cost savings aspects of a product rather than technical sophistication, since the purchase agent is likely to place a higher premium on cost than other product characteristics. In a journal read by engineers the converse emphasis would be appropriate. There is, however, little indication that suppliers do take their readership into account when devising advertising programmes, a blanket approach frequently being adopted.

Cell 4 concerns the relationship between the organization and its environment. Of importance here is the nature of the organization, its suppliers, and its buying practices. A study by Mogee and Bean[19] has indicated that the more rapid the rate of technological change faced by an organization, the less important is the role of the purchasing agent in organizational buying decisions. This suggests that suppliers marketing high technology products should ascertain which individual within the buying centre exerts the greatest influence on the decision-making process and orientate their promotional strategy accordingly. The nature of the supplying company will also influence the decision-making process. Large suppliers tend to present less risk than smaller suppliers. However, where security of supply is important, or where price competition between suppliers is desirable, purchase agents may prefer to deal with a number of small firms. In some industries, competition between suppliers is positively encouraged by the buying organization which will be prepared to provide capital equipment for small suppliers. Finally, in some sectors groups of firms may come together as a co-operative buying unit in order to obtain greater bargaining strength with suppliers. In such cases, the criteria on which buying decisions are based may differ from those adopted where the purchasing company acts independently.

This four-cell framework indicates the complex nature of the organizational buying process and the importance of understanding the behavioural relationships between the individuals involved in the decision-making process. A model which addresses itself to this question is the Sheth model of industrial buying behaviour. This model is principally concerned with Cell 2 of the framework discussed above, namely the buying centre. Environmental influences on the decision-making process are, however, also taken into account.

9.61 The Sheth Model[20] of Industrial Buyer Behaviour

This model, although similar to the Howard-Sheth model of buyer behaviour described in the last chapter, differs from it in three respects. First, it is a specific model relating only to organizational buying behaviour. Second, unlike the Howard-Sheth model, it specifically takes into account decision-making involving more than one person. Third, fewer variables are considered.

The Sheth model identifies three separate aspects of organizational buyer behaviour:

1. The psychological environments of the individuals involved in the buying decision.
2. The conditions which precipitate joint decision-making among individuals.
3. The joint decision-making process and the resolution of conflict among decision-makers.

A central feature of the Sheth model is the recognition that organizational buying decisions are rarely made by one person and that typically several different departments are involved. Sheth describes his model in relation to decisions involving purchasing agents, quality control engineers, and production management. He argues that because of differences in background, expertise, and exposure to information, the individuals involved may have different *expectations* of the product to be purchased. For example, manufacturing management, the product user, may be particularly interested in delivery performance, proper installation, and efficient service. Quality control engineers, on the other hand, may look for consistent high quality and engineering pretesting. The purchasing agent may have a completely different set of expectations, and may look for maximum price advantage and low transport costs.

It will be seen from the diagram of the model in Figure 9.4 that Sheth identifies five factors that influence the psychological environments of the individuals involved in organizational buying decisions. Each of these factors may lead to differences in expectations.

1. *Background of the individuals*. This includes the educational background of the individuals involved, the requirements of their roles within the organization, and their life-styles.
2. *Information sources*. Purchasing agents are likely to have much greater exposure to commercial sources of product information than either quality control engineers or manufacturing management. They are also likely to have greater contact with suppliers' salesmen. Engineering and production personnel may therefore have to rely on information obtained from trade magazines, professional meetings, and word-of-mouth.
3. *Active search*. Typically, active search for information on competing suppliers' products is carried out by purchasing personnel as this is considered part of the purchasing function.
4. *Perceptual distortion*. The differing values and goals of the three groups of individuals will exert an influence on their perception of available objective information so that there is consistency with prior knowledge and beliefs.
5. *Satisfaction with past purchases*. As the three parties involved may have different goals, they are likely to use different criteria in evaluating past experiences of products. The degree of satisfaction achieved with past purchases may therefore differ between the parties involved and this will affect their expectations in the current decision process.

Having identified the factors affecting expectations, Sheth examines those determining whether a particular buying decision will be *autonomous* or *joint*. These are divided into *product-specific* and *company-specific* factors.

Product-specific factors include the *perceived risk* in buying decisions, the *type of purchase*, and the *time pressure*. Sheth suggests that the higher the perceived risk attached to a particular buying decision, that is the greater the adverse consequences of being wrong, the more likely is the decision to be joint. Equally the nature of the purchase is important since a decision to purchase a one-off piece of capital equipment is more likely to involve several departments than a decision to re-order typewriter ribbons. Finally, if a decision has to be taken quickly then it is more likely to be delegated to one person.

Company-specific factors include *company size*, the *degree of centralization*, and the *company orientation*. The larger the company, the more likely are decisions to be joint. However, the more centralized a company's structure, the less likely are decisions to be joint. Company orientation will also influence the choice of those involved in a buying decision. In a production-orientated company buying decisions tend to be made by production

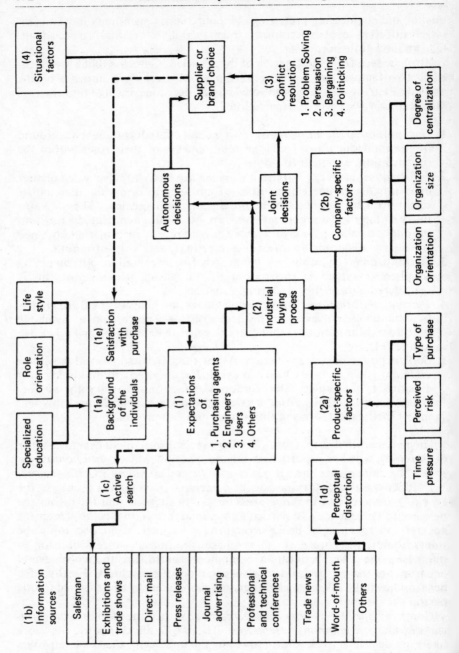

Figure 9.4 Source: Sheth, J.N. 'A Model of Industrial Buyer Behaviour', *Journal of Marketing* Vol. 37 No. 4 pp. 50–56, October 1973. (By kind permission of the American Marketing Association)

staff, while in technology-orientated companies purchase decisions tend to be made by engineering personnel.

The Sheth model of Industrial Buyer Behaviour does not examine in any detail autonomous buying decisions but rather concentrates on the joint decision-making process and the resolution of conflicts among decision-makers. Sheth argues that the existence of conflict between the departments involved in a buying decision is not in itself bad, since it reflects partly differences in the educational backgrounds of those involved, and partly the organization's policy of rewarding specialized skills and viewpoints. What is, however, important from the organization's point of view is the manner in which this conflict is resolved.

The model suggests four possible ways in which conflict may be resolved: *problem-solving, persuasion, bargaining,* and *politicking.* It is suggested that in cases where the basis of conflict is differences in expectations about suppliers or brands, the conflict is likely to be resolved by problem-solving behaviour. This will usually involve the active search for additional information and may lead to the collection of information about suppliers or brands not previously considered. In cases where the basis of conflict is the criteria used to evaluate alternative suppliers or brands, however, conflict is more likely to be resolved through persuasion. In this case, the dissenting member(s) is persuaded to adopt criteria which the majority believe to be more appropriate to the achievement of overall corporate objectives. Generally, no additional information is sought but there will be increased interaction and communication between the individuals involved. In extreme cases an independent observer may be brought in to reconcile outstanding differences.

Although time-consuming, the resolution of conflicts by problem-solving and persuasion is likely to lead to rational decision-making. Circumstances do arise, however, where the conflict is based on fundamental differences in buying objectives or goals. The individuals involved may recognize these differences and agree to differ. In these circumstances, conflict may be resolved by bargaining, where a single individual is empowered to make the decision in return for a favour or promise of reciprocity in the future. This is a non-rational means of resolving conflict. Equally irrational is the last of Sheth's methods of resolving conflict — politicking. This is often resorted to where the basis of disagreement involves the 'style of decision-making' and may arise where there is mutual dislike among the individuals concerned.

Although the model is based on the premise that the buying decision is the outcome of a systematic decision-making process, Sheth does point out that there is a great deal of evidence to suggest that in some cases industrial buying decisions are determined by *ad hoc* situational variables. Such cases would involve, for example, strikes, machine breakdowns, temporary economic conditions, and organizational changes such as a merger.

The model is interesting because it highlights the conflicts inherent in joint organizational buying decisions and identifies the factors which lead to differences in the expectations and perceptions of the individuals concerned. Further work is needed to clarify the nature of the linkages involved but it is

nonetheless an important model in an area where little research has bee
undertaken.

9.7 Implications for Marketing

We have seen in this chapter that organizations may be viewed as being com
posed of various interacting systems. Therefore, a major task is to ensure tha
the various parts of the organization are integrated in order to achiev
defined organizational goals. As organizations increase in size they becom
more complex and the task of integrating the various systems becomes mor
acute.

Marketing has a critical role in ensuring integration, for whilst it i
primarily concerned with revenue-producing activities, it also has a majo
part to play in the co-ordination and control of the various functional area
of the organization in order to ensure that revenue and profit goals ar
achieved. An important part of this function is the preparation of a market
ing plan which not only sets goals but is also a blueprint for their achieve
ment. In preparing such a plan the marketing department must consult wit
other parts of the organization so as to ensure that there are sufficien
internal resources to implement the targets set. For example, a sales target o
twice the production capacity of the organization is clearly impossible, unles
production can be sub-contracted to other organizations or furthe
production capacity can be quickly installed. Once agreed, the marketin
plan and any subsequent changes should be circulated to other depart
ments so that each part of the organization is fully aware of its expecte
role.

The marketing plan is, however, merely one aspect of the communicatio
process within the organization. It is vital that marketing, operating largely a
the interface between the external and internal environments, ensures ;
regular two-way flow of information within the organization. This can b
achieved in various ways, some of which are outlined below.

1. Meetings between departmental managers should be held regularly i
   order to discuss and resolve problem areas; decide courses of action result
   ing from changes in the internal and external environments; and eliminat
   duplication of effort. All decisions taken should be quickly communicate
   to subordinates.
2. Meetings with sales force personnel should be held at regular intervals i
   order to discuss problems; announce new products and pricing policies
   and ensure that the sales force is aware of company policy regardin
   various issues. Such meetings should be supplemented by an annual sale
   conference at which a broader framework is adopted; contributions bein
   made by production, finance, and personnel departments.
3. Salesmen and other personnel should be encouraged to report o
   competitors' activities. This information can then be analysed, its impli
   cations noted, and appropriate action taken.
4. News bulletins from the marketing department to the sales force and t
   other departments should be issued periodically. These can be used t

stimulate greater effort and to explain the implications of various internal and external changes. For example, the implications of the launch of a competing product can be analysed and the organization's reactions to this threat can be outlined. Typical reactions might include increased sales promotion and price reductions and it is obviously important for salesmen to have advance notice of these. Bulletins are necessary aids for they provide permanent reference documents for salesmen when presenting company policies to customers and can do much to alleviate the isolation experienced by personnel who have to operate some distance away from the mainstream of the organization's activities.

. In large organizations a company newspaper can be an important source of information about the company's activities. These publications can provide details of new products, company activities, recently recruited personnel, as well as reporting on various social activities. They can have an important effect in ensuring a feeling of 'belonging' and most large companies do produce such a publication, usually on a monthly basis.

The need for such communication efforts will, of course, depend on the ze and structure of the organization. In very small companies there is sually less need for formal methods of communication. In large companies, n the other hand, effective communication depends both on formal communication and on the way in which the structure of the organization allows or informal communication. However, as we have seen, there is no ideal eneralized structure for organizations. In multi-product, fast-moving con- mer goods organizations, such as Beechams or Gillette, the tall, marketing-rientated structure with its hierarchy of product group managers, product anagers, and brand managers seems to work very well and allows for dequate formal and informal communication. Such hierarchical structures em to be less effective, and even inappropriate, in service industries or gineering companies.

The complexity of organizational functioning and communication can be rther ascertained from the discussion on organizational buying behaviour. Vhereas in very small companies the responsibility and authority for the urchasing decision may be vested in one individual, in large, complex rganizations this is unlikely to be the case. Thus, time and effort must be evoted by the vendor to the identification of the decision-maker in each urchasing unit. Only after the level at which purchase decisions are made as been identified can the appropriate sales approach be formulated. For xample, if the actual purchase decision in a large organization is taken by a oard director, it could be inappropriate for negotiations to be undertaken y a sales representative. It should be noted that contract negotiations etween large organizations are often undertaken by board directors of the vo companies and, once agreed, the servicing of the contract is delegated to sales representative who then liaises with the customer's purchasing officer.

8 Summary

A key ingredient determining successful marketing is the extent to which the efforts of the entire organization are harnessed to achieve marketing goals. Organizations are complex entities and as they become larger th co-ordination and control functions of marketing become more difficult Effective performance in a marketing role therefore often depends on th marketer's skill in influencing change within the organization in order t cope with changes in the external environment.

2. The common features of organizations are: co-ordination of effort common goals or purpose; division of labour; hierarchy of authority an responsibility; and *Gestalt*.

3. There are several differing approaches to the study of organizations the most important being the classical approach, the human relation approach, and the systems approach.

4. The classical approach is particularly concerned with the need to clarif authority and responsibility, the efficient use of the division of labour and the standardization of working methods. The best known of th classical writers are Weber, Fayol, and Taylor.

5. The human-relations approach stemmed largely from the work of May at the Hawthorne plant. This approach focuses attention on the socia factors at work within organizations, particularly the influence o informal groups operating within the formal organization.

6. The systems approach concentrates on the interaction between the variou parts, or sub-systems, of an organization and the relationship between th organization and its external environment. Systems approaches are some times referred to as contingency theories because they see organizationa effectiveness as being contingent on the correct match between an organi zation's internal structure and its operating environment.

7. Central to an organization's efficient performance are effective communi cation and co-ordination. There is, however, no ideal communicatio pattern since the organization's objectives, structure, and external envi ronment will influence the nature of information flows. Effectiv co-ordination will help improve communication and reduce conflic between formal and informal groups existing within the organization.

8. The need for organizational change in order to meet organizational objec tives may arise through internal and external pressures. Factors that ar necessary to the organization being able to cope effectively with chang are: effective communication with the external environment and th dissemination of this information internally; internal flexibility an creativity; integration and commitment to organizational goals; a internal climate of support and freedom from threat.

9. Since many organizations sell their products or services to other organi zations it is important to have an appreciation of the various influences o organization buying decisions. The main influences are inter-firm, intra firm, interdepartmental, and those existing within the purchasing depart ment. The organizational buying process is complex and it is important t understand the behavioural relationships existing between the individual involved. The Sheth model of industrial buying behaviour attempts t explain these relationships as well as to account for environmenta influences.

References

1. Schein, E.H. *Organizational Psychology* (New Jersey: Prentice-Hall, 1970).
2. Weber, M. *The Theory of Social and Economic Organization* trans. A.M. Henderson and T. Parsons, edited by T. Parsons. (New York: Oxford University Press, 1947).
3. Fayol, H. *General and Industrial Management*, trans. C. Storrs. (London: Pitman, 1949).
4. Taylor, F.W. *Scientific Management* (New York: Harper & Row, 1911).
5. Mayo, E. *The Human Problems of an Industrial Civilization* (New York: Macmillan, 1933).
6. Roethlisberger, F.J. and Dickson, W.V *Management and the Worker – An Account of a Research Program Conducted by the Western Electric Co., Hawthorne Works, Chicago* (Cambridge, Mass.: Harvard University Press, 1939).
7. Porter, L.W. and Lawler, E.E. 'Properties of Organization Structure in Relation to Job Attitudes and Job Behaviour', *Psychol. Bulletin* 1965, 64.
8. Woodward, J. *Industrial Organization: Theory and Practice* (London: Oxford, 1965).
9. Burns, T. and Stalker, G.M. *The Management of Innovation* (London: Tavistock, 1961).
10. Lawrence, P.R. and Lorsch, J.W. *Organization and Environment: Managing Differentiation and Integration* (Boston: Harvard Business School, 1967).
11. Kahn, R.L. et al *Organizational Stress: Studies in Role Conflict and Ambiguity* (New York: John Wiley, 1964).
12. Walker, O.C. et al, 'Organizational Determinants of the Industrial Salesman's Role Conflict and Ambiguity.', *Journ. Marketing*, 1975, 39.
13. Lupton, T. 'Best Fit in the Design of Organizations', *Personnel Review*, 1974, 4.
14. Sherif, M. *et al. Inter-Group Conflict and Co-operation: The Robbers Cave Experiment* (Norman, Oklahoma: University Book Exchange, 1961).
15. Leavitt, H.J. 'Some Effects of Certain Communication Patterns on Group Performance' *Journ. Abnorm Soc. Psych.*, 1951, 46.
16. Shaw, M.E. 'Communication Networks', *Advances in Experimental Social Psychology*, L. Berkowitz, ed. (New York: Academic Press, 1964).
17. Lewin, K. 'Group Decision and Social Change', *Readings in Social Psychology*, E. Maccoby *et al*, eds. (New York: Holt, Rinehart, and Winston, 1958).
18. Bonoma, T.V. and Zaltman, G., eds. *Organizational Behaviour* (Chicago: American Marketing Association, 1978).
19. Mogee, M.E. and Bean, A.S. 'The Role of the Purchasing Agent in Industrial Innovation' in Bonoma and Zaltman, *ibid*.

20. Sheth, J.N. 'A Model of Industrial Buyer Behaviour' *Journ. Marketing*, 1973, 37.

Further Reading

Brown, J.A.C. *The Social Psychology of Industry* (Harmondsworth: Penguin, 1954).
Castles, F.G., Murray, D.J., Potter, D.C., eds. *Decisions, Organizations and Society* (Harmondsworth: Penguin, 1971).
Stewart, Rosemary *The Reality of Organizations* (London: Macmillan, 1970).

Past Examination Questions

1. What lessons can the sales force manager learn from the Hawthorne studies? (IM 1974)
2. Examine the relationship between organizational structures and organizational effectiveness. (IM 1976)
3. By reference to a business organization with which you are familiar, discuss how role-playing enhances or inhibits organizational effectiveness. (IM 1977)
4. Discuss the view that organizations are not sets of relationships among people but are relationships among sets of interlocking and interdependent groups. (IM 1978)
5. Does the work of F.W. Taylor have any relevance to modern marketing management? (IM 1979)

10. THE INDIVIDUAL IN THE ORGANIZATION

'In a unified company in which the objectives of managers and men (whom I regard as one group of people), of company and unions are identical, the probability of success is far higher.'

Tony Wilkinson,
Chairman, Wilkinson Group.

10.1 Introduction

One of the primary tasks of management is to recruit the right people for the right tasks and to motivate employees to a high level of performance; this is especially true for marketing management. Whilst it must be accepted that profits are made from catering for the needs of people, rather than merely by selling products, it must also be accepted that profits are made through the skills and efforts of the employees in an organization in catering for the demands of a market. As society is becoming more complex and sophisticated, so the required level of marketing skills and efforts must rise. Marketing management is responsible not only for the basic revenue-producing efforts but also for back-up services in terms of sales administration, distribution, and promotional activities. It follows, therefore, that the closer the goals of employees are to those of the organization, the greater will be the degree of cohesiveness of the members of the organization and the greater the ability of the organization as a whole to cater for the demands of a dynamic market and, hence, the greater the possibilities of profit.

In Chapter 4 it was shown that motivation is a complex subject and one that every manager should not only appreciate, but exploit, if the organization is to be effective. However, the problem is that individuals' needs are not the same and thus the motivating factors required to trigger various behaviours are different. In examining the behaviour of the individual within the organization, we are looking at behaviour within the constraints of organizations with different structures and different market philosophies, and which in terms of demands on employees are vastly different. But since all members of a society have been subject to the same basic social conditioning it would appear that the basic motivators of individuals must be similar. In terms of a very general theory such as that of Maslow this can be acknowledged to be true, but there remains the question of how an organization can best cater for an individual's particular needs in order to produce the required behaviour in the work environment.

In this chapter we shall examine approaches to recruitment, selection and training of personnel; the nature of the psychological contract; some of the theories that have been proposed to explain motivation mechanisms within the organizational environment; and the relationship between need fulfilment and the concept of job satisfaction. One of the problems is that man as an employee has too often been thought of as being motivated solely by money and it is only comparatively recently that the complexity of employee motivation in an organizational setting has been understood.

10.2 Recruitment, Selection, and Training

The success of an organization will to a large extent depend on the effective role performance of its employees. An important psychological problem facing the organization is therefore the recruitment, selection, and training of the people who fulfil the roles specified by the organization's structural framework.

There are two ways of approaching this problem: either to try to fit the man to the job, or to try to fit the job to the man.

Fitting the man to the job, as the term implies, means that job descriptions are taken as fixed and the organization is faced with the task of finding people with the right qualifications and experience to fill the available positions. For this reason it is often called the *selection approach*. Emphasis is placed on the choice and design of selection techniques and the needs of the organization assume paramount importance.

By comparison, *fitting the job to the man* starts from the assumption that the capacity of the human being is fixed; and emphasis is placed on designing the job and its physical environment to fit the limitations and capacities of humans. It is sometimes called the *classification approach* since it attempts to channel people into jobs which fully utilize their individual talents.

It would be incorrect to view these two approaches as strict alternatives as each has its individual merits. Clearly it would be unrealistic to establish a job description without first having ascertained that the job was capable of being performed by a human. Equally, it would be unproductive to expend a vast amount of effort in trying to tailor-make a job for each individual. It is, however, helpful to review the techniques involved in each approach and to examine their relevance to the selection and recruitment of marketing personnel.

10.21 The Selection Approach

Few organizations can afford to make many mistakes in the selection of employees because of the costs involved in the recruitment process; the loss of organizational effectiveness while a position remains unfilled, or filled by the wrong person; and the growing difficulty of shedding employees who fail to meet the organization's requirements. For this reason, increasing attention is being given to improving the accuracy of selection processes by the application of scientific techniques.

The task of selecting an individual to fill a specified position has two main aspects:

1. To determine the requirements of the job and to identify the mental, physical, and psychological characteristics needed for its successful performance.
2. To find and select an individual that matches these requirements.

Application of scientific techniques to both aspects of this task can aid the identification of valid selection criteria and assist in the elimination of bias.

In order to determine the attributes required by potential candidates it is first necessary to draw up a detailed job description and to identify criteria for measuring job performance. The job description should indicate the mental, physical, and psychological qualities required for the performance of the job. It should show the type of responsibility involved and any special working conditions that may affect the job holder's family circumstances; for example, are unsocial hours involved or will the job take its holder away from home? Equally important is the ability to measure job performance. For some jobs this may be relatively easy; for example, the performance of a machine operator may be related to levels of output achieved and the quality of the finished item. It is less easy, however, to measure the job performance of managers where the 'style' of management may be as important as the physical performance of certain tasks.

In the case of salesmen, difficulties exist both in describing the job to be performed and in identifying reliable measures of job performance. It is not possible to identify specific actions that are necessary to secure a sale as a variety of approaches can be used. There may also not be a high correlation between job performance in the short run and the long run. For example, a salesman may spend time getting to know his clients and his sales performance in the short run may bear no relation to his long run potential. In these circumstances, the job description may have to be rather loose and a variety of performance criteria employed.

Having drawn up a job description and identified a range of performance criteria, attributes which are considered relevant to successful job performance should be identified and tested against the performance criteria. It is important that this stage in the process is not overlooked, and that care is taken to ensure that the sample of candidates tested is sufficiently large and representative to allow unbiased correlation between individual personal attributes and the identified measures of job performance. Once this process has been completed, it should be possible to identify a few key personal variables that show a high correlation with job performance. These variables should then be used as a basis for selecting future candidates.

The reliability of the attributes selected as predictors of good job performance will, to a large extent, depend on the ability to measure individual personal variables and to relate them to a measure of job performance. Interviews used to be the principal way of evaluating potential candidates in terms of different attributes, but they tend to be unreliable since they depend a great deal on the quality of the interviewer. It is very difficult to ensure conformity in an interview situation and − as we have seen in earlier chapters − to eliminate bias caused, for example, by halo effects (see Chapter 7) and stereotyping (see Chapter 6).

By structuring interviews, it is posssible to ensure greater conformity between interviews and provide a standardized basis of evaluation. There are numerous ways of structuring interviews, but perhaps the best known is the 'Seven-Point Plan' designed by Professor Alec Rodger[1]. This established seven criteria against which the candidate is evaluated, a separate score being given by the interviewer for the candidate's performance against each criterion. The seven criteria identified by Rodger are set out below.

1. *Physique.* Some jobs require specific physical capabilities or the ability to withstand certain strains. Requirements are specified under the headings: health, hearing, eyesight, voice, appearance.
2. *Attainment.* This relates to the level of education, training, and experience.
3. *Intelligence.* The level of intelligence (which may be measured by means of tests) and the need for initiative or adaptability.
4. *Special aptitudes.* The job may require special skills, for example, verbal or figure fluency, manual dexterity, mechanical aptitude, or an ability to deal with spatial concepts (again, these skills may be measured by means of tests).
5. *Interests.* By eliciting information on a candidate's interests (for example, whether they are social, physically active, or practical or culturally orientated) it may be possible to assess whether he will fit in with the people with whom he will work or come into contact. This type of information can also help in making allowance for the stress a candidate may experience in the interview situation.
6. *Disposition.* The selection procedure may have identified certain general character traits (for example, steadiness, reliability, adaptability) which have an influence on job performance.
7. *Circumstances.* This factor takes account of the physical environment in which the job is to be performed (for example, does it require working in isolation or absences from home?) and the needs of the individual (for example, security, opportunities for promotion).

It will be seen that the Seven Point Plan provides a framework which copes well with the needs of most jobs and which can be easily modified to take account of special circumstances.

Increasingly, selection techniques are being evolved which reduce the scope for person perception errors. These take the form of scientifically evaluated standardized tests, or job samples, and can be used to measure intelligence, manual dexterity, special aptitudes (such as, numerical, spatial, clerical), temperament, and personality. Such techniques can be particularly helpful where the task to be performed is clearly defined and where success can be easily measured. They are, therefore, useful in selection for such jobs as machine operators, clerical staff, and pilots. They are less easily applied in cases where there is no clear-cut measure of performance and where the job holder has to show flexibility to deal with many, often unforseen, events. Tests and job samples are thus of limited value in the selection of managerial staff, teachers, and salesmen.

A recent Institute of Marketing study[2] showed that only 18% of the companies represented in the survey used personality assessment tests in the recruitment of salesmen. This report also concluded that 'there is no evidence . . . to suggest that the use of personality assessment tests leads to a higher proportion of satisfactory salesmen being recruited'. Despite this, the report recommends that such tests be used 'as an aid where the recruitment situation has proved particularly difficult'.

Tests, however, have the disadvantage that they may be seen by applicants as an impersonal form of evaluation. The company appears to be interested only in the correct performance of the given task and not to be concerned about the employee as an individual. Many applicants resent this approach and some may attempt to fake their answers and thus render the test useless. Others may develop an image of the company and its management as being unsympathetic to their needs and aspirations and this can lead to apathy and an unwillingness to accept change. Care has therefore to be taken in the selection process to ensure that potential employees are provided with a correct image of the company, since a person's first impressions can have an important influence on the formation of attitudes to the company which may affect his long-run contribution to it. Selection policies can also influence the image the public at large has of the company. For this reason, a number of companies continue to hold interviews, for good public relations, even though the basis of selection depends on test results.

10.22 The Classification Approach

An alternative to the selection approach is the classification approach which involves trying to design the job to fit the man. Traditionally this has taken the form of job design, or human engineering, where attention is focused on the potential and limitations of the worker in an attempt to maximize output from a given number of employees. Particular attention may be given to the development of patterns of movements which enable the worker to perform his job more quickly, but with less fatigue; to planning the layout of the factory floor to enable efficient transfers of work, raw materials, and waste; and to the design of machines to minimize errors and reduce the risk of accidents.

With the advent of behavioural science, however, it has become clear that it is not sufficient only to consider the individual worker, but it is also necessary to take account of the social interaction between individuals. Within every formal organization there are many informal organizations and these informal organizations between workers exert a significant influence on the way in which the individual worker fulfils his role in the formal organization of which he is part.

The Hawthorne Studies, discussed in the previous chapter, demonstrated the importance of the social factor in job performance and had a major influence on subsequent research into the role of social relationships within the formal organization. The Hawthorne Studies were not, however, designed to investigate social relationships within the organization and therefore did not examine the effect on job performance of changes in informal groups.

A study which did address itself to this question was the Tavistock

Institute's studies of the 'longwall method' of coal mining[3]. These studies investigated the effects on coal miners of a technological change involving the installation of mechanical coal-cutting equipment and conveyors. Prior to the installation of this equipment, individual teams of two to eight men were responsible for cutting, loading, and removing the coal from a short section of the coal-face (the shortwall method). Each team worked independently and, because of the teamwork involved and the intrinsic danger of the mining situation, strong emotional bonds were formed among team members. Teams competed to achieve the highest output and conflict between teams was not uncommon. With the installation of coal-cutting equipment, however, much larger teams were required, often involving fifty men under one supervisor. The nature of the work also changed, and, although the level of output still depended on each man fulfilling his given task, there was less close contact between the members of the team. New small groups emerged, but these tended to be composed of men responsible for performing the same task. There became a loss of 'meaning' between the work performed and the level of output achieved and this resulted in passivity and indifference; productivity suffered. The studies showed that the new work arrangement made it physically impossible for the men to meet their emotional needs through informal groupings that also favoured high levels of productivity.

These, and other studies, have shown the importance of catering for the social needs of employees within the formal organization. This may be done formally through a social club or less formally by designing the working environment in such a way that informal groupings assist, rather than operate against, the attainment of high levels of productivity. The company that shows indifference to the emotional needs of its employees may well find that the informal organizations within it may conspire to negate or defeat planned objectives.

10.23 Training

Having selected its employees, the organization must decide how to make the most effective use of their potential. Training is important in this respect. It may be undertaken to provide new employees with information about the company; to teach specific skills that enable employees to perform their job or to adjust to new technology; and to provide existing employees with the educational opportunity to progress within the organization. Whatever the reason for the training scheme, it is important at the outset that there is a clear idea of the training needs and goals, as the more clearly these can be specified the more likely is the training programme to succeed. Information must also be obtained on the level of intelligence and expertise of potential trainees as it is important that the training programme is correctly pitched; that is, it is neither so difficult that trainees are made to feel inadequate, or so easy that they become bored and frustrated.

The design of training schemes must take due account of learning theory. This means that the learner should be an active participant in the learning process and that new responses are 'reinforced', either by some reward or by recognition that the response has been made correctly. The training programme should be broken up into learnable units that are logically related to each other. There should also be sufficient opportunity to practice the newly learned responses and to generalize these responses to other appropriate situations. Where possible, care should be taken that the new responses do not conflict with old responses or attitudes. If this is unavoidable, the training scheme must be so designed to enable old responses to be unlearned before the new responses are learned. It is also important that the learner is motivated and this may be facilitated if the design of the training programme takes account of the motives which trainees bring with them into the learning situation. Finally, the training scheme must allow for individual differences in the speed and depth of learning.

Special problems arise in managerial and supervisory training programmes where attitudes, motives, and interpersonal relationships may need to be learned or developed. In general, participative techniques such as role play have been found to be useful in these situations. Videotape can play a useful part in such training programmes as the trainee is able to see his own role play and analyse for himself how well he performed.

It must be recognized, however, that if a training programme is to be successful in changing attitudes, the trainees must be encouraged to be open and frank about their own feelings towards a given situation. This can often unleash strong but previously concealed feelings towards the organization and the way it operates. If these feelings are widely held and management is seen not to react positively to them, then the training scheme may have the reverse effect to that intended and lead to increased dissatisfaction among key personnel. Sykes[4] provides a vivid example of this type of situation. A training course run by consultants for supervisors of a medium-sized contracting firm revealed deeply held grievances about the behaviour of senior management. After an internal enquiry, in which senior management blamed junior management and junior management blamed senior management, the Managing Director announced a number of changes based on the consultant's report. These changes were, however, slow to be implemented and some were made grudgingly. Within a few months foremen began to leave the company and within a year 29% of the 97 foremen had left and another 25% were looking for other jobs; in previous years staff turnover had been one or two men a year.

This study illustrates the need for training to be an integral part of organizational development. Enlightened management will see it as such and will be prepared to investigate ideas and grievances generated through the training process and to take the necessary action.

10.3 The Nature of the 'Psychological Contract'

There exists within all organizations an implied 'psychological contract' between the organization and its individual members. The psychological contract may take many forms depending on the type of organization, be it a company, a school, or a church, but it usually involves a pattern of rights, privileges, and obligations. A new employee joining a company will, for example, bring with him certain expectations regarding his level of pay, his working environment, job security, and the prospects for advancemen within the organization. The company, on the other hand, will have certai expectations of him; that he works hard and conscientiously, and that he doe not upset his colleagues or make it difficult for them to perform their give tasks within the organization. Some aspects of this contract may be writte down in a formal contract of employment, but there will be other less tangibl aspects of the psychological contract that cannot be clearly specified o paper.

An important aspect of the psychological contract from the point of view of the organization is that, by agreeing to become a member of the organi zation, the individual implicitly accepts the system of authority by which th various activities of the organization are co-ordinated and controlled. This i important since a hierarchy of authority is essential to the effective attain ment of the organization's objectives or goals. Also, authority, unlike power cannot be exercised against a person's will, but requires the consent, o willingness, of the individual to subordinate his rights in a given situation t his superior.

In subjecting himself to the authority system of an organization, th individual will usually expect the organization to take due account of hi needs and aspirations and must feel, or perceive, that he can exert sufficien influence on the organization to ensure that advantage is not taken of hi commitment to its authority system. The manner of influence will var according to the type of organization concerned, but will normally involv some form of consultation and grievance procedure which the individual car invoke either by himself or through a representative body.

The nature of the psychological contract between the organization and it members is affected by a host of factors, not least being the type of organi zation concerned, its objectives, its size, its history, the norms of the society within which it operates, and the attitudes and beliefs held by its members.

In Chapter 9 we reviewed some of the theoretical approaches to the study of organizations. Taylor's theories of 'rational economic man' epitomize the classical approach and suggest that adequate financial rewards alone are enough to ensure that the individual meets the organization's work require ments. This philosophy has been applied successfully over a number of years in assembly line operations. It has, however, become clear in recent years, as jobs have become more complex and competition more severe, that working to the rule book is not sufficient. The modern commercial and industrial organization requires a greater commitment by its workforce to its goals and objectives; it seeks from its workforce the exercise of creativity, judgement, and loyalty.

The concept of 'social man' stemming from the work of Mayo suggests a different kind of psychological contract, where the manager, instead of ini tiating work and controlling the manner in which it is performed, acts as an intermediary between management as a whole and the group. He uses his authority to specify goals, but delegates to the group the responsibility to determine how best these goals are to be achieved. In this way, the employee becomes identified with the goals of the organization and obtains emotional satisfaction from being identified with the organization's achievements.

Numerous studies have been undertaken to determine the applicability of the human-relations approach, but the results are generally inconclusive. Many studies have shown that an employee-related approach to the psychological contract can lead to significant improvements in productivity; other studies have failed to show any improvements.

The lack of evidence for the general validity of either the concept 'rational economic man' or 'social man' led other researchers to suggest that man is too complex and variable to be categorized in this way. All individuals are different and bring with them to the work situation varying needs and expectations. This view supports the systems approach to the study of organizations which suggests that we cannot understand the behavioural dynamics of organizations by looking solely at either the individual's motivations or the organization's structure and authority system. The two are interrelated and interact in a complex manner. For 'complex man' there can be no generalized psychological contract. Two men working side-by-side may have totally different views on the psychological contract between themselves and the organization. For one the level of wages may be the prime motivating factor, while for the other it may be some intrinsic satisfaction in the job itself. This suggests that management systems must be flexible and that the individual manager must be prepared to respond in different ways according to the people concerned and the situations that present themselves.

10.4 Theories of Employee Motivation

We shall now examine some of the more recent theories that have been developed to explain employee motivation.

10.41 McGregor's 'Theory X' and 'Theory Y'.

McGregor's view[5] of the organization's approach to the individuals it employs is linked closely to Maslow's theory of motivation (see Chapter 4). He argued that the classical concept of 'rational economic man', which he labelled 'Theory X', takes no account of the individual's need for self-fulfilment. It is based on the premise that workers are passive, indolent, unambitious, and gullible, and that workers can only be controlled by the use of coercion and the threat of punishment. McGregor argued that management should abandon the Theory X concept of workers in favour of Theory Y, which takes the view that man is indifferent to organizational goals only because past experiences have so taught him. Theory Y suggests that employees can achieve personal psychological development if the organizational structure provides for the integration of individual and organizational goals.

The assumptions underlining Theory X and Theory Y are summarized below.

THEORY X
1. Man has an inherent dislike of work and will avoid it if he can.
2. The average worker must be forcefully directed and threatened with punishment to get him to do a fair day's work.

3. The average worker likes to be directed, wants to avoid responsibility, and above all else seeks security.
4. Few workers have either the imagination or the ingenuity to solve organizational problems.

It should be noted that the last assumption implies that men are divided into two distinct classes; those who direct and those who are to be directed.

THEORY Y
1. Man does not have an inherent dislike of work. Work is as natural as play or rest. Depending on the situational variables involved, it can be a source of satisfaction and will therefore be sought, or can be a source of punishment and will therefore be avoided.
2. The average worker likes to, and will, exercise self-direction and self control in the pursuit of goals to which he is committed.
3. The average worker not only likes responsibility but will seek and accept it
4. Many workers have the capacity to solve organizational problems and given the opportunity and motivation, they will use this capacity.

McGregor's theory is descriptive rather than predictive and was used to support his belief that job enlargement programmes, decentralization of organizational power, and participative leadership would provide scope for individual self-fulfilment.

10.42 The Two-Factor Theory

This theory was proposed by Herzberg, Mausner, and Snyderman in 1959[6] although it is generally referred to as 'Herzberg's Theory'. The work is based on a study of the causes of job satisfaction and dissatisfaction among 200 engineers and accountants. Each respondent was interviewed independently and was asked to describe specific events and job incidents which had resulted in him feeling exceptionally good or exceptionally bad about his job. The results were then content analysed and it was found that things which were associated with high satisfaction (termed 'satisfiers') were rather different from those things which were associated with situations of low satisfaction (termed 'dissatisfiers'). From this analysis two groups of work variables were postulated:

1. *Satisfiers*. Factors which result in job satisfaction and are generally motivating factors.
2. *Dissatisfiers*. Factors which result in job dissatisfaction and are generally 'hygiene' factors.

The factors identified under these two headings were stated to be:

Satisfiers (Motivating factors)	Dissatisfiers (Hygiene factors)
Achievement	Financial reward
Recognition	Interpersonal relations with supervisors
The work itself	Interpersonal relations with fellow-workers
Responsibility	Technical aspects of supervision
Advancement	Company policy and administration
	General working conditions

This analysis resulted in the 'Two-factor' Theory which states that:

1. job satisfaction factors are satisfying but their absence does not necessarily produce job dissatisfaction;
2. the absence of job dissatisfaction factors does not lead to job satisfaction.

In other words, job satisfaction results not only from the presence of hygiene factors at an acceptable level but also from the presence of motivating factors. The employee normally expects to find hygiene factors present and, without motivators, he would merely find that the job is tolerable. Thus, attempts at improving the work situation will only reduce or prevent dissatisfaction. But employees can be motivated to greater effort if the work itself is designed to increase responsibility or provide a sense of achievement. It is this latter approach that has formed the basis of job enrichment and job enlargement programmes which many organizations have sought to implement.

Herzberg's theory is controversial and has drawn a great deal of criticism, especially with regard to the method of recording critical incidents as the basis for determining satisfaction/dissatisfaction factors. The theory does, in fact, appear to be an artefact of the method used for obtaining the data. In this regard, Argyle[7] points out that 'numerous studies have now shown that if any other method is used these results are not obtained, so it seems that the theory is simply wrong'.

On the other hand, even if the theory has major flaws, Herzberg and his colleagues deserve credit for the contribution they have made to the understanding of ideal conditions of work. Prior to this research, little attention had been given to the intrinsic features of work such as achievement or recognition.

10.43 Expectancy Theory

This is a general theory of motivation framed in the context of the work situation and was proposed by Vroom in 1964[8]. It uses as its basis the concept of *valence* which Vroom defines as 'the attractiveness of a goal or outcome' or 'the anticipated satisfaction from an outcome'. Outcomes can be positive or negative in valence. Thus an individual would wish to achieve an outcome with a positive valence and would prefer not to attain an outcome with a negative valence. Generally, the individual is faced with a trade-off between various outcomes. Thus, to earn more money (positive valence) an individual may have to work overtime which would given him less time available to spend with his family (negative valence). The decision to work overtime therefore depends on the net attractiveness of the outcome.

An important part of the decision between choices is the factor of expectancy, since it is a combination of both expectancy and valence that determines the decision that will be taken. Thus, in a choice between something with a high positive valence that is unlikely (low expectancy), and something that has low, or even negative, valence but is likely (high expectancy), or something with reasonable expectancy and positive valence, then the latter is likely to be chosen.

Unlike the Two-Factor Theory, Expectancy Theory has received good support from subsequent studies. Mitchell and Beach[9] have reviewed sixteen different studies using expectancy theory as a method of predicting occupational choice and job satisfaction and, in each case, there was significant support for the theory.

Vroom suggests that job satisfaction is a reflection of how desirable an individual finds his job; it is a measure of the individual's valence for his work situation. The implications of this for management are:

1. Expectancy is the important factor. Individuals make choices based on what they expect, not on previous outcomes (rewards).
2. Outcomes need to be identified with behaviour that is regarded as desirable by management.
3. Valence is subjective and, since what may have a high valence for one individual may have a low valence for another, there should be an attempt to match outcomes with the goals of different employees.

10.44 Equity Theory

This was developed by Adams in 1965[10]. The basic premise is that employees will attempt to achieve equity between their inputs (training, effort, ability) and their outcomes (salary, status, 'perks') and in so doing will also compare their outcome/input ratio with that of other employees. If there is little difference between these comparisons, then a state of equity exists; the individual is comfortable with the situation and there is unlikely to be any change. However, if there is an imbalance, it will create a state of tension proportional to the magnitude of the inequity, which in turn creates a desire to reduce the inequity. The alternatives available to the individual in adjusting inputs would be as follows:

Outcome/Input Ratio Too High (i.e. over-reward)	*Outcome/Input Ratio Too Low* (i.e. under-reward)
1. Increase input (e.g. more effort)	1. Reduce input (e.g. less effort)
2. Decrease outcome (e.g. accept lower salary)	2. Increase outcome (e.g. obtain higher salary)
3. Change external standard (e.g. increase quality)	3. Change external standard (e.g. produce lower quality)

Subsequent studies have tended to support this theory. Generally, subjects decreased their output when they felt underpaid and increased their output when they felt overpaid. But there was a different result when the basis of payment varied. When the outcome/input ratio was perceived as being too high, the quantity of output increased when hourly paid and the quality of output increased when paid on a piece-rate basis. A study of Adams and Jacobsen[11] neatly illustrated this; subjects employed on a piece-rate basis to undertake proofreading, upon being told that they were overpaid, read fewer pages in an hour but also detected more errors than others who felt more fairly paid.

The implications of this theory for management would appear to be:

1. Organizations must provide equitable rewards, otherwise employees may reduce effort or find alternative employment.
2. Employees view rewards in a relative rather than in an absolute way. The important factor is the reward compared with that received by others doing the same type of work. This implies that it is the social or interpersonal comparison that is the vital factor.

10.5 The Role of Money as a Motivating Factor

The above studies, and others, provide strong support for the view that the financial incentive is not nearly as powerful as is sometimes thought. Money is clearly necessary in order for people to survive and ensure an adequate standard of living for their families. Once these basic needs are fulfilled however, individuals seek other satisfactions from their working environments. The satisfaction of these higher order needs may therefore replace financial incentives as the immediate prime motive in the work situation. The perceived absence of adequate financial reward may be a source of dissatisfaction but the presence of a high financial reward may not be an important motivating factor. In considering the evidence for this view one must consider the time perspective in relation to the various studies and the changes that have occurred in society as a whole.

When Taylor undertook his work there were few social security benefits and often the only alternative to work was starvation; life was more basic, society more stratified and, in terms of Maslow's theory discussed in Chapter 4, work was vital to satisfy the lower order needs such as the physiological and safety needs. However, it can be argued that by the time of the Hawthorne studies, society had changed; the lower order needs had become comparatively less important and the significance of the higher order needs in the work environment became more apparent.

Herzberg's theory supports this view. He considered money to be a 'hygiene factor' which causes dissatisfaction when absent but contributes little to satisfaction when present. In parallel, Expectancy Theory suggests that money acquires valence due to its attractiveness in obtaining other desired outcomes. What is important here is the net attractiveness of the outcome and therefore the valence of money would be compared with the valence of other outcomes. Similarly, Equity Theory suggests that money has a relative rather than an absolute importance and financial rewards must therefore be measured in their social context. Equity Theory can be seen as the basis for the insistence of the maintenance of differentials by various trade unions in wage bargaining.

Perhaps one of the reasons for the persistence of the belief in the importance of financial reward is that, whilst the individual may feel that he personally is not highly motivated by money, this is not true of his co-workers and subordinates. This was illustrated by Kahn[12] in a study of workers and supervisors in a factory in the American Midwest. General foremen,

foremen, and workers were not only asked what they personally considered to be the important factors in a job but also what they considered their immediate subordinates felt were the important factors. The results are shown in Table 10.1.

Table 10.1

Factor (Numbers interviewed in brackets)	Men (2,499)	Foremen (196)		General Foremen (45)	
	Perception of self	Perception of men	Perception of self	Perception of foremen	Perception of self
Steady work, and steady wages	61	79	62	86	52
Getting along well with the people I work with	36	17	39	22	43
High wages	28	61	17	58	11
Getting along well with my supervisor	28	14	28	15	24
Good chances of promotion	25	23	42	24	47
Good chance to do interesting work	22	12	38	14	43
Good physical working conditions	21	19	18	4	11
Good chance to turn out good quality work	16	11	18	13	27
Pensions and other old-age security benefits	13	17	12	29	15
Not having to work too hard	13	30	4	25	2

% Rating each factor 1st, 2nd, and 3rd

Source: Kahn, 1958. Reproduced by kind permission of the North Holland Publishing Company

It can be seen that, although high wages was overall ranked third by the men, their supervisors, the foremen, felt that the men put a far higher value on this factor. Similarly the foremen's supervisors, the general foremen, in turn felt that the foremen placed a higher personal emphasis on high wages than was the case. The results also show the high value placed on social factors by the three groups and it is interesting to note that the self-perception of the various factors is similar for all groups.

At executive level, status and role tend to be important factors and, in this sense, remuneration may be regarded as a symbol or yardstick of success. In the U.K. the higher rates of income tax have led companies to pay salaries partly as benefits in kind. Such benefits have principally taken the form of prestigious motor cars and other status symbols. They can be viewed as not only part of a remuneration package but as contributing to the status of an individual among his peer groups outside the work environment.

A study which sheds some light on the various motivating factors affecting managers was that conducted by Elliott and Margerison[13]. Using a self-completion questionnaire they analysed the replies of 791 managers in various functions, of whom 103 identified themselves as marketing managers. The self-perceptions of marketing and other functional managers in relation to need requirements are summarized in Table 10.2.

The conclusions that are drawn in this study relate to comparative scores for different functional managers, rather than to absolute scores. It can be seen from the table that, in comparison with other managerial groups, marketers score high on the needs for achievement, power, and self-actualization but score low on the needs for financial reward and for security. Given the assumptions that marketers have a greater need for pursuing their ideas and for creativity, perhaps these results are not surprising. However, the low score on need for financial reward is seen by Elliott and Margerison as most surprising but they conclude that the rewards for marketers 'lie in intrinsic things such as self-actualization . . . more than in financial rates. This is *not* to say that marketing men are uninterested in money, but that they see their job as the main motivation'.

The emphasis placed on various motivating factors will however be influenced by the kind of society in which the individual has been socialized and now operates. In a free market economy, money is likely to be more important than in a Socialist society, where status and role are the main goals sought. But even within a capitalist economy there may be factors limiting the incentive power of financial rewards. Lawler,[14] for example, suggested that one of the major reasons that salary is not often found as the most important factor is that, in many instances, it is not related to merit in the actual job situation. In one study he carried out, when managers were asked to list factors that they saw as determining salary, he found that training and experience were considered as being the most important. One conclusion here is that if the system does not use job performance as a criterion for determining salary then it is doubtful if salary can ever be an incentive for better job performance.

10.6 Implications for Marketing

In the first part of this chapter we examined a number of strategies that the organization may employ to obtain an appropriate match between an individual's aptitudes and skills and the requirements of the job. Unfortunately, it has so far proved difficult to establish a link between specific personality attributes and effective job performance in the marketing function. It does, however, seem clear that successful marketing personnel show high need achievement and personality testing techniques may therefore be a useful supplement to the conventional selection interview.

The motivation of employees must be a priority of marketing management, but, as we have seen, there are no simple answers to this vexing problem. Most companies view the remuneration system as being a key element in the motivation of their employees. This is particularly true in the

Table 10.2

Ratings Given by Managers to Needs

Factor	Marketing	Personnel	Finance	Production	Consultancy	Administration	Research & Development
Need for Self-actualization	11.7	10.6	10.6	11.0	10.8	10.2	11.5
Need for Reward	4.6	5.3	5.3	5.1	5.3	5.2	5.0
Need for Security	9.2	9.0	10.8	9.0	10.1	10.9	9.9
Need for Achievement	43.9	42.4	41.6	43.1	42.9	41.7	44.3
Need for Power	10.4	10.5	10.4	11.0	10.0	10.5	9.9

case of sales staff; here companies operate a wide variety of payment systems, ranging from commission-only to salary-only.

The commission-only system has the advantage that it reduces overheads to a minimum, while allowing the successful salesman to earn a great deal of money. The salesman is, however, placed in a position of insecurity as he is under pressure to ensure that he makes sufficient sales to meet his basic living expenses. It is therefore not surprising that this method of remuneration has fallen dramatically in popularity, although it is still used in areas where aggressive selling is required, for example, life assurance, encyclopaedias, and cosmetics. Staff turnover does, however, tend to be high.

Most companies employ a salary-plus-commission remuneration system for their sales forces; the basic salary providing the employee with the security of being able to meet his basic living expenses, while the commission provides for additional luxuries. An increasing number of firms are, however, moving over to a salary-only system and this is particularly the case in companies where the salesmen, in addition to their selling skills, are required to have the technical expertise to match the company's products with the customer's requirements.

Expectancy Theory suggests that there is a direct link between behaviour and the nature of rewards, and this means that a remuneration system that is flexible and provides a range of rewards is more likely to be effective than one that is rigid. This is recognized, particularly in the remuneration of sales staff, and many companies offer a wide variety of incentive schemes including sales competitions with prizes such as visits to the U.S.A. for those exceeding specific sales targets.

Despite the emphasis given to methods of remuneration as a key motivating factor, there is increasing evidence to suggest that management have taken an over-simplistic view of employee motivation and have laid too much stress on tangible rewards. While financial reward is clearly of importance, its significance appears to be relative rather than absolute. This poses problems for management as it is clearly somewhat easier to reward employees with money than it is to respond to less clearly defined needs such as the need for achievement and the need for self-actualization.

Table 10.3 summarizes the results of the Institute of Marketing study[2] in 1979 to ascertain the factors, other than money, that sales managers considered most effective in the motivation of salesmen. It shows that meetings with supervisors to discuss career and job problems were ranked most important overall. Regular accompaniment by the sales manager was ranked

Table 10.3
Most Effective Motivating Factors
(mentioned in first three choices)
TYPE OF COMPANY

	All Companies	Repeat Consumer	Durable Intermediate	Repeat Industrial	Repeat Equipment	Services
Meetings with supervisor	1	3	3	1	2	1
Regular accompaniment by sales manager	2	2	2	2	1	4
Merit promotion system	3	4	6	4	3	2
Participation in setting sales targets	3	6	4	2	4	5
Sales force meetings/ conventions	5	5	5	5	5	3
Sales contests/ competitions	6	1	1	6	6	6
Bigger car for higher turnover	7	7	7	7	7	7
Fear of dismissal/ unemployment	8	8	8	8	8	8

second most important. This result is not unduly surprising; it suggests that salesmen have a need for regular feedback on the results of their efforts and this is consistent with McClelland's findings for individuals having a high need for achievement.

An interesting feature of the results of this survey is the variations between product categories. Incentive schemes are ranked the most significant motivating factor in consumer and durable product categories, but are not considered particularly important in other product areas. Participation in the setting of sales targets is considered to be particularly effective for repeat industrial products; and merit promotion systems are considered important in service industries.

For marketing employees generally it must be recognized that individuals will have different needs and expectations of the organization and management must, as far as possible, cater for these differences. Successful marketing requires the use of talented and creative individuals and it is important that such individuals are given sufficient freedom of action to exercise their talents. Clear guidelines must, however, be established on the boundaries of action if effective performance is to result. If the boundaries are too rigid then creativity and initiative may be stifled and the organization will receive only 'minimal effort and minimal creativity from its members'[15]. However, if the boundaries are too wide then there may be a lack of effective discipline. Obviously, the organization must set rules defining acceptable behaviour as this is an essential part of the system of authority and control. If the individual is aware of the limits imposed on his behaviour, and receives regular feedback on his performance, then he is better able to match his expectations with the organization's system of rewards and punishments. There can be no absolute guidelines since much will depend on the nature of the organization and its goals, the individual's role within the organization, the nature of his needs and expectations, and the extent to which the organization is able to satisfy his needs, both intrinsic and extrinsic.

Summary

1. The success of an organization largely depends on the efforts of its employees. It is therefore important that the organization uses suitable recruitment, selection, and training techniques and is able to motivate its employees to a high level of performance.
2. There are two approaches to recruitment and selection: fitting the man to the job (the selection approach) and fitting the job to the man (the classification approach). Each has its individual merits and they should not be viewed as strict alternatives.
3. Training is important in order to provide new employees with information about the company, to teach specific skills, and to provide the basis for career progression within the organization. Training schemes should take account of learning theory if they are to achieve maximum effectiveness.
4. For every employee there exists a 'psychological contract' between him and his organization. This encompasses the variety of expectations that each party will have regarding the other. Some aspects of the contract will be formally stated in a written contract of employment but others are less tangible, and need to be understood if good industrial relations are to be maintained.
5. Employee motivation is an important feature of organizational success. Several theories have been proposed, some of which are: McGregor's 'Theory X' and 'Theory Y'; Herzberg's Two-Factor Theory; Vroom's Expectancy Theory; and Adam's Equity Theory. Each has made a contribution to our understanding of the motivating factors affecting the work situation but no single theory offers a comprehensive explanation.
6. Financial reward has often been held to be the single most important motivating influence. However, various studies indicate that money is not as important as has been thought and that its influence is diluted by the need to fulfil higher order needs such as self-actualization and achievement.

References

1. Williams, A. 'The Human Element', *A First Course in Business Organization* A. Davies, ed. (London: Allen and Unwin, 1971).
2. Dunkeld, S.P. and Cashin, M.R. *Sales Force Practice Today* (Cookham: Institute of Marketing, 1979).
3. Trist, E.L. and Bamforth, K. 'Some Social and Psychological Consequences of the Longwall Method of Coal-getting', *Human Relations*, 1951, 4.

4. Sykes, A.J.M. 'The Effect of a Supervisory Training Course in Changing Supervisors' Perceptions and Expectations of the Role of Management', *Human Relations*, 1962, 15.

5. McGregor, D. *The Human Side of Enterprise* (New York: McGraw Hill, 1960).

6. Herzberg, F. *et al. The Motivation to Work* (New York: Wiley, 1959).

7. Argyle, M. *The Social Psychology of Work* (Harmondsworth: Penguin, 1974).

8. Vroom, V.H. *Work and Motivation* (New York: Wiley, 1964).

9. Mitchell, T.R. and Beach, L.R. 'A Review of Occupational Preference and Choice Research using Expectancy Theory and Decision Theory', *Journ. Occupational Psych.* 1976, 49.

10. Adams, J.S. 'Inequity in Social Exchange', *Advances in Experimental Social Psychology*, Vol. 2 L. Berkowitz, ed. (New York: Academic Press, 1965).

11. Adams, J.S. and Jacobsen, P.R. 'Effects of Wage Inequities on Work Quality', *Journ. Abnorm. and Social Psych.* 1964, 69.

12. Kahn, R. 'Human Relations on the Shop Floor', *Human Relations and Modern Management* H. Jones, ed. (Amsterdam: North Holland 1958).

13. Elliott, K. and Margerison, C. 'The Marketing Man's Image of Himself and his Work Relationships', *European Journal of Marketing,* 1979, p. 11.

14. Lawler, E.E. *The Mythology of Management Compensation* (New Haven, Conn: Yale University Press, 1965).

15. Katz, R.L. 'Management Assumptions and Organizational Consequences' *Organizational Behaviour and Administration*, P.R. Lawrence *et al*, eds. (Homewood, Illinois: Dorsey Press, 1961).

Further Reading

Davies, D.R. and Shackleton, V.J. *Psychology and Work* (London: Methuen, 1975).

Jessup, G. and Jessup H. *Selection and Assessment at Work* (London: Methuen, 1975).

Past Examination Questions

1. Are psychological tests of any value in the selection of salesmen? (IM 1974)

2. Have theories of motivation created rather than solved employee behavioural problems and demands? (IM 1975)

3. A firm who provide a wide range of benefits to their staff (for example: canteens, sports facilities, good pensions, above average holidays) are nevertheless encountering severe industrial relations problems.

   You have been appointed as a consultant in human relations to make recommendations. Outline the problems which you would expect to have to investigate. (CAM 1976)

4. What common errors are made by interviewers in the selection interview situation? How can they be overcome? (IM 1977)
5. What does the work of either (a) Vroom or (b) Herzberg tell us about the determination of suitable employee incentives in the sphere of marketing? (IM 1978)
6. 'Work provides the individual with much of his status and identity within society'. Discuss in relation to the determination of suitable employee incentives in the sphere of marketing. (IM 1979)

11. *THE CHALLENGE OF THE FUTURE*

'The consumer is, so to speak, the king . . . each is a voter who uses his votes to get things done that he wants done.'

Samuelson

'The general effect of sales effort . . . is to shift the locus of decision in the purchase of goods from the consumer where it is beyond control to the firm where it is subject to control.'

Galbraith

11.1 Introduction

Marketing has emerged in recent decades as a co-ordinating function which acts as a bridge between the needs of the organization, to make a profit and stay in business, and the needs of the consumer, that the right goods are made available at the right time and at the right price. This concept of marketing is well expressed in the 1952 Annual Report of the U.S. General Electric Company:

[The marketing concept] . . . introduces the marketing man at the beginning rather than at the end of the production cycle and integrates marketing in each phase of business. Thus, marketing, through its studies and research, will establish for the engineer, the design and manufacturing man, what the consumer wants in a given product, what price he is willing to pay, and where and when it will be wanted. Marketing will have authority in product planning, production scheduling, and inventory control, as well as in sales distribution and servicing of the product.

This traditional concept of marketing has, however, come under criticism in recent years as being both too narrow and too shallow in approach — too narrow because it concentrates on profit-motivated companies which exchange consumers goods for money, and too shallow because it fails to take account of the social and environmental effects of these transactions. In this chapter we will examine these criticisms in further detail and, in doing so, will look at the roles of both consumerism and social marketing. Finally, we will examine the usefulness of a behavioural approach to marketing problems in the future.

11.2 Widening the Market Concept

Kotler and Levy[1] were among the first to draw attention to the narrowness of the traditional marketing concept. They argued that business and non-business organizations are functionally similar and that there was no reason why the concept of marketing could not be extended and a more generalized approach taken to the concepts of 'product' and 'consumer'. Rejecting the traditional view that a market transaction must be the ultimate result of marketing activity, they argued that 'the crux of marketing lies in a general idea of exchange rather than in the narrow idea of market transactions'.

This view suggests that marketing is an organizational activity that can be embraced by all organizations, whether or not their prime objective is to make profits. It also means that a marketing philosophy could be applied to organizational objectives other than the sale of products, and marketing effort directed towards groups other than consumers.

11.21 Widening the concept of 'consumer'

If one accepts a behavioural approach to organizations, then there is much to commend a widening of the traditional concept of marketing to include groups other than consumers. In Chapter 9 we saw that an effective organization was one that responds to the needs of both its internal and external environments. Even for profit-motivated companies this does not entail solely the successful fulfilment of customer needs, although this is clearly important. The modern organization operates in an increasingly complex environment and the relationships it establishes with diverse groups such as suppliers, employees, unions, environmental groups, and governments can be vital to the successful attainment of its prime objectives. By widening the marketing concept to include these groups, and thereby identifying their needs and expectations of the organization, unnecessary and damaging conflicts of interest may be avoided. Also, by establishing a closer rapport with these groups, the organization will be better placed to identify and respond to changes in its internal and external environment.

Such an approach would require the adoption of the marketing philosophy by all areas of management and not only those concerned directly with the product and the final consumer. Table 11.1 below shows the principal management functions of an organization and identifies the groups to which marketing activity might be directed.

11.22 Widening the concept of 'product'

In recent years there has been a noticeable extension of marketing effort to include, in addition to physical products, services, organizations, people, places, and ideas and causes. Although many of the traditional tools of product marketing can be applied in these areas, particular problems do arise.

In the case of services, for example, the intangible nature of the product precludes the customer from sampling or testing the product before purchase. This means that the seller must appeal to the buyer's imagination when promoting his product or rely on testimonials from opinion leaders. Many personal services, such as hairdressing, however, are orientated to the individual and it is therefore difficult for the consumer to make generalizations from the experiences of others. In many cases services cannot be

Table 11.1
A Wider Definition of 'Consumer'

	Management Function	Target Market
Traditional Definition	Marketing	Customers
Wider Definition	Personnel	Employees Unions
	Public Relations	General public Governments Pressure groups
	Production	Suppliers Research institutions
	Administration (legal, accounting, finance)	Governments Professional bodies Trade associations

standardized and must be tailor-made to suit the individual's needs; many must also be consumed on the spot. This creates problems for pricing and distribution, particularly as an unconsumed service cannot be sold off at a discount. Thus, although service marketing can make use of many of the traditional tools of product marketing, such as market research and segmentation analysis, other tools such as promotion, distribution, and pricing decisions will often require unique solutions.

In addition to marketing its products an organization might decide to market itself, either for public relations purposes or as a means of drawing attention to lesser-known brands. Very often successful marketing of a leading brand name will lead to a reputation for quality and reliability. In many cases, however, the consumer will be unaware of the name of the company producing the brand or of other brands that the company manufactures. Organizational marketing therefore provides a tool by which the organization as a whole can capitalize on the successes of its individual parts. It can also be used to bolster or amend an existing public image. For example, a company concerned that it has developed an image of being rather staid and unadventurous may decide to develop a more progressive image by drawing attention to those areas where it is working at the forefront of technology. Organizational marketing can therefore be defined as those 'activities undertaken by an organization to create, maintain or alter attitudes and/or behaviour of various audiences towards the organization as a whole to stimulate exchange'. (Kotler)[2]

The link with traditional product marketing becomes less strong when the concept of 'product' is widened to include exchanges that are not related to profit. One of the first difficulties that has to be faced is the selection of new criteria for measuring success. If, for example, the police wished to embark on an organizational marketing campaign to improve their public image,

they would need some yardstick by which they could measure the effectiveness of different strategies. If no single criterion could be readily established, it would be necessary to use a number of different measures and this
would make the interpretation of results open to subjective assessment.

Person and place marketing are concerned with creating, maintaining, and
changing public and consumer attitudes towards a particular person or place.
Quite often, however, the objective of the exchange is not money. A
politician, for example, is concerned to maintain and enhance his public
image and he may promote this image through speeches and articles. In this
case, the basis of exchange is the promise of future actions and policies, in
return for an electoral vote. Again, a government promoting a depressed
region may offer various financial inducements to companies in return for
the creation of a specified number of jobs.

Marketing of ideas and causes rarely involves financial considerations.
People are encouraged to spend time and effort in support of a particular
cause in return for a possible improvement in their perceived 'quality of life'.
Nonetheless marketing strategies can be applied to such 'products'; as Kotler
and Zaltman[3] point out 'Marketing men by their training are finely attuned to
market needs, product development, pricing and channel issues, and mass
communication and promotion techniques, all of which are critical in the
social area.'

Table 11.2 gives some examples of the marketing mix for non-profit-
motivated organizations.

Table 11.2
Non-Profit-Motivated Organizations and the Marketing Mix

| | ORGANIZATION | | |
	Political Party	*Sporting Club*	*Community Environmental Action Group*
Basic Customer Need	Voice in govt.	Affiliation, leisure, enjoyment, exercise	Quality of life
Target Market	Electorate	Sporting public	Environmentally concerned public
Product	Party membership	Sporting club & facilities	The environmental cause
Price	Subscription to party fund, attendance at meetings, vote	Membership fee	Donations, time
Principal Promotional Tools	Publicity, advertising, personal selling	Club journal and newsletters	Publicity, petitions
Distribution	Branches, committee rooms	Club house & facilities	Demonstrations

Source: O'Leary & Iredale.[4] Reproduced by kind permission of MCB (European
Consumer Studies) Ltd.

11.3 Deepening the Marketing Concept

We have seen that the traditional concept of marketing has been challenged for being too shallow in approach, because it does not take into account the wider social and environmental effects of consumer transactions. Advocates of this view argue that business organizations must do more than assess the profitability of their actions. Should, for example, car manufacturers continue to produce large cars if these cars will during their lifetime consume more of society's scarce oil resources than smaller cars? Or, should manufacturers build obsolescence into their products when at only a little more expense they could produce more durable goods? Questions of this kind are clearly important and it is right that society should demand answers. Whether or not the marketer is the right person to respond is, however, questionable. Unfortunately, much of the literature in this area is of a philosophical nature and provides little guidance to the practising marketer.

All product decisions involve compromises and it is the job of the marketer to decide where the trade-off lies between individual features of product design, quality, and price. He does this by researching the needs of his market and makes a judgement on where the correct balance lies. This balance will depend to a large extent on his objective; whether this is to maximize profit, market share, cash flow, votes, membership, donations, etc. At the end of the day the marketer will judge his success by the extent to which he was able to meet his objectives.

These objectives may not always be acceptable to other members of society and pressure groups may be formed, and efforts made, to encourage the organization to change its product. If these efforts receive sufficient support the organization may voluntarily respond to public pressure; alternatively, governments or other regulatory bodies may step in and impose restrictions.

Many consumerists have argued that it should not be necessary to resort to such lengths to force manufacturers to produce socially responsible products. They believe that in responding to the needs of the market, companies should also take account of the needs of society as a whole. There is, therefore, some similarity of view between the consumer lobby and those that advocate the deepening of the marketing concept. The latter argue that the traditional marketing concept concentrates on short term objectives at the expense of longer term interests. As Feldman[5] argues:

A continuation of the present stress on [materialistic consumption] will result in individual short-term benefits, but may ultimately strain the resources of society, perhaps to breaking point. On the other hand, by shifting the emphasis to nonmaterial consumption and societal considerations, marketing will be acting on the long-run interests of society and will be facilitating the preservation of its future freedom of action.

Allied to this view is the concept of *demarketing* which was first put forward by Kotler and Levy in 1971[6]. This suggests that marketers could use their skills in advertising, sales, distribution, and pricing to discourage consumption at times of temporary shortage. In this way marketing could respond positively to a future of increasing scarcity of resources.

At their extreme, advocates of a deepening of the marketing concep appear to be suggesting that marketers, and the companies they represent should abandon their traditional objectives and instead adopt the role o social reformers. Clearly this is unrealistic. Nonetheless, as most organi zations have survival as one of their key objectives, it would be irresponsibl for the marketer to ignore changes in the social environment that may affec the success of the organization in the longer term. Thus, it would be unreal istic to expect a supermarket chain to add to its distribution costs, and there fore its prices, by deciding not to use larger, more cost effective trucks because society believes they are detrimental to the environment. It would however, be right for truck manufacturers to respond to this concern by try ing to produce less environmentally damaging vehicles, as the cost of failur may be untenable restrictions on the use of their product. Similarly, most o companies are now actively embracing the concept of demarketing and ar trying to encourage energy conservation. Their motives are not, however wholly altruistic but arise from a farsighted reappraisal of their longer term objectives.

An understanding of the social influences on behaviour will help th marketer to analyse the wider consequences of his actions. He must then as himself to what extent he could, by varying his actions, influence behaviou patterns in furtherance of his longer term survival. There will, however inevitably be actions that he could take in the interests of society as a whol that would not be perceived as being cost effective by the individua consumer. In such cases, the conflict of interest between the individua consumer and society as a whole will need to be resolved through th democratic system.

11.4 Consumerism

Consumerism has been described by Kotler[2] as a 'social movement seeking t augment the rights of buyers in relation to sellers'. As a movement it had it origins in the United States in the early 1960s. It rapidly gained momentum in both the U.S.A. and Sweden and has since spread to Japan, Netherlands, and the United Kingdom, and in more recent years to France and West Germany In the early days of the movement, consumerists and businessmen viewed each other with mutual suspicion and hostility. This led to a situation of claim and counter-claim by both sides, with each having little sympathy for the opposing view. The situation has now changed and the consumeris movement has become part of the environment which the marketer must take into account in his planning.

The *raison d'être* for the consumerist movement is the inherent conflict of interest between the seller and the consumer. The seller is interested in promoting his product at the expense of other competing products, while the consumer is interested in receiving unbiased information on the relative merits of competing products so that he can make a rational decision. Two prime objectives of the consumerist movement have therefore been to improve the amount of information available to the consumer and to educate the consumer to use the information made available. Consumer organizations have produced magazines, such as *Which?*, that provide comparative test data on consumer durables, and have campaigned for more information to be made available on product packaging. They have also been successful in convincing some local authorities of the need for comparative price information on products sold by local retailers.

The second plank of the consumerist movement has been the recognition of the rights of the consumer in law, so that buyer and seller can stand with one another on equal terms in the market place. Their efforts in this area have led to a significant strengthening of the rights of the consumer to demand redress if products are not of merchantable quality or fit for their intended purpose. There has also been a noticeable increase in the amount of legislation in the field of product safety and health risks; and stricter standards have been introduced to ensure that advertising material is factually correct and not misleading.

No part of the marketing strategy has been left unchallenged by the consumer lobby. Product policy has been challenged because it leads to a proliferation of similar products with only cosmetic differences; packaging, because it is wasteful, polluting, dangerous, expensive, deceitful and lacking information on contents, conditions of use, date of manufacture, etc. Pricing strategies have been criticized for being confusing to the consumer and psychologically orientated, and for introducing illusory innovations at higher prices. Communication methods have also been slated for encouraging excessive materialism and planned obsolescence, for creating unnecessary needs, and for promoting the psychological rather than the performance characteristics of products. Last but not least, distribution policies have been criticized for encouraging high pressure selling and deceitful promotions, while providing insufficient in-store service and poor after sales service.

For the reader who has patiently worked his way through this book the above category of complaints must appear to undermine the whole concept of marketing and its attempts to recognize the behavioural needs of the consumer. Indeed, opponents of the consumerist movement have argued that 'Consumerists have frequently misunderstood the realities of consumer behaviour and have consequently advocated or introduced measures aimed at protecting buyers against imaginary evils or assisting buyers in ways they do not notice' (Foxall)[7]. They argue that consumerists do not appreciate the real power the consumer exerts in the market place, as by his buying decisions the consumer will, in the long run, determine the products that succeed and those that fail. Many critics of the consumerist movement believe that the net result of consumer pressure will be more and more controls on business freedom, and that this will lead to higher prices, reduced consumer choice, and more standardized products.

Increasingly, however, marketers are coming to terms with the consumerist movement, recognizing that it is a feature of the market place that will not disappear very easily. Many companies within industry groups have come to realize that by joint voluntary action they can improve consumer information and standards of health and safety without damaging the market or their competitive positions. In this way they have avoided pre-emptive actions by government bodies that would not be in the interests of their industry, the consumer, or society as a whole. The consumerist movement has therefore, in part, been responsible for the growing interest shown by marketers in the social and environmental consequences of their actions.

Marketers are beginning to realize that if they do not include items such as safety, health, quality, information, and education in the marketing mix, then consumer pressure will cause government bodies to step in and redress the balance. A positive modern marketing strategy must therefore take account of these wider needs of the market. This does not mean that we should adopt the consumerist view that buyers always strive to make rational decisions, for, as we have seen in the earlier chapters of this book, this is not the case. Rather, the fact that these issues have drawn such vocal support, albeit from a relatively narrow and predominantly middle class section of the buying public, suggests that marketers have to some extent failed in their job to identify fully the needs of their target market. The astute marketer will realize that there is a group of needs seeking fulfilment and that new product opportunities may be found in consumer concern for higher standards of safety, health, quality, and information.

Nonetheless, it must be recognized that the consumerist movement as a whole represents only a small, although vocal, section of the population. The marketer must therefore take care to ensure that in responding to consumerist pressure he does not alienate other sections of his market or act against their best interests. Many of the actions advocated by the consumer lobby would add to product costs and in many cases it is not clear that the benefits to society would be commensurate with their costs. As Foxall[8] quite rightly argues, 'To the extent that consumerism leads to decisions being made on behalf of consumers rather than by consumers, it can only harm consumers. If we are really to be concerned to further the interests of buyers, we cannot honestly disregard this.'

11.5 Social Marketing

The concept of *social marketing* has featured a great deal in marketing literature in recent years, but unfortunately it has no clear or generally accepted definition. Individual authors have described social marketing in terms either of a widening of the definition of marketing to include social exchanges or a deepening of the market concept to include the social consequences of these exchanges. Bagozzi[9] rejects both these approaches and argues that social marketing is the answer to the question 'Why and how are exchanges created and resolved in social relationships?'. By this he refers to what in economics are termed transfer payments, such as the provision of welfare services, where part of society's general tax revenue is used to help the needy and dependent in society. Bagozzi is not principally concerned with the transfer of money but with the social exchanges that take place, both tangible and intangible. The extent to which marketing itself can aid our understanding and control of such exchanges is a subject of much debate and controversy. It is, however, clear that the behavioural sciences themselves could make an important contribution in this field.

11.6 Quo Vadis?

Marketing is a relatively new discipline and it is not surprising that there should be some debate on the nature of the problems on which it is brought to bear. Indeed such informed debate should be welcomed as it indicates that our thinking has not become stultified and narrow. No discipline can be compartmentalized on the narrow basis of subject matter because problems have a knack of cutting across the boundaries of subject. Rather, we should try to use the tools of analysis that are available to us and apply them to the problems that confront us.

In this way marketing has drawn heavily on the behavioural sciences as a means of explaining and helping our understanding of the problems that confront the marketer. We have seen that a number of the concepts developed by psychologists and sociologists, such as perception, motivation, attitude, and social groups, norms and roles have been of immense assistance to the marketer. Others, such as personality, although interesting fields of academic study, have so far proved of little practical assistance. We are, however, still only scratching the surface of a complex and many-sided problem. Marketers are just beginning to develop their own tools of analysis and have much more to learn about the factors that lead up to and determine whether a purchase decision will be made. Behavioural analysis must therefore continue to be a topic of major concern to the marketer. For, as we said at the outset, *marketing is about people, not products.*

References

1. Kotler, P. and Levy, S.J. 'Broadening the Concept of Marketing,' *Journal of Marketing*, January 1969.
2. Kotler, P. *Marketing Management: Analysis, Planning and Control,* 2nd Ed. (Englewood Cliffs, N.J.: Prentice Hall, 1972).
3. Kotler, P. and Zaltman, G. 'Social Marketing: An Approach to Planned Social Change', *Journal of Marketing*, July 1971.
4. O'Leary, R. and Iredale, 1. 'The Marketing Concept: Quo Vadis?', *European Journal of Marketing* 1976, 10.
5. Feldman, L.P. 'Societal Adaptation. A New Challenge for Marketing'. *Journal of Marketing* 1971, 35.
6. Kotler, P. and Levy, S.J. 'Demarketing, Yes, Demarketing', *Harvard Business Review* November, 1971.
7. and 8. Foxall, G. 'Towards a Balanced view of Consumerists' *European Journal of Marketing* 1979, 12.
9. Bagozzi, R.P. 'Marketing as an Exchange' *Journal of Marketing* October, 1975.

Past Examination Questions

1. Write notes on any four of the following:
   (a) The Halo Effect

    (b) Stereotyping
    (c) Sociometry
    (d) The Structured Interview
    (e) The Primary Group
    (f) TAT (IM 1974)

2. Write notes on any four of the following:
    (a) Conditioning
    (b) Associations and Institutions
    (c) The Concept of Authority
    (d) Stratification in Society
    (e) Self-actualization
    (f) The Primary Group. (IM 1975)

3. Differentiate between:
    (a) Inter-role conflict and intra-role conflict,
    (b) Intrinsic motivation and extrinsic motivation, and
    (c) Institutions and Associations. (IM 1976)

4. Write notes on any two of the following:
    (a) Cognitive dissonance or the cognitive process
    (b) Recognition and recall
    (c) Reference and membership (peer) groups
    (d) Propaganda
    (e) The extended family (CAM 1976)

5. Write notes on any three of the following:
    (a) Reference groups
    (b) Opinion Leadership
    (c) Forgetting
    (d) Frustrated behaviour
    (e) Traits
    (f) Group norms. (IM 1977).

6. Define and write brief notes about any two of the following:
    (a) *Gestalt* as a concept in perception
    (b) The nuclear and extended family
    (c) Maslow's hierarchy of needs
    (d) Class and status
    (e) Sociometry
    (f) Persuasion (CAM 1978).

7. In what ways can a knowledge of the behavioural sciences (sociology, psychology) help the marketing advertising executive to have a better understanding of consumer choices and purchasing behaviour? (CAM 1978)

8. 'A possible reason why some businessmen are willing to tolerate a psychologist underfoot is that they may have made a good profit by following his advice about advertising and selling the company's product.' Discuss the role of the psychologist in the marketing of consumer goods. (IM 1978)

9. In what ways can psychology and sociology help provide a scientific basis for the practice of marketing? (IM 1979)

10. Write notes on three of the following:-
    (a) Self-actualization
    (b) Family life cycle
    (c) Semantic differential scales
    (d) Role Conflict
    (e) Prejudice
    (f) Short term memory (IM 1979)

INDEX

231

BOOKS FOR MANAGERS
AND STUDENTS

MARKETING PLANS
How to prepare them, How to use them

Malcolm H. B. McDonald

A major new book on this crucial and often neglected area. It demonstrates how the marketing planning process works, how to carry out a marketing audit, how to set marketing objectives and strategies, how to schedule and how to cost out what has to be done to achieve the objectives and how to design and implement a simple marketing planning system.

This book will be helpful to DIPLOMA students of both the Institute of Marketing and the CAM Foundation

MARKETING
COMMUNICATIONS

Colin J. Coulson-Thomas

Provides students with a knowledge of the ways in which a business communicates with its market and the ways in which these can be evaluated. Contents include: communications; people, organization and communication; marketing management; innovation; marketing communications; buyer behaviour and motivation; the purchase decision; the promotion mix; sales management; brand/product management; distribution; relationships with external organizations; public relations; advertising; media; the advertising campaign; sales promotion; social marketing; market research; competitors; communications from the market.

Recommended Text **IM DIPLOMA – Marketing Communications**

BUSINESS ORGANIZATION

R. J. Williamson

Provides students with a lucid and comprehensive picture of this fundamental topic.

Aspects of the subject covered include: the manager's role, communications, control, business law, finance, purchasing, production, human resources, industrial relations, marketing, and change. The revision exercises on each chapter will be especially helpful to students preparing for examinations. 'It is written in a clear, concise style, which makes for easy reading, and has the benefit of topicality, in respect of references to legislation, institutions and attitude trends.' *The Quarterly Review of Marketing*

Recommended Text **IM CERTIFICATE Part I – Business Organization**